S0-ACM-063

DINARCHUS, HYPERIDES, AND LYCURGUS

THE ORATORY OF CLASSICAL GREECE

Translated with Notes • Michael Gagarin, Series Editor

VOLUME 5

DINARCHUS, HYPERIDES, AND LYCURGUS

Translated by Ian Worthington, Craig R. Cooper, & Edward M. Harris

UNIVERSITY OF TEXAS PRESS, AUSTIN

Printed in the United States of America

First edition, 2001

Requests for permission to reproduce material from this work should be sent to Permissions, University of Texas Press, Box 7819, Austin, TX 78713-7819.

∞ The paper used in this book meets the minimum requirements of ANSI/NISO Z39.48-1992 (R1997) (Permanence of Paper).

Library of Congress Cataloging-in-Publication Data

Dinarchus, Hyperides, and Lycurgus / translated by Ian Worthington, Craig R. Cooper & Edward M. Harris.
p. cm. — (The oratory of classical Greece v. 5)
Includes bibliographical references and index.
ISBN 0-292-79142-9 (hardcover : alk. paper) —
ISBN 0-292-79143-7 (pbk. : alk. paper)
1. Speeches, addresses, etc., Greek—Translations into English. 2. Dinarchus—Translations into English. 3. Hyperides—Translations into English. 4. Lycurgus—Translations into English. I. Worthington, Ian. II. Cooper, Craig R. (Craig Richard), 1960– III. Harris, Edward Monroe. IV. Title. V. Series.
PA3633 .D56 2001
885′.0108—dc21 00-012082

This book has been supported by an endowment dedicated to classics and the ancient world, funded by grants from the National Endowment for the Humanities, the Gladys Krieble Delmas Foundation, the James R. Dougherty, Jr. Foundation, and the Rachael and Ben Vaughan Foundation, and by gifts from Mark and Jo Ann Finley, Lucy Shoe Meritt, Anne Byrd Nalle, and other individual donors.

CONTENTS

ACKNOWLEDGMENTS

This is the fifth volume in a series of translations of *The Oratory of Classical Greece.* The aim of the series is to make available primarily for those who do not read Greek up-to-date, accurate, and readable translations with introductions and explanatory notes of all the surviving works and major fragments of the Attic orators of the classical period (ca. 420–320 BC): Aeschines, Andocides, Antiphon, Demosthenes, Dinarchus, Hyperides, Isaeus, Isocrates, Lycurgus, and Lysias. This volume is devoted to a trio of orators, Dinarchus, Hyperides, and Lycurgus, who together represent a good range of the material from the last decades of our period.

On behalf of all the translators, I would like to thank Alan Boegehold, who read the volume for the Press and made many helpful comments and suggestions. Let me also acknowledge once again the help and support of the University of Texas Press, especially Director Joanna Hitchcock, Humanities Editor Jim Burr, Managing Editor Carolyn Wylie, and Copyeditor Nancy Moore.

—M.G.

For this, my swan song on Dinarchus I would think, I thank Michael Gagarin for his comments and eye for detail and also my wife Tracy for her continued support.

—I.W.

I would like to extend my thanks to my colleagues and friends in the Department of Classics at the University of Winnipeg for their continued support and especially to Michael Gagarin for the many suggestions he made to improve this translation.

—C.R.C.

I would like to thank my friend Frederick Naiden for reading over the entire translation with a sharp eye and saving me from several mistakes and Michael Gagarin for his careful attention to each and every word of the translation. In a day when philological expertise is rare, he maintained the highest standards of our profession.

—E.M.H.

SERIES INTRODUCTION

Greek Oratory

By Michael Gagarin

ORATORY IN CLASSICAL ATHENS

From as early as Homer (and undoubtedly much earlier) the Greeks placed a high value on effective speaking. Even Achilles, whose greatness was primarily established on the battlefield, was brought up to be "a speaker of words and a doer of deeds" (*Iliad* 9.443); and Athenian leaders of the sixth and fifth centuries,[1] such as Solon, Themistocles, and Pericles, were all accomplished orators. Most Greek literary genres—notably epic, tragedy, and history—underscore the importance of oratory by their inclusion of set speeches. The formal pleadings of the envoys to Achilles in the *Iliad,* the messenger speeches in tragedy reporting events like the battle of Salamis in Aeschylus' *Persians* or the gruesome death of Pentheus in Euripides' *Bacchae,* and the powerful political oratory of Pericles' funeral oration in Thucydides are but a few of the most notable examples of the Greeks' never-ending fascination with formal public speaking, which was to reach its height in the public oratory of the fourth century.

In early times, oratory was not a specialized subject of study but was learned by practice and example. The formal study of rhetoric as an "art" (*technē*) began, we are told, in the middle of the fifth century in Sicily with the work of Corax and his pupil Tisias.[2] These two are

[1] All dates in this volume are BC unless the contrary is either indicated or obvious.

[2] See Kennedy 1963: 26–51. Cole 1991 has challenged this traditional picture, arguing that the term "rhetoric" was coined by Plato to designate and denigrate an activity he strongly opposed. Cole's own reconstruction is not without prob-

scarcely more than names to us, but another famous Sicilian, Gorgias of Leontini (ca. 490–390), developed a new style of argument and is reported to have dazzled the Athenians with a speech delivered when he visited Athens in 427. Gorgias initiated the practice, which continued into the early fourth century, of composing speeches for mythical or imaginary occasions. The surviving examples reveal a lively intellectual climate in the late fifth and early fourth centuries, in which oratory served to display new ideas, new forms of expression, and new methods of argument.[3] This tradition of "intellectual" oratory was continued by the fourth-century educator Isocrates and played a large role in later Greek and Roman education.

In addition to this intellectual oratory, at about the same time the practice also began of writing speeches for real occasions in public life, which we may designate "practical" oratory. For centuries Athenians had been delivering speeches in public settings (primarily the courts and the Assembly), but these had always been composed and delivered impromptu, without being written down and thus without being preserved. The practice of writing speeches began in the courts and then expanded to include the Assembly and other settings. Athens was one of the leading cities of Greece in the fifth and fourth centuries, and its political and legal systems depended on direct participation by a large number of citizens; all important decisions were made by these large bodies, and the primary means of influencing these decisions was oratory.[4] Thus, it is not surprising that oratory flourished in Athens,[5] but it may not be immediately obvious why it should be written down.

The pivotal figure in this development was Antiphon, one of the fifth-century intellectuals who are often grouped together under the

---

lems, but he does well to remind us how thoroughly the traditional view of rhetoric depends on one of its most ardent opponents.

[3] Of these only Antiphon's Tetralogies are included in this series. Gorgias' *Helen* and *Palamedes*, Alcidamas' *Odysseus*, and Antisthenes' *Ajax* and *Odysseus* are translated in Gagarin and Woodruff 1995.

[4] Yunis 1996 has a good treatment of political oratory from Pericles to Demosthenes.

[5] All our evidence for practical oratory comes from Athens, with the exception of Isocrates 19, written for a trial in Aegina. Many speeches were undoubtedly delivered in courts and political forums in other Greek cities, but it may be that such speeches were written down only in Athens.

name "Sophists."[6] Like some of the other sophists he contributed to the intellectual oratory of the period, but he also had a strong practical interest in law. At the same time, Antiphon had an aversion to public speaking and did not directly involve himself in legal or political affairs (Thucydides 8.68). However, he began giving general advice to other citizens who were engaged in litigation and were thus expected to address the court themselves. As this practice grew, Antiphon went further, and around 430 he began writing out whole speeches for others to memorize and deliver. Thus began the practice of "logography," which continued through the next century and beyond.[7] Logography particularly appealed to men like Lysias, who were metics, or noncitizen residents of Athens. Since they were not Athenian citizens, they were barred from direct participation in public life, but they could contribute by writing speeches for others.

Antiphon was also the first (to our knowledge) to write down a speech he would himself deliver, writing the speech for his own defense at his trial for treason in 411. His motive was probably to publicize and preserve his views, and others continued this practice of writing down speeches they would themselves deliver in the courts and (more rarely) the Assembly.[8] Finally, one other type of practical oratory was the special tribute delivered on certain important public occasions, the best known of which is the funeral oration. It is convenient to designate these three types of oratory by the terms Aristotle later uses: forensic (for the courts), deliberative (for the Assembly), and epideictic (for display).[9]

---

[6] The term "sophist" was loosely used through the fifth and fourth centuries to designate various intellectuals and orators, but under the influence of Plato, who attacked certain figures under this name, the term is now used of a specific group of thinkers; see Kerferd 1981.

[7] For Antiphon as the first to write speeches, see Photius, *Bibliotheca* 486a7–11 and [Plut.], *Moralia* 832c–d. The latest extant speech can be dated to 320, but we know that at least one orator, Dinarchus, continued the practice after that date.

[8] Unlike forensic speeches, speeches for delivery in the Assembly were usually not composed beforehand in writing, since the speaker could not know exactly when or in what context he would be speaking; see further Trevett 1996.

[9] *Rhetoric* 1.3. Intellectual orations, like Gorgias' *Helen*, do not easily fit into Aristotle's classification. For a fuller (but still brief) introduction to Attic oratory and the orators, see Edwards 1994.

THE ORATORS

In the century from about 420 to 320, dozens—perhaps even hundreds—of now unknown orators and logographers must have composed speeches that are now lost, but only ten of these men were selected for preservation and study by ancient scholars, and only works collected under the names of these ten have been preserved. Some of these works are undoubtedly spurious, though in most cases they are fourth-century works by a different author rather than later "forgeries." Indeed, modern scholars suspect that as many as seven of the speeches attributed to Demosthenes may have been written by Apollodorus, son of Pasion, who is sometimes called "the eleventh orator."[10] Including these speeches among the works of Demosthenes may have been an honest mistake, or perhaps a bookseller felt he could sell more copies of these speeches if they were attributed to a more famous orator.

In alphabetical order the Ten Orators are as follows:[11]

- AESCHINES (ca. 395–ca. 322) rose from obscure origins to become an important Athenian political figure, first an ally, then a bitter enemy of Demosthenes. His three speeches all concern major public issues. The best known of these (Aes. 3) was delivered at the trial in 330, when Demosthenes responded with *On the Crown* (Dem. 18). Aeschines lost the case and was forced to leave Athens and live the rest of his life in exile.

- ANDOCIDES (ca. 440–ca. 390) is best known for his role in the scandal of 415, when just before the departure of the fateful Athenian expedition to Sicily during the Peloponnesian War (431–404), a band of young men mutilated statues of Hermes, and at the same time information was revealed about the secret rites of Demeter.

[10] See Trevett 1992.

[11] The Loeb volumes of *Minor Attic Orators* also include the prominent Athenian political figure Demades (ca. 385–319), who was not one of the Ten; but the only speech that has come down to us under his name is a later forgery. It is possible that Demades and other fourth-century politicians who had a high reputation for public speaking did not put any speeches in writing, especially if they rarely spoke in the courts (see above n. 8).

Andocides was exiled but later returned. Two of the four speeches in his name give us a contemporary view of the scandal: one pleads for his return, the other argues against a second period of exile.

- ANTIPHON (ca. 480–411), as already noted, wrote forensic speeches for others and only once spoke himself. In 411 he participated in an oligarchic coup by a group of 400, and when the democrats regained power he was tried for treason and executed. His six surviving speeches include three for delivery in court and the three Tetralogies—imaginary intellectual exercises for display or teaching that consist of four speeches each, two on each side. All six of Antiphon's speeches concern homicide, probably because these stood at the beginning of the collection of his works. Fragments of some thirty other speeches cover many different topics.

- DEMOSTHENES (384–322) is generally considered the best of the Attic orators. Although his nationalistic message is less highly regarded today, his powerful mastery of and ability to combine many different rhetorical styles continues to impress readers. Demosthenes was still a child when his wealthy father died. The trustees of the estate apparently misappropriated much of it, and when he came of age, he sued them in a series of cases (27–31), regaining some of his fortune and making a name as a powerful speaker. He then wrote speeches for others in a variety of cases, public and private, and for his own use in court (where many cases involved major public issues), and in the Assembly, where he opposed the growing power of Philip of Macedon. The triumph of Philip and his son Alexander the Great eventually put an end to Demosthenes' career. Some sixty speeches have come down under his name, about a third of them of questionable authenticity.

- DINARCHUS (ca. 360–ca. 290) was born in Corinth but spent much of his life in Athens as a metic (a noncitizen resident). His public fame came primarily from writing speeches for the prosecutions surrounding the Harpalus affair in 324, when several prominent figures (including Demosthenes) were accused of bribery. After 322 he had a profitable career as a logographer.

- HYPERIDES (390–322) was a political leader and logographer of so many different talents that he was called the pentathlete of orators.

He was a leader of the Athenian resistance to Philip and Alexander and (like Demosthenes) was condemned to death after Athens' final surrender. One speech and substantial fragments of five others have been recovered from papyrus remains; otherwise, only fragments survive.

- ISAEUS (ca. 415–ca. 340) wrote speeches on a wide range of topics, but the eleven complete speeches that survive, dating from ca. 390 to ca. 344, all concern inheritance. As with Antiphon, the survival of these particular speeches may have been the result of the later ordering of his speeches by subject; we have part of a twelfth speech and fragments and titles of some forty other works. Isaeus is said to have been a pupil of Isocrates and the teacher of Demosthenes.

- ISOCRATES (436–338) considered himself a philosopher and educator, not an orator or rhetorician. He came from a wealthy Athenian family but lost most of his property in the Peloponnesian War, and in 403 he took up logography. About 390 he abandoned this practice and turned to writing and teaching, setting forth his educational, philosophical, and political views in essays that took the form of speeches but were not meant for oral delivery. He favored accommodation with the growing power of Philip of Macedon and panhellenic unity. His school was based on a broad concept of rhetoric and applied philosophy; it attracted pupils from the entire Greek world (including Isaeus, Lycurgus, and Hyperides) and became the main rival of Plato's Academy. Isocrates greatly influenced education and rhetoric in the Hellenistic, Roman, and modern periods until the eighteenth century.

- LYCURGUS (ca. 390–ca. 324) was a leading public official who restored the financial condition of Athens after 338 and played a large role in the city for the next dozen years. He brought charges of corruption or treason against many other officials, usually with success. Only one speech survives.

- LYSIAS (ca. 445–ca. 380) was a metic—an official resident of Athens but not a citizen. Much of his property was seized by the Thirty during their short-lived oligarchic coup in 404–403. Perhaps as a result he turned to logography. More than thirty speeches survive in whole or in part, though the authenticity of some is doubted.

We also have fragments or know the titles of more than a hundred others. The speeches cover a wide range of cases, and he may have delivered one himself (Lys. 12), on the death of his brother at the hands of the Thirty. Lysias is particularly known for his vivid narratives, his *ēthopoiïa,* or "creation of character," and his prose style, which became a model of clarity and vividness.

THE WORKS OF THE ORATORS

As soon as speeches began to be written down, they could be preserved. We know little about the conditions of book "publication" (i.e., making copies for distribution) in the fourth century, but there was an active market for books in Athens, and some of the speeches may have achieved wide circulation.[12] An orator (or his family) may have preserved his own speeches, perhaps to advertise his ability or demonstrate his success, or booksellers may have collected and copied them in order to make money.

We do not know how closely the preserved text of these speeches corresponded to the version actually delivered in court or in the Assembly. Speakers undoubtedly extemporized or varied from their text on occasion, but there is no good evidence that deliberative speeches were substantially revised for publication.[13] In forensic oratory a logographer's reputation would derive first and foremost from his success with jurors. If a forensic speech was victorious, there would be no reason to alter it for publication, and if it lost, alteration would probably not deceive potential clients. Thus, the published texts of forensic speeches were probably quite faithful to the texts that were provided to clients, and we have little reason to suspect substantial alteration in the century or so before they were collected by scholars in Alexandria (see below).

In addition to the speaker's text, most forensic speeches have breaks for the inclusion of documents. The logographer inserted a notation

---

[12] Dover's discussion (1968) of the preservation and transmission of the works of Lysias (and perhaps others under his name) is useful not just for Lysias but for the other orators too. His theory of shared authorship between logographer and litigant, however, is unconvincing (see Usher 1976).

[13] See further Trevett 1996: 437–439.

in his text—such as *nomos* ("law") or *martyria* ("testimony")—and the speaker would pause while the clerk read out the text of a law or the testimony of witnesses. Many speeches survive with only a notation that a *nomos* or *martyria* was read at that point, but in some cases the text of the document is included. It used to be thought that these documents were all creations of later scholars, but many (though not all) are now accepted as genuine.[14]

With the foundation of the famous library in Alexandria early in the third century, scholars began to collect and catalogue texts of the orators, along with many other classical authors. Only the best orators were preserved in the library, many of them represented by over 100 speeches each (some undoubtedly spurious). Only some of these works survived in manuscript form to the modern era; more recently a few others have been discovered on ancient sheets of papyrus, so that today the corpus of Attic Oratory consists of about 150 speeches, together with a few letters and other works. The subject matter ranges from important public issues and serious crimes to business affairs, lovers' quarrels, inheritance disputes, and other personal or family matters.

In the centuries after these works were collected, ancient scholars gathered biographical facts about their authors, produced grammatical and lexicographic notes, and used some of the speeches as evidence for Athenian political history. But the ancient scholars who were most interested in the orators were those who studied prose style, the most notable of these being Dionysius of Halicarnassus (first century BC), who wrote treatises on several of the orators,[15] and Hermogenes of Tarsus (second century AD), who wrote several literary studies, including *On Types of Style.*[16] But relative to epic or tragedy, oratory was little studied; and even scholars of rhetoric whose interests were broader than style, like Cicero and Quintilian, paid little attention to the orators, except for the acknowledged master, Demosthenes.

Most modern scholars until the second half of the twentieth century continued to treat the orators primarily as prose stylists.[17] The

---

[14] See MacDowell 1990: 43–47; Todd 1993: 44–45.

[15] Dionysius' literary studies are collected and translated in Usher 1974–1985.

[16] Wooten 1987. Stylistic considerations probably also influenced the selection of the "canon" of ten orators; see Worthington 1994.

[17] For example, the most popular and influential book ever written on the orators, Jebb's *The Attic Orators* (1875) was presented as an "attempt to aid in giving

reevaluation of Athenian democracy by George Grote and others in the nineteenth century stimulated renewed interest in Greek oratory among historians; and increasing interest in Athenian law during that century led a few legal scholars to read the orators. But in comparison with the interest shown in the other literary genres—epic, lyric, tragedy, comedy, and even history—Attic oratory has been relatively neglected until the last third of the twentieth century. More recently, however, scholars have discovered the value of the orators for the broader study of Athenian culture and society. Since Dover's groundbreaking works on popular morality and homosexuality,[18] interest in the orators has been increasing rapidly, and they are now seen as primary representatives of Athenian moral and social values, and as evidence for social and economic conditions, political and social ideology, and in general those aspects of Athenian culture that in the past were commonly ignored by historians of ancient Greece but are of increasing interest and importance today, including women and the family, slavery, and the economy.

GOVERNMENT AND LAW IN CLASSICAL ATHENS

The hallmark of the Athenian political and legal systems was its amateurism. Most public officials, including those who supervised the courts, were selected by lot and held office for a limited period, typically a year. Thus a great many citizens held public office at some point in their lives, but almost none served for an extended period of time or developed the experience or expertise that would make them professionals. All significant policy decisions were debated and voted on in the Assembly, where the quorum was 6,000 citizens, and all significant legal cases were judged by bodies of 200 to 500 jurors or more. Public prominence was not achieved by election (or selection) to public office but depended rather on a man's ability to sway the

---

Attic Oratory its due place in the history of Attic Prose" (I.xiii). This modern focus on prose style can plausibly be connected to the large role played by prose composition (the translation of English prose into Greek, usually in imitation of specific authors or styles) in the Classics curriculum, especially in Britain.

[18] Dover (1974, 1978). Dover recently commented (1994: 157), "When I began to mine the riches of Attic forensic oratory I was astonished to discover that the mine had never been exploited."

majority of citizens in the Assembly or jurors in court to vote in favor of a proposed course of action or for one of the litigants in a trial. Success was never permanent, and a victory on one policy issue or a verdict in one case could be quickly reversed in another.[19] In such a system the value of public oratory is obvious, and in the fourth century, oratory became the most important cultural institution in Athens, replacing drama as the forum where major ideological concerns were displayed and debated.

Several recent books give good detailed accounts of Athenian government and law,[20] and so a brief sketch can suffice here. The main policy-making body was the Assembly, open to all adult male citizens; a small payment for attendance enabled at least some of the poor to attend along with the leisured rich. In addition, a Council of 500 citizens, selected each year by lot with no one allowed to serve more than two years, prepared material for and made recommendations to the Assembly; a rotating subgroup of this Council served as an executive committee, the Prytany. Finally, numerous officials, most of them selected by lot for one-year terms, supervised different areas of administration and finance. The most important of these were the nine Archons (lit. "rulers"): the eponymous Archon after whom the year was named, the Basileus ("king"),[21] the Polemarch, and the six Thesmothetae. Councilors and almost all these officials underwent a preliminary examination (*dokimasia*) before taking office, and officials submitted to a final accounting (*euthynai*) upon leaving; at these times any citi-

---

[19] In the Assembly this could be accomplished by a reconsideration of the question, as in the famous Mytilenean debate (Thuc. 3.36–50); in court a verdict was final, but its practical effects could be thwarted or reversed by later litigation on a related issue.

[20] For government, see Sinclair 1988, Hansen 1991; for law, MacDowell 1978, Todd 1993, and Boegehold 1995 (Bonner 1927 is still helpful). Much of our information about the legal and political systems comes from a work attributed to Aristotle but perhaps written by a pupil of his, *The Athenian Constitution* (*Ath. Pol.*—conveniently translated with notes by Rhodes 1984). The discovery of this work on a papyrus in Egypt in 1890 caused a major resurgence of interest in Athenian government.

[21] Modern scholars often use the term *archōn basileus* or "king archon," but Athenian sources (e.g., *Ath. Pol.* 57) simply call him the *basileus*.

zen who wished could challenge a person's fitness for his new position or his performance in his recent position.

There was no general taxation of Athenian citizens. Sources of public funding included the annual tax levied on metics, various fees and import duties, and (in the fifth century) tribute from allied cities; but the source that figures most prominently in the orators is the Athenian system of liturgies (*leitourgiai*), by which in a regular rotation the rich provided funding for certain special public needs. The main liturgies were the *chorēgia,* in which a sponsor (*chorēgos*) supervised and paid for the training and performance of a chorus which sang and danced at a public festival,[22] and the trierarchy, in which a sponsor (trierarch) paid to equip and usually commanded a trireme, or warship, for a year. Some of these liturgies required substantial expenditures, but even so, some men spent far more than required in order to promote themselves and their public careers, and litigants often try to impress the jurors by referring to liturgies they have undertaken (see, e.g., Lys. 21.1–5). A further twist on this system was that if a man thought he had been assigned a liturgy that should have gone to someone else who was richer than he, he could propose an exchange of property (*antidosis*), giving the other man a choice of either taking over the liturgy or exchanging property with him. Finally, the rich were also subject to special taxes (*eisphorai*) levied as a percentage of their property in times of need.

The Athenian legal system remained similarly resistant to professionalization. Trials and the procedures leading up to them were supervised by officials, primarily the nine Archons, but their role was purely administrative, and they were in no way equivalent to modern judges. All significant questions about what we would call points of law were presented to the jurors, who considered them together with all other issues when they delivered their verdict at the end of the trial.[23] Trials were "contests" (*agōnes*) between two litigants, each of whom presented his own case to the jurors in a speech, plaintiff first,

---

[22] These included the productions of tragedy and comedy, for which the main expense was for the chorus.

[23] Certain religious "interpreters" (*exēgētai*) were occasionally asked to give their opinion on a legal matter that had a religious dimension (such as the prosecution of a homicide), but although these opinions could be reported in court

then defendant; in some cases each party then spoke again, probably in rebuttal. Since a litigant had only one or two speeches in which to present his entire case, and no issue was decided separately by a judge, all the necessary factual information and every important argument on substance or procedure, fact or law, had to be presented together. A single speech might thus combine narrative, argument, emotional appeal, and various digressions, all with the goal of obtaining a favorable verdict. Even more than today, a litigant's primary task was to control the issue—to determine which issues the jurors would consider most important and which questions they would have in their minds as they cast their votes. We only rarely have both speeches from a trial,[24] and we usually have little or no external evidence for the facts of a case or the verdict. We must thus infer both the facts and the opponent's strategy from the speech we have, and any assessment of the overall effectiveness of a speech and of the logographer's strategy is to some extent speculative.

Before a trial there were usually several preliminary hearings for presenting evidence; arbitration, public and private, was available and sometimes required. These hearings and arbitration sessions allowed each side to become familiar with the other side's case, so that discussions of "what my opponent will say" could be included in one's speech. Normally a litigant presented his own case, but he was often assisted by family or friends. If he wished (and could afford it), he could enlist the services of a logographer, who presumably gave strategic advice in addition to writing a speech. The speeches were timed to ensure an equal hearing for both sides,[25] and all trials were completed within a day. Two hundred or more jurors decided each case in the popular courts, which met in the Agora.[26] Homicide cases and

---

(e.g., Dem. 47.68–73), they had no official legal standing. The most significant administrative decision we hear of is the refusal of the Basileus to accept the case in Antiphon 6 (see 6.37–46).

[24] The exceptions are Demosthenes 19 and Aeschines 2, Aeschines 3 and Demosthenes 18, and Lysias 6 (one of several prosecution speeches) and Andocides 1; all were written for major public cases.

[25] Timing was done by means of a water-clock, which in most cases was stopped during the reading of documents.

[26] See Boegehold 1995.

certain other religious trials (e.g., Lys. 7) were heard by the Council of the Areopagus or an associated group of fifty-one Ephetae. The Areopagus was composed of all former Archons—perhaps 150–200 members at most times. It met on a hill called the Areopagus ("rock of Ares") near the Acropolis.

Jurors for the regular courts were selected by lot from those citizens who registered each year and who appeared for duty that day; as with the Assembly, a small payment allowed the poor to serve. After the speakers had finished, the jurors voted immediately without any formal discussion. The side with the majority won; a tie vote decided the case for the defendant. In some cases where the penalty was not fixed, after a conviction the jurors voted again on the penalty, choosing between penalties proposed by each side. Even when we know the verdict, we cannot know which of the speaker's arguments contributed most to his success or failure. However, a logographer could probably learn from jurors which points had or had not been successful, so that arguments that are found repeatedly in speeches probably were known to be effective in most cases.

The first written laws in Athens were enacted by Draco (ca. 620) and Solon (ca. 590), and new laws were regularly added. At the end of the fifth century the existing laws were reorganized, and a new procedure for enacting laws was instituted; thereafter a group of Law-Givers (*nomothetai*) had to certify that a proposed law did not conflict with any existing laws. There was no attempt, however, to organize legislation systematically, and although Plato, Aristotle, and other philosophers wrote various works on law and law-giving, these were either theoretical or descriptive and had no apparent influence on legislation. Written statutes generally used ordinary language rather than precise legal definitions in designating offenses, and questions concerning precisely what constituted a specific offense or what was the correct interpretation of a written statute were decided (together with other issues) by the jurors in each case. A litigant might, of course, assert a certain definition or interpretation as "something you all know" or "what the lawgiver intended," but such remarks are evidently tendentious and cannot be taken as authoritative.

The result of these procedural and substantive features was that the verdict depended largely on each litigant's speech (or speeches). As one speaker puts it (Ant. 6.18), "When there are no witnesses, you (jurors) are forced to reach a verdict about the case on the basis of the prosecutor's and defendant's words alone; you must be suspicious and examine their accounts in detail, and your vote will necessarily be cast on the basis of likelihood rather than clear knowledge." Even the testimony of witnesses (usually on both sides) is rarely decisive. On the other hand, most speakers make a considerable effort to establish facts and provide legitimate arguments in conformity with established law. Plato's view of rhetoric as a clever technique for persuading an ignorant crowd that the false is true is not borne out by the speeches, and the legal system does not appear to have produced many arbitrary or clearly unjust results.

The main form of legal procedure was a *dikē* ("suit") in which the injured party (or his relatives in a case of homicide) brought suit against the offender. Suits for injuries to slaves would be brought by the slave's master, and injuries to women would be prosecuted by a male relative. Strictly speaking, a *dikē* was a private matter between individuals, though like all cases, *dikai* often had public dimensions. The other major form of procedure was a *graphē* ("writing" or "indictment") in which "anyone who wished" (i.e., any citizen) could bring a prosecution for wrongdoing. *Graphai* were instituted by Solon, probably in order to allow prosecution of offenses where the victim was unable or unlikely to bring suit himself, such as selling a dependent into slavery; but the number of areas covered by *graphai* increased to cover many types of public offenses as well as some apparently private crimes, such as *hybris.*

The system of prosecution by "anyone who wished" also extended to several other more specialized forms of prosecution, like *eisangelia* ("impeachment"), used in cases of treason. Another specialized prosecution was *apagōgē* ("summary arrest"), in which someone could arrest a common criminal (*kakourgos,* lit. "evil-doer"), or have him arrested, on the spot. The reliance on private initiative meant that Athenians never developed a system of public prosecution; rather, they presumed that everyone would keep an eye on the behavior of his political enemies and bring suit as soon as he suspected a crime, both to harm his opponents and to advance his own career. In this way all public officials would be watched by someone. There was no disgrace in admitting that a prosecution was motivated by private enmity.

By the end of the fifth century the system of prosecution by "any one who wished" was apparently being abused by so-called sykophants (*sykophantai*), who allegedly brought or threatened to bring false suits against rich men, either to gain part of the fine that would be levied or to induce an out-of-court settlement in which the accused would pay to have the matter dropped. We cannot gauge the true extent of this problem, since speakers usually provide little evidence to support their claims that their opponents are sykophants, but the Athenians did make sykophancy a crime. They also specified that in many public procedures a plaintiff who either dropped the case or failed to obtain one-fifth of the votes would have to pay a heavy fine of 1,000 drachmas. Despite this, it appears that litigation was common in Athens and was seen by some as excessive.

Over the course of time, the Athenian legal and political systems have more often been judged negatively than positively. Philosophers and political theorists have generally followed the lead of Plato (427–347), who lived and worked in Athens his entire life while severely criticizing its system of government as well as many other aspects of its culture. For Plato, democracy amounted to the tyranny of the masses over the educated elite and was destined to collapse from its own instability. The legal system was capricious and depended entirely on the rhetorical ability of litigants with no regard for truth or justice. These criticisms have often been echoed by modern scholars, who particularly complain that law was much too closely interwoven with politics and did not have the autonomous status it achieved in Roman law and continues to have, at least in theory, in modern legal systems.

Plato's judgments are valid if one accepts the underlying presuppositions, that the aim of law is absolute truth and abstract justice and that achieving the highest good of the state requires thorough and systematic organization. Most Athenians do not seem to have subscribed to either the criticisms or the presuppositions, and most scholars now accept the long-ignored fact that despite major external disruptions in the form of wars and two short-lived coups brought about by one of these wars, the Athenian legal and political systems remained remarkably stable for almost two hundred years (508–320). Moreover, like all other Greek cities at the time, whatever their form of government, Athenian democracy was brought to an end not by internal forces but by the external power of Philip of Macedon and his son Alexander. The legal system never became autonomous, and the rich sometimes complained that they were victims of unscrupulous litigants, but there is no indication that the people wanted to yield control of the legal process to a professional class, as Plato recommended. For most Athenians—Plato being an exception in this and many other matters—one purpose of the legal system was to give everyone the opportunity to have his case heard by other citizens and have it heard quickly and cheaply; and in this it clearly succeeded.

Indeed, the Athenian legal system also served the interests of the rich, even the very rich, as well as the common people, in that it provided a forum for the competition that since Homer had been an important part of aristocratic life. In this competition, the rich used the courts as battlegrounds, though their main weapon was the rhetoric of popular ideology, which hailed the rule of law and promoted the ideal of moderation and restraint.[27] But those who aspired to political leadership and the honor and status that accompanied it repeatedly entered the legal arena, bringing suit against their political enemies whenever possible and defending themselves against suits brought by others whenever necessary. The ultimate judges of these public competitions were the common people, who seem to have relished the dramatic clash of individuals and ideologies. In this respect fourth-century oratory was the cultural heir of fifth-century drama and was similarly appreciated by the citizens. Despite the disapproval of intellectuals like Plato, most Athenians legitimately considered their legal system a hallmark of their democracy and a vital presence in their culture.

THE TRANSLATION OF GREEK ORATORY

The purpose of this series is to provide students and scholars in all fields with accurate, readable translations of all surviving classical Attic oratory, including speeches whose authenticity is disputed, as well as the substantial surviving fragments. In keeping with the originals, the language is for the most part nontechnical. Names of persons and places are given in the (generally more familiar) Latinized forms, and names of officials or legal procedures have been translated into English equivalents, where possible. Notes are intended to provide the nec-

---

[27] Ober 1989 is fundamental; see also Cohen 1995.

essary historical and cultural background; scholarly controversies are generally not discussed. The notes and introductions refer to scholarly treatments in addition to those listed below, which the reader may consult for further information.

Cross-references to other speeches follow the standard numbering system, which is now well established except in the case of Hyperides (for whom the numbering of the Oxford Classical Text is used).[28] References are by work and section (e.g., Dem. 24.73); spurious works are not specially marked; when no author is named (e.g., 24.73), the reference is to the same author as the annotated passage.

ABBREVIATIONS:

Aes.	=	Aeschines
And.	=	Andocides
Ant.	=	Antiphon
Arist.	=	Aristotle
Aristoph.	=	Aristophanes
Ath. Pol.	=	*The Athenian Constitution*
Dem.	=	Demosthenes
Din.	=	Dinarchus
Herod.	=	Herodotus
Hyp.	=	Hyperides
Is.	=	Isaeus
Isoc.	=	Isocrates
Lyc.	=	Lycurgus
Lys.	=	Lysias
Plut.	=	Plutarch
Thuc.	=	Thucydides
Xen.	=	Xenophon

NOTE: The main unit of Athenian currency was the drachma; this was divided into obols and larger amounts were designated minas and talents.

1 drachma	=	6 obols
1 mina	=	100 drachmas
1 talent	=	60 minas (6,000 drachmas)

[28] For a listing of all the orators and their works, with classifications (forensic, deliberative, epideictic) and rough dates, see Edwards 1994: 74–79.

It is impossible to give an accurate equivalence in terms of modern currency, but it may be helpful to remember that the daily wage of some skilled workers was a drachma in the mid-fifth century and 2–2½ drachmas in the later fourth century. Thus it may not be too misleading to think of a drachma as worth about $50 or £33 and a talent as about $300,000 or £200,000 in 1997 currency.

BIBLIOGRAPHY OF WORKS CITED

Boegehold, Alan L., 1995: *The Lawcourts at Athens: Sites, Buildings, Equipment, Procedure, and Testimonia.* Princeton.

Bonner, Robert J., 1927: *Lawyers and Litigants in Ancient Athens.* Chicago.

Cohen, David, 1995: *Law, Violence and Community in Classical Athens.* Cambridge.

Cole, Thomas, 1991: *The Origins of Rhetoric in Ancient Greece.* Baltimore.

Dover, Kenneth J., 1968: *Lysias and the Corpus Lysiacum.* Berkeley.

———, 1974: *Greek Popular Morality in the Time of Plato and Aristotle.* Oxford.

———, 1978: *Greek Homosexuality.* London.

———, 1994: *Marginal Comment.* London.

Edwards, Michael, 1994: *The Attic Orators.* London.

Gagarin, Michael, and Paul Woodruff, 1995: *Early Greek Political Thought from Homer to the Sophists.* Cambridge.

Hansen, Mogens Herman, 1991: *The Athenian Democracy in the Age of Demosthenes.* Oxford.

Jebb, Richard, 1875: *The Attic Orators,* 2 vols. London.

Kennedy, George A., 1963: *The Art of Persuasion in Greece.* Princeton.

Kerferd, G. B., 1981: *The Sophistic Movement.* Cambridge.

MacDowell, Douglas M., 1978: *The Law in Classical Athens.* London.

———, ed. 1990: *Demosthenes, Against Meidias.* Oxford.

Ober, Josiah, 1989: *Mass and Elite in Democratic Athens.* Princeton.

Rhodes, P. J., trans., 1984: *Aristotle, The Athenian Constitution.* Penguin Books.

Sinclair, R. K., 1988: *Democracy and Participation in Athens.* Cambridge.

Todd, Stephen, 1993: *The Shape of Athenian Law.* Oxford.

Trevett, Jeremy, 1992: *Apollodoros the Son of Pasion.* Oxford.
———, 1996: "Did Demosthenes Publish His Deliberative Speeches?" *Hermes* 124: 425–441.
Usher, Stephen, 1976: "Lysias and His Clients," *Greek, Roman and Byzantine Studies* 17: 31–40.
———, trans., 1974–1985: *Dionysius of Halicarnassus, Critical Essays.* 2 vols. Loeb Classical Library. Cambridge, MA.
Wooten, Cecil W., trans., 1987: *Hermogenes' On Types of Style.* Chapel Hill, NC.
Worthington, Ian, 1994: "The Canon of the Ten Attic Orators," in *Persuasion: Greek Rhetoric in Action,* ed. Ian Worthington. London: 244–263.
Yunis, Harvey, 1996: *Taming Democracy: Models of Political Rhetoric in Classical Athens.* Ithaca, NY.

ADDENDA

Carey, Christopher, 1997: *Trials from Classical Athens.* London.
Usher, Stephen, 1999: *Greek Oratory: Tradition and Originality.* Oxford.

SUPPLEMENTARY BIBLIOGRAPHY FOR VOLUME 5

Badian, Ernst, 1961: "Harpalus," *Journal of Hellenic Studies* 81: 16–43.
Blass, Friedrich, 1898: *Die attische Beredsamkeit*², vol. 3.2. Leipzig.
Bosworth, A. B., 1988: *Conquest and Empire: The Reign of Alexander the Great.* Cambridge.
Davies, J. K., 1971: *Athenian Propertied Families.* Oxford.
Faraguna, Michele, 1992: *Atene nell' eta di Alessandro: problemi politici, economici, finanziari.* Rome.
Goldstein, J. A., 1968: *The Letters of Demosthenes.* New York.
Hansen, Mogens H., 1975: *Eisangelia: The Sovereignty of the People's Court in Athens in the Fourth Century B.C. and the Impeachment of Generals and Politicians.* Odense.
Harris, Edward M., 1995: *Aeschines and Athenian Politics.* Oxford.
Kennedy, George A., 1994: *A New History of Classical Rhetoric.* Princeton.
Sealey, Rafael, 1993: *Demosthenes and His Time.* New York.

Worthington, Ian, 1992: *A Historical Commentary on Dinarchus: Rhetoric and Conspiracy in Later Fourth-Century Athens.* Ann Arbor.

———, ed., 1994a: *Persuasion. Greek Rhetoric in Action.* London.

———, ed., 1994b: *Ventures into Greek History. Essays in Honour of N. G. L. Hammond.* Oxford.

———, 1999: *Greek Orators 2, Dinarchus 1 and Hyperides 5 and 6.* Warminster.

———, ed., 2000: *Demosthenes: Statesman and Orator.* London.

DINARCHUS

Translated with introduction by Ian Worthington

INTRODUCTION TO DINARCHUS

Dinarchus, the son of Sostratus, was born in Corinth in about 361/0.[1] He moved to Athens, by then the leading city for the study of rhetoric, when he was relatively young. This was probably a little before 338, for he fought at the battle of Chaeronea, at which a combined force of Greek cities, including Athens, was defeated by Philip II of Macedon (see 1.78n). In Athens he was a pupil of Theophrastus, Aristotle's successor as head of the Lyceum, and he also apparently attended the lectures of Demetrius of Phalerum. His career as a logographer would certainly have started by the mid 330s, and his metic status allowed him to devote himself entirely to it while he lived in Athens. As a result, he amassed considerable wealth.

In 323 Dinarchus was commissioned by the state to write speeches for one of the prosecutors appointed by the people in the politically charged Harpalus trials, which were set against a background of intrigue in the time of Alexander the Great of Macedon (see further below). This was a turning point in his career, elevating him to the status of one of the leading logographers of the day, and he flourished especially during the ten-year regime (317–307) of Demetrius of Phalerum, the puppet king of Cassander of Macedon. His friendship with Macedonians and Macedonian sympathizers in this period

[1] We do not have much information about Dinarchus' life. What little we have comes from four later and often contradictory sources: Dionysius of Halicarnassus' essay on Dinarchus, Pseudo-Plutarch's brief life (*Moralia* 850b–e), Photius, and the *Suda* (*s.v.* Dinarchus). Dionysius is the most reliable of these. This point and many others in the Introduction and in the notes to the Translation are treated more fully in Worthington 1992. The reader is referred to this work for further details throughout.

would be his undoing, however. When Demetrius Poliorcetes ousted Demetrius of Phalerum from Athens in 307, Dinarchus was forced to leave the city. He went to Chalcis, where he lived in exile for fifteen years. He returned to Athens in 292/1 with the consent of Demetrius Poliorcetes, who may have been persuaded to recall him by Theophrastus.

While lodging in Athens with his friend Proxenus, Dinarchus lost a large amount of money. He then sued his host for two talents, stating that when he arrived in Proxenus' house he had with him 285 gold staters and silver articles to the value of twenty minas. This was the first time, so we are told, that Dinarchus himself delivered a speech, but the outcome of the trial is unknown. We do not know when, how, or where Dinarchus died.

Dinarchus was a prolific writer; he had expertise in many branches of the law and wrote prosecution and defense speeches (see the list of genuine public and private speeches given by Dionysius at the end of his essay). Although some later writers mention 160 speeches of his, the figure of 61 speeches given by Dionysius (who cites titles and opening words in his list at *Dinarchus* 10 and 12) is probably more accurate. Aside from scattered fragments, only 3 speeches survive, those written against Demosthenes, Aristogeiton, and Philocles (1, 2, and 3), when the three men were brought to trial (along with others) in 323 for their role in the Harpalus scandal. The first has survived almost in full, but the latter two are incomplete.

Despite being a leading logographer, Dinarchus' rhetorical style has been condemned since antiquity, with the notable exceptions of Callimachus (*Suda, s.v.* Kallimachos; cf. Athenaeus 15.669c) and Cicero (*De oratore* 2.23.94; cf. *Brutus* 9.36). To Dionysius, for example, Dinarchus was a "rustic Demosthenes," inferior to someone like Demosthenes in his disjointed arrangement of material and incoherent composition (*Dinarchus* 8). Modern opinion spanning a century concurs.[2] However, it must be stressed that Dinarchus was included in the Canon of the Ten Attic Orators, and that since so

---

[2] For example, Blass 1898: 289–333; Jebb 1875: 2.374; J. F. Dobson, *The Greek Orators* (London, 1919), 302–307; Kennedy 1963: 256–257; and M. Nouhaud and L. Dors-Méary, *Dinarque Discours,* Budé text (Paris: 1990), xvi.

many orators must have been excluded from it, his inclusion can testify only to his literary merits and reputation.[3] Indeed, there is much about Dinarchus' style that is worthy of commendation, in particular his use of ring composition.

Ring composition is a stylistic device for organizing subject matter within a particular work (be it a poem, play, history, or speech) into a pattern with echoes of language and themes. The device operates on a series of levels: a work is divided into a number of parts, which may be called the main framework or primary level. Each of these primary-level parts may then be subdivided, and each of these secondary-level parts may be further subdivided, and then subdivided again, each division having a structure of ring composition. The result is a number of stories or narratives within "the" story or "the" narrative (which is the primary level). The technique is used at highly sophisticated levels by Dinarchus in the speech *Against Demosthenes,* where reiteration of a theme tends to enclose a particular structural unit. The sophistication of this technique tells against criticisms of his poor compositional abilities or incoherent arrangement of material.

When Alexander became king in 336 he was faced with a revolt by the Greek states, which had been under the control of Philip II since the battle of Chaeronea in 338. Alexander stormed into Greece with such unexpected speed that in a matter of months he had subdued the Greeks and reimposed his father's League of Corinth (only Sparta remained aloof).[4] Alexander was duly proclaimed its leader, and the Persian invasion, first put forward by his father, was again endorsed. Then in 335 Thebes revolted, supported by some states (including initially Athens) and by money from the Persian king. Alexander swept against the Thebans, and, when they defied him, he forced the city to surrender and razed it to the ground.

From that time on until Alexander's death in 323 Greece remained passive; the lesson of Thebes had been well learned, as Alexander intended. The only deviation from this passivity was the abortive war of Agis III of Sparta from 331 to 330. He attempted to unite the Greeks

---

[3] See Ian Worthington, "The Canon of the Ten Attic Orators," in Worthington 1994a.

[4] On the historical background, see Bosworth 1988: 28–34.

against Macedon but failed to do so.[5] Despite the obvious cost to Greek autonomy, Macedonian hegemony of Greece brought with it a period of peace, which more importantly allowed the Greeks some prosperity after their many decades of fighting. Nowhere was this prosperity more evident than in Athens, thanks to the administration of Lycurgus, the treasurer of the Theoric Fund, who was even able to initiate a building program and make other reforms. In 330 Athens was the venue for two trials of no small political interest, the prosecution of Leocrates by Lycurgus (see Lyc. 1) and the great clash between Demosthenes and Aeschines (see Dem. 18 and Aes. 3). These trials were not, however, linked to the issue of Macedonian domination but were personal and linked to domestic politics.[6] Athens, thanks to Demosthenes, prudently kept a low profile internationally for most of the 330s and 320s.

Then in 324 as Alexander returned from the East, his imperial treasurer Harpalus, the son of Machatas, absconded to Athens with a powerful force of six thousand mercenaries, five thousand talents of stolen money, and thirty warships to be deployed against Alexander. His debauchery at his financial headquarters in Babylon made him an obvious candidate for Alexander's retribution, and inciting a revolt of the Greeks was his only chance for survival.

The Athenians—and the Greeks as a whole—had cause to welcome Harpalus' offer and revolt, owing to the recent arrival of Nicanor of Stagira, who had brought Alexander's Exiles Decree for proclamation at Olympia. Under the terms of the decree, all Greek cities (excluding Thebes) were to receive back their exiles, and the Athenians were also required to return the strategically important island of Samos to the native Samians. Though the Greeks refused to receive back their exiles (cf. Din. 1.58 and 94), resistance was futile: the Macedonians controlled Greece, as demonstrated in the final clause of the decree, in which Alexander stated that Antipater would have authority

[5] To the bibliography in Worthington 1992: 185–189 add E. Badian, "Agis III: Revisions and Reflections" in Worthington 1994b: 258–292.

[6] See N. Sawada, "Athenian Politics in the Age of Alexander the Great: A Reconsideration of the Trial of Ctesiphon," *Chiron* 26 (1996): 57–82 and Worthington, "Demosthenes' (In)activity in the Reign of Alexander the Great" in Worthington 2000: 90–113.

to coerce any Greek city to receive back its exiles. Also playing a factor on the political scene now was the debate whether Alexander should be worshipped as a god by the mainland Greeks.[7]

Despite the outcry against the Exiles Decree, which clearly flouted the autonomy of the Greek poleis, and the debate over worshipping a living Alexander, Demosthenes advised the Athenians against using Harpalus' force in a revolt against the king. The Assembly ordered the general Philocles not to allow Harpalus into the city, and consequently he was forced to make for the mercenary base at Taenarum in the southern Peloponnese. Not long after (about June 324),[8] he returned to Athens, this time as a suppliant, with a much reduced force and less money, and was admitted into the city by Philocles. A second Assembly meeting was held, at which Hyperides spoke in favor of accepting Harpalus' offer of support, but again Demosthenes won the day. Harpalus was imprisoned, the money he had brought with him, allegedly seven hundred talents, was impounded on the Acropolis the same day (Din. 1.70 and 89; cf. 90; Hyp. 5.9–10), and a guard posted over the money (cf. Din. 1.62). Demosthenes' course was no doubt influenced by the fact that the Athenians were about to send an embassy to Alexander over the Exiles Decree—as other states were doing—and to accept Harpalus' offer might jeopardize its success.

Demosthenes was then sent to Olympia as *architheōros* (head of the Athenian religious delegation) to the festival in order to discuss the terms of the Exiles Decree with Nicanor. Soon after he returned he spoke in favor of recognizing Alexander's divine status, a *volte face* that was seen as the result of his accepting a bribe (Din. 1.94, 103, Hyp. 5.31–32). While Demosthenes may have taken a bribe, it is more likely that he supported the apotheosis simply to placate Alexander and to bolster the chances of success of the Athenian embassy to Alexander. After all, did it matter whether Alexander was called a god if he ruled in the Athenians' favor? The remark of Demades that may be connected to the Samian issue, that the Athenians were so concerned

[7] To the bibliography in Worthington 1992: 262–265 add G. L. Cawkwell, "The Deification of Alexander the Great: A Note" in Worthington 1994b: 293–306.

[8] On chronology, see Ian Worthington, "The Chronology of the Harpalus Affair," *Symbolae Osloenses* 61 (1986): 63–76.

about heaven that they stood to lose the earth, sums up the situation nicely.

Ultimately Demosthenes' strategy did not pay off. After he returned from Olympia, Harpalus escaped. He fled first to Taenarum and thence to Crete, where he was murdered. In Athens, accusations were leveled against Demosthenes and several others that they had taken bribes from Harpalus in order to facilitate his escape, and when only half of his alleged seven hundred talents was found on the Acropolis, the case seemed open and shut. At a meeting of the Assembly Demosthenes struck a counter blow: protesting his innocence, he proposed that the Areopagus investigate the matter under the procedure known as *apophasis,* which had developed in the fourth century.[9] He also offered to submit to the death penalty if the Areopagus found him guilty, and others also suspected followed suit, such as Philocles (Din. 3.2, 5, 16, 21; cf. Hyp. 5.34 for unnamed others). As the inquiry progressed, he issued a challenge (*proklēsis*) to the people to present the Areopagus with evidence for their accusation (Din. 1.5, Hyp. 5.2). At this point, he confessed to taking some money from Harpalus, not for himself but for the Theoric Fund (Hyp. 5.12–13).

After six months (Din. 1.45) the Areopagus issued its report accusing Demosthenes and several others of receiving bribes from Harpalus (in Demosthenes' case, twenty talents of gold). Around the same time news arrived that Alexander had rejected the Athenian embassy's pleas over the Exiles Decree. The coincidence is too much. The Areopagites were reacting angrily at Demosthenes' failed diplomatic strategy over the Exiles Decree; they may even have hoped that their action would curry favor with Alexander, should they appeal again. Demosthenes himself pleaded that he had been sacrificed to please the king (Hyp. 5.14) and resorted to a second *proklēsis,* aimed this time at the Areopagites, to produce the evidence on which their findings had been based (Din. 1.6, 61, Hyp. 5.3). However, he was brought to trial in about March 323. Others accused of complicity in the affair, and also tried then, included Aristogeiton, Aristonicus, Cephisophon,

[9] The Areopagus inquired into those suspected of treason and delivered a preliminary verdict (*apophasis*) under this procedure. Anyone found guilty at this stage was then brought to trial for a final verdict in an ordinary lawcourt. See R. W. Wallace, *The Areopagos Council* (Baltimore, 1989), 198–201.

Charicles (the son-in-law of the general Phocion), Demades, Hagnonides, the general Philocles, and Polyeuctus of Sphettus, some of whom are mentioned in Dinarchus' and Hyperides' speeches. There were probably others also indicted for taking bribes, whose names are lost to us. Almost all were acquitted, apart from Demosthenes.[10] After one week he fled into self-imposed exile, not to return until after Alexander's death when the Lamian War (323–322) was in full swing.

The three extant speeches of Dinarchus, along with Hyperides' speech against Demosthenes (Hyp. 5, translated below in this volume),[11] are our only surviving contemporary sources for the Harpalus affair and indeed the only relatively complete ones we have from the trials of those accused in it. Small fragments exist of Dinarchus' speeches against three others accused, Aristonicus and Hagnonides (Dionysius of Halicarnassus, *Dinarchus* 10), and Polyeuctus of Sphettus (cf. Din. 1.100), but these furnish no additional information. It is possible that we have a fragment of a speech by Stratocles, another prosecutor at Demosthenes' trial, since he uses the same imagery about Thebes' destruction as Dinarchus at 1.24.[12]

The implications of the Harpalus affair (and Exiles Decree) as they affect the Greek attitude to Macedonian rule are significant, since they must have tested the subservience of the Greeks. However, there was no rebellion, and that Demosthenes' counsel prevailed at the meeting of the Assembly held when Harpalus had been admitted into the city shows that the majority of the Athenians had no wish to wage war against Alexander then. They sent a diplomatic envoy to the king about Harpalus and joined the rest of the Greeks who resorted to diplomacy in order to counter the decree. Thus, the Greeks were not ready to seize the first chance to revolt against their Macedonian mas-

---

[10] Except for Demosthenes, probably only Philocles was condemned (Dem., *Epistle* 3.31). Aristogeiton was acquitted (Dem., *Epistle* 3.37, 42), as were Hagnonides and Polyeuctus of Sphettus (Pseudo-Plut., *Moralia* 846c–d), and Demades was probably fined (Din. 1.29, 104).

[11] See also Worthington 1999: 94–113, 184–204 for a text, translation, and commentary on Hyp. 5.

[12] See Blass 1898: 319–320. The fragment says: "The city of the Thebans, which fought on the same side in the war against Philip with you, is being ploughed and sown."

ters but came to accept Macedonian rule, under which life was not so harsh, and were more willing to resort to diplomacy than to revolt.[13] Until, that is, the news came of Alexander's death (10 June 323), and then, with the exception of the Boeotian and the Euboean Leagues, Greece revolted. While Alexander was alive, the force of his own personality made rebellion out of the question; Alexander dead, however, was another matter.

BIBLIOGRAPHY

Major Ancient Sources: Dinarchus 1–3 (primarily of value for the Harpalus affair), Hyperides 5 (again, primarily of value for the Harpalus affair), Diodorus Siculus 17.108.4–109, Plutarch, *Demosthenes* 25–27 and *Phocion* 21–22, Pseudo-Plutarch, *Moralia* 846, and Quintus Curtius Rufus 10.1.45–2.4.

Commentaries: Worthington 1992 and Worthington 1999.

Oratory/Law: Kennedy 1963, Kennedy 1994, MacDowell 1978, Worthington 1994a.

Historical Background: Badian 1961, Bosworth 1988, Goldstein 1968, Sealey 1993, Worthington 1992, Worthington 1994b (especially the chapters by Badian, Cawkwell, and Worthington), Worthington 2000 (especially the chapters by Buckler and Worthington).

The text used is the Teubner edition of Dinarchus by N. C. Conomis (Leipzig: 1975). See also Worthington 1999 for a text.

---

[13] See Ian Worthington, "The Harpalus Affair and the Greek Response to the Macedonian Hegemony" in Worthington 1994b: 307–330; see too Worthington, "Demosthenes' (In)activity in the Reign of Alexander the Great" in Worthington 2000: 90–113, which considers Demosthenes' policy throughout the entire reign of Alexander.

1. AGAINST DEMOSTHENES

INTRODUCTION

The speech against Demosthenes is Dinarchus' only complete speech, though even it has three minor lacunae at chapters 33/34, 64, and 82. Like the other two speeches, it was written for a trial in the notorious Harpalus affair (on which see the Introduction to Dinarchus).

Demosthenes was the first to be tried (1.105). The charge was taking a bribe of twenty talents of gold from Harpalus. Ten men, including Himeraeus, Hyperides, Menesaechmus, Patrocles or Procles, Pytheas, and Stratocles, prosecuted him. Stratocles of Diomeia spoke first in the prosecution line-up, followed by Dinarchus' client (either Himeraeus or Menesaechmus), but the remaining order is unknown. Hyperides wrote and delivered his own speech; Dinarchus, being a metic (resident alien), of course could not speak in court but was commissioned by the state to write speeches for one of the formal prosecutors.

Demosthenes faced a serious charge, namely, treason for accepting a bribe that jeopardized the best interests of the city. The prescribed penalty was either a fine of ten times the amount of bribe taken (with *atimia* until paid) or death (*Ath. Pol.* 54.2, Din. 1.60, Hyp. 5.24; cf. Andoc. 1.73–79, Dem. 21.113, Aes. 3.232); however, he was fined only fifty talents and was imprisoned. Soon after he fled into exile for several months.

The Areopagus' report into the affair significantly cited no evidence against those it accused of taking a bribe, but merely gave their names together with the amounts supposedly taken (Hyp. 5.6). Thus, the strategy of Dinarchus (and of Hyperides) against Demosthenes (and against the others accused) revolved around the premise that the Areopagus did not need to cite any evidence to support its findings because its prestige and reputation alone should be sufficient for the jurors (Din. 1.55). This point comes at the very center of Dinarchus' speech, as the ring composition reveals (for structures, see Worthington 1992). He also makes much use of Athens' past history to argue that the good and bad fortunes of a city stem from the policies of its leaders. Demosthenes' corruption and worthlessness have made Athens' prosperity and power decline, he says, and Athens will continue to suffer unless Demosthenes' influence in the city is ended. He urges the execution of Demosthenes by often referring to Demosthenes' decree subjecting himself to the death penalty if found guilty.

It is significant that although the Areopagus also gave no proof against the others indicted in the affair, most were acquitted (see the Introduction to Dinarchus). Since there was the same lack of evidence in all the cases, all those accused should have been either condemned or acquitted—a fact also recognized by the prosecution (Din. 1.113, 2.21, Hyp. 5.5–7). Thus, the case can be made that Demosthenes was a political scapegoat.

1. AGAINST DEMOSTHENES

[1] Athenians, your popular leader has pronounced a sentence of death on himself if it be proved that he took any sum from Harpalus, and he has been unequivocally convicted of taking bribes from those whom in the past he claimed he opposed. Since Stratocles has said a great deal and the majority of the charges have already been detailed, and as for the actual report, the Council of the Areopagus has published fair and true findings, and Stratocles has already outlined the consequences of this matter and has read out the pertinent decrees, [2] it remains for us, Athenians, especially when engaged in a case as important as this—the magnitude of which has never been encountered in the city—to make a common plea to all of you. Firstly, be sympathetic to those of us still to speak should we repeat points previously made. We will not do so to annoy you but to whip up your

anger by our repetition. Secondly, do not betray the common rights of the entire city nor trade the public safety for the pleadings of the defendant. [3] You should consider, Athenians, that just as this man Demosthenes is on trial before you, so are you before your peers. These are waiting to see what decision you will bring concerning the country's interests: whether you will surrender yourselves to the personal corruption and venality of these men or will make clear to all mankind that you detest those who take bribes to the detriment of the country. You did not order the Areopagus' investigation so that you could acquit them but in order to exact suitable punishment for their crimes when its findings were declared. [4] This decision is now up to you. When the Assembly voted in favor of a lawful decree and when all the citizens wanted to determine which politicians dared to take money from Harpalus to the disgrace and danger of the city, and, further, when you and many others, Demosthenes, proposed in the decree that the Areopagus should investigate these men—as is its traditional right—to see if any have taken gold from Harpalus, the Council of the Areopagus began its inquiry.

[5] Regardless of your challenges, it made the right decision, and it did not wish to subvert the truth and its own prestige because of you. Yet, gentlemen, as the Areopagites themselves said, the Council well knew beforehand the power of these men and their influence as orators and politicians. But if any harm or danger was threatening its country, it did not think that it should pay attention to any slander that would be directed against it. [6] Although it seemed to the people that the investigation was conducted fairly and with expediency, accusations, challenges, and charges have come from Demosthenes since he has been shown to have taken twenty talents of gold. Shall the Council, which is sufficiently trustworthy to establish justice and truth in cases of willful murder, and which has the right to pass life and death judgments on each citizen, and to champion those who died a violent death, and to expel or punish by execution those who have transgressed any law in the city, shall it now be powerless to exact justice in connection with the money that Demosthenes has been shown to have taken?

[7] "Yes! The Council has lied against Demosthenes"—this is the overriding argument in his defense. Has it lied against you and De-

mades?[1] It is not safe even to speak the truth against you men, so it seems! Did you not order that body to investigate many public affairs in the past and, because of its findings, praise its methods? Has the Council made false declarations against these men, whom the entire city cannot force to act rightly? Dear Heracles! [8] Why then, Demosthenes, did you agree in the Assembly to the death penalty on yourself if the Council should report against you? Why have you yourself destroyed many others by steadfastly endorsing the reports of the Council? What body shall the people now approach, or whom shall it order to investigate puzzling and major crimes if it is to find out the truth? [9] Despite claiming to be the people's man, you are dishonoring the Council, previously held in high repute. People trusted their lives to it; they often entrusted the constitution and democracy to it, which—although you are about to slander it—has protected your life from the many threats you say have been made against it and which guards the sacred deposits on which the safety of the city lies.

[10] In one way the Council is suffering a just retribution—for I shall say what I think. It had two alternatives before it. Either it should conduct the previous investigation over the three hundred talents which came from the Persian King, as the Assembly ordered.[2] In this way, by convicting this monster and exposing those who shared in that money and the treachery over Thebes—which this man betrayed—we would be free of this demagogue, who would be duly punished. [11] Or, if you wanted to pardon Demosthenes for these things and have many men in the city ready to take bribes against you, the Coun-

---

[1] Demades is paired with Demosthenes elsewhere (1.11, 45, 89, 101, 104, 2.14; cf. Hyp. 5.25–26), perhaps because he was the next to be tried in the order of prosecution (cf. 2.15). He played an influential role in political life and received the state benefactions of a statue and *sitēsis* (free meals from the city) for his mission to Alexander the Great after the fall of Thebes in 335 when the king had demanded the surrender of several leading Athenian statesmen (see 1.32n). He proposed Alexander's apotheosis, for which he was later prosecuted and fined ten talents.

[2] A reference to the money given by the Persian King to help the revolt of Thebes in 335; cf. 1.18. Aeschines (3.156–157, 239–240) and Hyperides (5.17, 25) also connect Demosthenes with receiving money from Persia and betraying Thebes to its destruction. However, only the oratorical sources accuse Demosthenes of this.

cil should not have undertaken an investigation into the money recently reported, since it knew your wishes in the previous case. Yet despite the excellence and justice of these recent reports against this man and the others, and despite the fact that the Council of the Areopagus has not been swayed by the influence of either Demosthenes or Demades but has deemed justice itself and truth of more consequence, [12] Demosthenes nevertheless goes around slandering the Council and telling stories about himself that he will perhaps tell you in an effort to deceive you. Things like: "I made the Thebans your allies."[3] No, Demosthenes, you harmed the common interests of both our states. Or, "I brought everyone into line at Chaeronea." No again; on the contrary, you yourself and no one else fled from the line there.[4] Or, "I was an ambassador on many embassies on your behalf." [13] I do not know what he would have done or said if what he had advocated on these missions had turned out to be successful! After touring the whole world arranging these misfortunes and disasters, he thinks he should be given the greatest privileges: to take bribes against the country and to say and do what he wishes against the people.

[14] Athenians, you did not take into account the actions of Timotheus, who sailed around the Peloponnese and defeated the Spartans in a naval battle off Corcyra.[5] He was the son of Conon[6] who freed the

---

[3] The alliance achieved by Demosthenes between Athens and Thebes in 339, shortly before the battle of Chaeronea (on which see 1.78n); cf. Dem. 18.153.

[4] That Demosthenes deserted his post at Chaeronea (cf. 71, 81; Aes. 3.7, 148, 151–152, 159, 175–176, 181, 187, 244, 253) is untrue. In Athenian law, those who fled and were then found guilty in a court of law lost their personal rights (Andoc. 1.73), but this situation clearly did not befall Demosthenes.

[5] Cf. 3.17. Timotheus defeated a Spartan fleet off Corcyra in 375, and in 367/6 he besieged Samos, then occupied by a Persian garrison. It capitulated ten months later, and Athenian cleruchs (colonists; cf. Hyp. 1.17n) were sent there. He was then appointed to the campaign to retake Amphipolis, and while campaigning in Macedonia he was occupied with the sieges to which Dinarchus refers here. However, in 356/5 he was tried for alleged negligence and fined one hundred talents, which forced him into an exile in Chalcis, where he died two or three years later.

[6] Cf. Dem. 20.69. In 394 Conon, with Persian help, annihilated the Peloponnesian fleet at the battle of Cnidus (Dem. 20.68, 70), which was a major blow to the Spartan hegemony of the Greeks.

Greeks, and he took Samos, Methone, Pydna, Potidaea, and twenty other cities as well. You did not let such services affect the trial then taking place or the oaths by which you cast your votes, but you fined him one hundred talents because Aristophon[7] said he took money from the Chians and the Rhodians. [15] Will you not then punish this despicable creature and Scythian[8]—I'm almost speechless with rage—whom not just one man but the entire Areopagus Council investigated and showed that he possessed money against your interests and accepted bribes against the city? He has been proved guilty. Make him an example to others. Not only is he known to have taken money from the Great King but also he enriched himself at the city's own expense, and just recently he even helped himself to some of the money brought into Athens by Harpalus. [16] And yet the embassies upon which Demosthenes served are but a fraction of the noble deeds performed by Timotheus. Which one of you would not ridicule anyone presuming to listen to this man, when he proudly boasts and compares his deeds to those of Timotheus and Conon? You must not compare this outcast to those whose deeds on your behalf were worthy of the city and your ancestors. I shall now produce the decree concerning Timotheus, and then return to my case against Demosthenes. Read it.

[DECREE]

[17] Such was the nature of this citizen,[9] Demosthenes, who might rightly have gained the sympathy and gratitude of his fellow politicians. He performed great deeds for the city by actions and not by words, and he stayed loyal to the same policy rather than switching back and forth like you. When he was put to death, he asked for no special benefits that would make him superior to the laws and did not think that those who have sworn to vote according to the laws should regard anything as more important than their duty. But he was ready to be condemned, if the jurors so decided, and did not plead circumstances or voice opinions in public that he did not hold.

[18] Gentlemen of Athens, will you not execute this accursed man?

---

[7] The leading prosecutor of Timotheus at his trial.

[8] A reference to Demosthenes' alleged illegitimacy (cf. Aes. 3.171–172), although most scholars reject the charge.

[9] That is, Timotheus.

On top of many other great errors he ignored the destruction of the city of Thebes, even though he had taken three hundred talents from the Persian King for its defense.[10] The Arcadians came to the Isthmus and sent away the embassy from Antipater—it had no success—but they welcomed the embassy from the hard-pressed Thebans, which had reached them with difficulty by sea and was bearing a suppliant's olive-branch and heralds' wands plaited, as they said, from young shoots. [19] The Thebans came to tell the Arcadians that they had not revolted from a desire to break their friendship with the Greeks, nor did they not want to do anything in opposition to Greece, but they were no longer able to bear the conduct of the Macedonians in the city, or to suffer slavery, or to witness the abuses committed against free people. [20] Although the Arcadians were willing to help them and pitied them in their misfortunes, they made it clear that although they were constrained because of circumstances to follow Alexander with their bodies, in spirit they supported the Thebans and the freedom of the Greeks. Since their general Astylus[11] was open to bribery, as Stratocles also has said, and demanded ten talents to bring the relief force to the Thebans, the envoys sought out this man, who they knew had the King's gold, and begged and beseeched him to give the money for the deliverance of their city. [21] But this miserable, impious, and mercenary man had no desire to part with a mere ten talents from the huge capital that he had, even though he saw such high hopes dawning for the safety of Thebes. Instead, he allowed others to furnish this money, just as Stratocles said, so as to persuade the Arcadians who had marched out to go back home and not help the Thebans.

[22] Do you think the evils that Demosthenes and his venality have been responsible for are minor or have little effect on the rest of Greece? Do you think that he should get any pity from you for such transgressions, rather than the ultimate penalty for his recent crimes and those of the past? Athenians, all mankind will hear the judgment that you deliver today: they will take note of you the judges and how you deal with the man who has committed such iniquities. [23] You

---

[10] See 1.10n.

[11] Little is known of the Arcadian leader Astylus. Here and in 21 Dinarchus tells us that Astylus demanded a bribe of ten talents to secure Arcadian support for Thebes, but Aes. 3.240 gives the sum as nine talents of silver.

imposed extreme and inexorable penalties on others for crimes of much less import than those perpetrated by this man. You executed Menon the miller because he had a free boy from Pallene in his mill.[12] You inflicted death on Themistius of Aphidna because he assaulted the Rhodian lyre player at the Eleusinia,[13] and on Euthymachus because he put the Olynthian girl in his brothel.[14] **[24]** But thanks to this traitor, the children and wives of the Thebans were divided among the tents of the barbarians, a neighboring and allied city has been torn from the middle of Greece, and the city of Thebes, which shared the war against Philip with you, is being ploughed and sown.[15] I repeat: it is being ploughed and sown! I tell you this contemptible man had no pity for a city so piteously destroyed, even though he went there as your envoy, many times sharing the food and drink with its people, and claims he made them your ally. He often turned to them when they were affluent, but he has betrayed them when they were struck by misfortune. **[25]** When the democracy in our city had been overthrown,[16] and the exiles were being mustered in Thebes by Thrasybulus for the seizure of Phyle, the Thebans, as our elders say, despite the strength of the Spartans and their refusal to let any Athenian enter or leave, nevertheless aided the return of the democrats and passed the decree, so many times read out to you, that they would overlook any Athenian bearing arms passing through their territory.[17] **[26]** But this man, who is so closely associated with our allies, as he will presently

---

[12] The details are unknown; evidently it was illegal to confine an Athenian citizen, a violation of a citizen's rights that the Athenians valued so highly, hence the death penalty was imposed on Menon for his crime.

[13] Nothing is known about Themistius.

[14] This episode is probably to be connected to the betrayal of Olynthus, the chief city of the Chalcidian League, to Philip II in 348 (cf. 1.26 and 1.28).

[15] On the razing of Thebes in 335 by Alexander, see the Introduction to Dinarchus.

[16] In 404/3 by the Thirty.

[17] The restoration of democracy in 403 after the oligarchic rule of the Thirty was a favorite topos among the orators (cf. Lyc. 1.61, Aes. 3.191–192, 195, 208). When Athens was ruled by the Thirty (404/3), the Spartans ordered that anyone discovering an exile was to return him to Athens and the Thirty or be liable to a fine of five talents. The Thebans, however, decreed that Boeotia would offer refuge to any Athenian exile and imposed a fine of one talent on any who contra-

tell you, did no such thing in return, and did not want to part with any of the money that he received for their safety. Gentlemen, remember these things, and bear in mind the disasters that came about when Olynthus and Thebes fell because of traitors.[18] Decide wisely now for your own best interests: get rid of those wanting to take bribes against their country, and fix your hopes of safety on yourselves and on the gods. [27] For by only one way, gentlemen of Athens, and one way alone will you make mankind better: if you expose those criminals who are famous and punish them as befits their crimes. In the case of ordinary defendants no one knows—or wants to learn—how they have been punished when convicted, but everyone will know about eminent men, and they praise the jurors when they do not sacrifice justice to the reputation of the defendants. Read the decree of the Thebans. Quote the evidence. Read the letters.

[DECREE; EVIDENCE; LETTERS]

[28] Athenians, this man is a hireling, a hireling with a long history. This was the man who summoned from Thebes the embassy from Philip and was responsible for the termination of the first war.[19] This man helped to defend Philocrates,[20] who proposed peace with Philip (because of which you exiled him). He hired a carriage for the envoys who came here with Antipater, and taking them with him he first

---

vened this decree. They also helped the exiled Thrasybulus of Stiria to seize Phyle, from where he set out to win victory over the Thirty at the battle of Munychia.

[18] Olynthus, the final Chalcidian city to resist Philip, fell to him in 348. The citizens were either enslaved or fled into exile. Philip achieved success at Olynthus apparently by bribing two of the city's hipparchs, Euthycrates and Lasthenes, to open the gates to him (cf. Dem. 8.40, 9.56–57, 19.265, 342, and 18.48).

[19] The "first war" was waged between Athens and Philip from 357 to 346. According to Demosthenes (2.6), Philip had agreed to hand over the Athenian colony of Amphipolis to the Athenians in return for their surrendering Pydna to him. When he reneged on his alleged agreement, war followed (Aes. 2.21, 70, 72, 3.54). With Philip's invasion of the Chalcidice in 349, Olynthus sued for a treaty with Athens. The city fell in 348 (see 1.26n) and the Chalcidice was annexed to Macedonia. The war ended in 346 with the Peace of Philocrates (see next note).

[20] Philocrates proposed that Athens send envoys to discuss Philip's peace terms in 348/7, but he was indicted under the *graphē paranomōn* procedure (Aes. 2.13–14, 3.62). Demosthenes successfully defended him (Aes. 2.14; cf. 3.62). The even-

introduced into the city the custom of fawning on the Macedonians. [29] Gentlemen of Athens, do not acquit him, do not let him go unpunished, for he is responsible for the misfortunes of the city and the rest of Greece and has been caught red-handed taking bribes to harm the city. Since good fortune has brought you prosperity and the expulsion of one of the two who has defiled the country, and has handed this one over to you for execution, do not oppose the common interests. Instead, procure happier omens for the affairs of state and divert our misfortunes onto these leaders. [30] For what occasion will you keep Demosthenes, thinking that he will be of value to you? Could any one of you or of the bystanders[21] say what private or public matter this man has undertaken and not ruined? Did he not go to the home of Aristarchus and plan with him the death of Nicodemus, which they accomplished—you all know about this—and then expel Aristarchus on disgraceful charges?[22] And did Aristarchus not find Demosthenes to be such a friend that he considered him an evil spirit come to visit him and the source of his misfortunes? [31] When he began to advise the people, and would he had never done so—I will pass over his private affairs, for time does not allow me to speak at length—is it not true that absolutely no good has come to the city and that not only the city but all Greece has fallen into danger, misfortune, and disgrace? Has he not let slip every opportunity to help you, despite having many opportunities to do so in his speeches? On

---

tual peace between Philip and the Athenians in 346 was named the Peace of Philocrates, but in 343 Philocrates was impeached by Hyperides for having made proposals (in 346) contrary to the common good (cf. Hyp. 4.29–30). Although this charge had no legal grounds, Philocrates fled into exile before the trial (not exiled as Dinarchus states here) and was condemned to death *in absentia* (Dem. 19.114–119, Aes. 2.6, 3.79–82).

[21] Many trials were attended by spectators, who were separated from the litigants and jurors by a fence. This trial in particular would have attracted a huge crowd.

[22] Aristarchus, a well-to-do orphan, was apparently persuaded by Demosthenes to murder Nicodemus of Aphidna, a supporter of Meidias and Eubulus who had charged Demosthenes with desertion in 348 during the Euboean campaign (cf. Din. 1.44; Aes. 2.148). Yet Nicodemus had failed to prosecute, so Aeschines (2.48) alleged, because Demosthenes had bought him off. This gives us the scenario for Demosthenes' vengeance on Nicodemus and his involvement with Aristarchus.

those occasions when some caring and patriotic man would have elected to do something for the city, this demagogue, who will soon say how useful he has been to you, so far from taking positive action has diverted his own bad fortune onto those doing something on your behalf. [32] Charidemus sailed to the Persian King, wanting to be of service to you with actions not words and to secure safety for you and the other Greeks at his own personal risk.[23] But Demosthenes walked around the market place making speeches and pledged himself a partner in the undertaking. Fortune so upset the plan that it turned out the opposite to what was anticipated. [33] Although Ephialtes hated him, he was compelled to be a partner in the undertaking and sailed off.[24] Fortune also took Ephialtes from the city. Euthydicus promised beneficial deeds on behalf of the people.[25] Demosthenes said he was this man's friend, but he also perished. Think about these things, which you see and understand far better than I, and you will see, weighing up future prospects in the light of the past, that this man is of no benefit except to enemies plotting against the city.[26] [34] Is it not necessary for us to raise up another force such as we had in the time of Agis,[27] when all the Spartans had taken the field, joined by the Achaeans and Eleans and ten thousand mercenaries? Alexander, so they said, was in India,[28] and because of traitors in each city, the whole of Greece was unhappy with the situation and was hoping for some

[23] On Charidemus, see Dem. 23.144–195. He was originally from Oreus on Euboea and was awarded Athenian citizenship in 357/6 for his military services.

[24] Ephialtes was an ambassador to Persia in 341/0 and returned with money for distribution among leading public officials in order to provoke war against Philip. He was later killed in battle.

[25] Nothing is known of Euthydicus, apart from the mention at Dem., *Epistle* 3.31.

[26] There is a lacuna in the text at this point. Perhaps only a few words are missing.

[27] In 331, Agis III of Sparta led an abortive war against the Macedonian hegemony of Greece. He received support from several states, including most of the Peloponnese, but never from Athens (cf. Aes. 3.165–166), and he was defeated and killed by Antipater the next year.

[28] Alexander was in Persia during Agis' war and did not leave for India until summer 327. Dinarchus would have known this, but he has distorted the facts here for rhetorical effect.

relief from misfortunes. What happened? [35] What did Demosthenes do then? He who has the power to advise and make proposals, and who will soon tell us that he hates our current state of affairs? Leaving aside the other dangers, did you make any proposals concerning these? Did you offer advice? Did you contribute money? Were you of any value at all to those working for the common safety? Not at all: you went around recruiting speechwriters. You wrote a letter at home, shaming the dignity of the city, and strolled around dangling it from your fingertips. [36] You lived well in the midst of the city's hardships, traveled in a sedan chair to Piraeus, and abused the needy for their poverty. Shall Demosthenes, then, be of benefit to you on future occasions when he has let slip all previous ones? By our Lady Athena and Zeus the Protector, if only the enemies of the city could have such advisers and leaders and not better ones! [37] Gentlemen, will you not remember the deeds of your ancestors? When great and numerous dangers were befalling the city, they risked peril for the well-being of the people and proved worthy of the city, their own freedom, and their just reputation. It would be a long task to tell of these great men of the past, Aristeides and Themistocles,[29] who built the walls of the city and brought the tribute paid freely and willingly by the Greeks to the Acropolis. [38] You will remember the deeds shortly before the present time performed by Cephalus the orator, Thrason of Herchia, Eleus, and Phormisius,[30] and other fine men, some of whom even now are still alive. Some of these lent help to the exiles so that they could return to Thebes when the Spartans had garrisoned the Cadmea and at their

---

[29] Themistocles was responsible for the increase in the Athenian navy in 483 and for the rebuilding of the city walls after 480 and the building of those at Piraeus. Aristeides played a prominent role in the organization of the Delian League in 478 after the Persian Wars and was responsible for the assessment of the tribute payable to Athens by its allies.

[30] Cephalus of Collytus was an orator (Dem. 18.219) who helped to overthrow the Thirty in Athens (404/3) and was responsible for sending an Athenian force to expel the Spartan garrison from Thebes in 379/8 (see below). Thrason was a Theban *proxenos* (Aes. 3.138) and served as an ambassador to Cetriporis in Thrace in 356/5. Eleus may be the trierarch mentioned in *IG* II^2 1632, 144–145. Phormisius is cited at *Ath. Pol.* 34.3 with others who were not members of the Thirty (cf. Xen., *Hellenica* 2.3.2).

own peril freed a neighboring city so long enslaved.[31] [39] Others of your ancestors were persuaded by Cephalus, who proposed a decree and was not swayed by the power of Sparta. He did not think of the danger of taking risks and making proposals on behalf of the city but proposed that the Athenians should march out and lend support to the exiles who had seized Thebes. And when your fathers went there a few days later, the commander of the Spartan garrison was expelled and the Thebans were set free, and your city had acted in a manner worthy of your ancestors. [40] Those men, Athenians, those men were worthy advisers and leaders for you and the people, not, by Zeus, rogues such as these, who have done and will do nothing of value for the city; they just look after their own safety and make money anywhere they can. They have given the city a worse reputation than they themselves have, and now, convicted of taking bribes, they deceive you and after such behavior think nothing of seeking their own gain from you. According to their own decree, they should have been put to death long ago for acts such as these.

[41] Gentlemen of Athens, are you not ashamed to think that Demosthenes' punishment should be decided from only our speeches? Do you not know that he takes bribes, steals, and betrays his friends and that he and the fortune associated with him are hardly good for the city? From what decrees or laws has he not made money? [42] Are there any of you in court who were among the three hundred when he introduced the law concerning trierarchs?[32] Tell those sitting next to you that he took three talents to change and redraft the law for each Assembly meeting, that he resold measures for which he had taken payment, and that he did not make good those for which he had been

---

[31] In 382 the Spartans illegally seized the Theban Cadmea and exiled three hundred leading citizens (Diodorus Siculus 15.20, Xen., *Hellenica* 5.2.28–31). The Theban exiles took refuge in Athens and in midwinter 379/8, with Athenian help proposed by Cephalus (see preceding note), expelled the Spartan garrison (Diodorus Siculus 15.25–27, Xen., *Hellenica* 5.4.1–20).

[32] In 354 Demosthenes proposed an increase in the number of citizens liable for the trierarchy, from 1,200 to 2,000 (14.16), and in 340/39 he introduced his trierarch law (to which Dinarchus refers), which threw the whole burden of the trierarchy onto the three hundred richest citizens of Athens (Dem. 18.102–109; cf. Aes. 3.55, 222, Dem. 36.45).

paid. [43] Gentlemen, tell me, by Zeus, do you think he was not paid to propose public maintenance in the Prytaneum and a statue in the Agora for Diphilus?[33] Or to confer your citizenship on Chaerephilus, Pheidon, Pamphilus, and Pheidippus,[34] or again on Epigenes and Conon the bankers?[35] Or to erect bronze statues in the Agora of Paerisades, Satyrus, and Gorgippus, the tyrants of the Pontus,[36] who send him one thousand medimni of grain per year? And he will presently tell you he cannot take refuge anywhere! [44] Was he not paid to introduce the proposal that Taurosthenes become an Athenian, although he had enslaved his own countrymen, and with his brother Callias had betrayed the whole of Euboea to Philip?[37] The laws do not

---

[33] Diphilus, son of Diopeithes of Sunium, may have been a syntrierarch before 325/4 and the man who proposed a naval law in (or immediately before) 323/2 (*IG* II[2] 1631, 511 and 1632, 19). Dinarchus refers to the right to dine at state expense (*sitēsis*) for life in the Prytaneum (Town Hall). This grant was normally combined with *proedria* (a front seat in the theater) and the erection of a bronze statue of the individual, presumably life-size, in the Agora.

[34] Chaerephilus was a salt-fish seller (see Hyp. Frs. 61–62), who owed his citizenship and that of his three sons (whose names follow) to Demosthenes, since they were enrolled in his deme of Paeania and it was customary for a new citizen to be enrolled in the deme of his *prostatēs* (sponsor). Little is known of Pheidon; he was certainly not as active liturgically as his brothers were. Pamphilus contributed one hundred drachmas to the *eutaxia* liturgy (*IG* II[2] 417, 14) in about 330. Pheidippus was trierarch before 322, since in that year, *IG* II[2] 1631, d622–624 records him as owing 1,200 drachmas for a trierarchy.

[35] Epigenes and Conon are largely unknown characters; they were originally metics and evidently owed their citizenship to Demosthenes. Conon is commonly believed to be the person accused in 1.56 and by Hyperides (5.26) of fraudulently obtaining theoric money, but see 1.56n.

[36] Paerisades I was ruler of Bosporus from 344/3 to 309; Satyrus and Gorgippus were two of his sons, later to rule with their father until his death (cf. Diodorus Siculus 20.22). The Bosporan area was important for its grain exportation to Athens, but relations between there and Athens had deteriorated in the fourth century, and the exploitation of Demosthenes' ties with the Spartocids indicates ill feeling towards the dynasty.

[37] Neither Taurosthenes nor Callias betrayed Euboea to Philip. In 341 Callias sought an alliance with Athens that would guarantee Euboean allegiance. Demosthenes secured its acceptance and was later accused of accepting a bribe for his

allow him to set foot on Athenian soil; if he does, then he is subject to the same penalties as someone exiled by the Areopagus who returns.[38] And this democrat proposed to make this man a citizen! [45] Do I need to summon witnesses about these men or the others whom he proposed as *proxenoi*[39] and citizens? By Athena, do you think that when he happily takes silver he would not take twenty talents of gold? Or when he receives bribes in small amounts he would not take such a large sum all at once? Or that the Council of the Areopagus, which investigated Demosthenes, Demades, and Cephisophon[40] for six months, has given you unfair reports? [46] Gentlemen, as I've said before, there are many citizens and other Greeks watching how you will judge this case: will you make the taking of bribes by others subject to prosecution by law or allow bribes to be taken against your interests without restraint? Will matters previously considered as trustworthy and assured now become untrustworthy because of Demosthenes' trial? He should have been executed for all his policies. He is subject to all the curses imposed by the city, [47] since he has sworn falsely on the Areopagus by the awful goddesses[41] and the other gods, by whom it is traditional to swear there, and has become accursed at every Assembly.[42] He has been proved to have taken bribes against the city; he has deceived both the people and the Council, defying the curse; he speaks one thing and thinks another; and he recommended a cruel and illegal course in private to Aristarchus.[43] For these crimes—if

---

part (Aes. 3.85–103). In probably the period 336–330, Taurosthenes and Callias were made Athenian citizens, for which Dinarchus accuses Demosthenes of taking a bribe (cf. Aes. 3.85, Hyp. 5.20).

[38] That is, he can be killed by anyone with impunity.

[39] These were individuals appointed by another state to look after their ambassadors and important visitors when in Athens.

[40] On Demades, see 1.7n. Cephisophon's identity is disputed, but he probably supported the Peace of Philocrates (Dem. 18.21 and 75).

[41] On the "awful goddesses," see 1.87n.

[42] Meetings of the Assembly and of the Boule were preceded by the herald reciting a prayer (Aes. 1.23, Din. 2.14) and invoking a curse on all traitors and enemies of the state (Andoc. 1.31, Dem. 19.70–71, 20.107, 23.97, Lyc. 1.31; cf. Din. 2.16). The curse is parodied in Aristoph., *Thesmophoriazusae* 295–310.

[43] See 1.30n.

there is any power to exact a just penalty from perjurers and criminals, as there surely is—this man will today meet with justice. Gentlemen of the jury, listen to the curse.

[CURSE]

[48] Nevertheless, gentlemen of the jury, Demosthenes is so ready to lie and speak dishonestly, and so unconcerned about shame or disgrace or a curse, that I hear he will dare to say that the Council previously convicted me. I am now being utterly inconsistent, so he says, because previously I opposed the report of the Areopagus and pleaded my own case, and now I am appearing on its behalf and accusing this man based on the report. This story is contrived, and never happened, but he dares to lie to you. [49] But, so that you can disregard him if he tells this story, and be certain that the Council did not report against me nor intended to do so, but rather that I have been wronged by one miserable man who was punished by you—let me briefly tell you. Then I will get back to him.

[50] Gentlemen, the Council of the Areopagus has to produce all its reports following two procedures. What are these? It can investigate either on its own initiative or when the people in Assembly order it. Apart from these, there is no other procedure it could follow. If then, you vile creature, you say that the Council investigated me on the orders of the people and published its report, [51] show the decree and who my prosecutors were when the report was made. In the present case both exist: the decree by which the Council was to investigate and prosecutors elected by the people, from whom the jurors are now learning about the crimes. If what you say is true, then I am ready to die; but if you say the Council reported me on its own initiative, then summon the Areopagites as witnesses, just as I shall produce them to say that I was not reported. [52] Moreover, having impeached a criminal and traitor who had slandered me and the Council,[44] like you Demosthenes, and proving before 2,500[45] citizens

---

[44] The speaker's former prosecutor is Pistias, a member of the Areopagus, who is named in 53. We know next to nothing about the case.

[45] The number 2,500 is large, but greater numbers of juries are known, and we are told at 1.107 that the jury at Demosthenes' trial numbered 1,500.

that this traitor had taken this action against me by hiring himself to Pythocles,[46] I avenged myself with those who were jurors then. Will you take up the deposition that previously I placed before the jurors as evidence—and no one denounced it as false—and which I shall now again produce? Read the deposition.

[DEPOSITION]

[53] Athenians, is it not shocking that because one man, Pistias an Areopagite, said I was a criminal and lied against me and the Council, that fabrication would have been stronger than the truth, if the trumped-up lies against me had been accepted because of my weakness and isolation then? But when the truth has been admitted by the entire Council of the Areopagus, that Demosthenes took twenty talents of gold against you and having done so is a criminal, and your popular leader, on whom some fix their hopes, has been caught in the act of taking bribes, [54] will the traditions of that body and justice and truth now be weaker than the word of Demosthenes? Will the slander of this man against the Council—how it reported many men for wronging the people, but when they came into court they were acquitted, the Council in some cases not obtaining one-fifth of the votes—be stronger than the truth?[47] There is an explanation for this, which all of you will easily understand. [55] The Council, gentlemen, considers cases that have been assigned to it by you and crimes committed within itself, not like you—and don't get angry at me—who at times tend to be swayed by mercy more than justice in deciding cases. But the Council simply reports anyone who is subject to the findings or who has broken any traditional rules of conduct, considering that someone who is used to committing small offenses will more easily welcome large-scale crimes. [56] Consequently, it reported to you and fined one of its members who robbed the ferryman of his

---

[46] Pythocles, an opponent of Demosthenes and a supporter of Aeschines (Dem. 19.225, 314, 18.285), was probably executed in 318 for supporting Phocion.

[47] If an accuser in a *graphē* failed to obtain at least one-fifth of the votes cast, he lost his citizen rights and so no longer had redress to the legal system (Andoc. 1.33, 4.18, Dem. 21.47, Plato, *Apology* 36a–b).

fare.[48] Again, the man who claimed the five-drachma allowance in the name of someone not present—this man also was reported to you.[49] And in the same way, it fined and expelled the man who dared to sell the Areopagite portion of meat contrary to the laws.[50] [57] You tried these men and acquitted them. You were not accusing the Council of the Areopagus of lying, but you gave more feeling to mercy than to justice and considered the penalty greater than the crime committed by the accused. Demosthenes, do you think that the Council made a false report? Not at all. Nevertheless, gentlemen, you yourselves acquitted these men and others like them, even though the Council reported them guilty. [58] When the people in the Assembly ordered the Areopagus to investigate whether Polyeuctus of Cydantidae[51] was accompanying the exiles to Megara, and to report back to you the results of the investigation, the Council reported he had gone there. You selected prosecutors in accordance with the law, he came into court, and you acquitted him, since Polyeuctus admitted that he went to Megara to Nicophanes, who was the husband of his mother. You did not think that he was doing anything odd or terrible by maintaining contact with his mother's husband, who had fallen on hard times,

---

[48] The man in question was an Areopagite, and so he would have been the subject of an investigation on the Areopagus' own initiative, which was only undertaken if the subject were an Areopagite. Nothing else about him is known.

[49] Dinarchus alludes to theoric money, which was used to enable the poor to attend the festivals. It is unlikely that the culprit here is Conon of Paeania, despite the similarity between this case and that cited at Hyp. 5.26, since in 57 we learn that the court acquitted him, whereas the Conon mentioned by Hyperides was fined one talent.

[50] Each Areopagite received a daily meat allowance.

[51] Polyeuctus was acquitted, after an *apophasis,* of accompanying the exiles to Megara, which would have been regarded as a treasonable crime (*prodosia*), hence the involvement of the Areopagus. The common belief is that Polyeuctus was the prosecutor in the case of Hyp. 4, but this is not certain. At 4.12, Hyperides mentions that when Polyeuctus was prosecuted by Alexander of Oeon he asked for at least ten *synēgoroi* from the tribe Aigeis, and this passage and that of Dinarchus here may well refer to the same occasion. Doubt is cast on the connection between Hyp. 4.12 and Din. 1.58 on chronological grounds, though, since the exiles are presumably those journeying to Olympia in anticipation of Alexander's Exiles Decree (cf. 81–82 and 103).

and helping him, as much as he could, when he was banished from his country. [59] This report of the Council was not proved false, Demosthenes, it was quite true, but the jurors thought fit to acquit Polyeuctus. I say again, the discovery of the truth was entrusted to the Council, but the court judged what was worthy of pardon. Because of this, should one not trust the Council over the present reports, when it has stated that you and your cronies have the gold? That would indeed be terrible!

[60] Now, Demosthenes, convince the jurors that any one of these violations is the same as your crimes and that to accept bribes against the country is worthy of pardon, so that you would justly be acquitted by these men. The laws lay down that double damages are owed for other crimes involving money, but concerning the taking of bribes they have laid down only two penalties: either death, so that by meeting this penalty the guilty party is made an example to others, or tenfold the original amount received as the penalty for bribes, so that those who dare to do this shall not gain by it.[52]

[61] Or will you not try to say that, but insist that the penalty imposed by the Council on those it previously reported has been considered fitting by others, but that you alone protested against it? But of all those ever reported, you alone of your own volition requested that these men be your judges and examiners, and you proposed the decree against yourself and made the people witnesses of what was agreed, laying down the death penalty on yourself if the Council should report that you had taken any of the money brought into the country by Harpalus. [62] You yourself, Demosthenes, proposed previously that the Council of the Areopagus should have power over all these men and other Athenians to punish anyone violating the law and to enforce the laws of the land. You yourself gave and entrusted the entire city to this body, which you will soon tell us is oligarchic. Two of the citizens, a father and son, were handed over to the execu-

[52] Hyperides (5.24) tells us that a simple fine punished ordinary crimes (excluding bribery), and ordinarily if a fine remained outstanding by a certain date the amount was doubled or the person imprisoned (*Ath. Pol.* 48.1). At 2.17, Dinarchus declares that bribery was punished by a fine ten times greater than the amount taken (cf. Dem. 24.112, Hyp. 5.24, *Ath. Pol.* 54.2), but here he adds the death penalty.

tioner and put to death in accordance with your decree.[53] [63] One of the descendants of Harmodius was imprisoned in keeping with your command.[54] These men, induced by the report of the Areopagus, tortured and executed Antiphon.[55] You yourself banished Charinus from the city for treason,[56] in accordance with the report and punishment of the Council. Will you now invalidate the decree, you who proposed it against yourself? How can that be just and lawful?

[64] Gentlemen of Athens, I call to witness the awful goddesses and the place in which they live, and the heroes of the land, and Athena Polias, and the other gods who have taken our city and land as home:[57] now that the people have handed over to you for punishment the man who took some of the imported money against the interests of his country,[58] corrupted and destroyed the well-being of the city, and betrayed the country he once claimed to have fortified by his diplomacy, [65] enemies and those ill disposed to the city would wish that man alive, considering this a misfortune for the city. But those who are sympathetic to your current circumstances, and hope that the affairs of the city would improve with a change of fortune, wish to exact a penalty worthy of his deeds, namely, death, and they pray to the gods for this. And I myself join in beseeching them to save

---

[53] The two men were probably the guards posted to watch Harpalus' money on the Acropolis, and when only 350 talents were found, they were executed on Demosthenes' order. They are probably also the subjects of the decree read out in 82.

[54] This was Proxenus, a descendant of the sixth-century "tyrannicide" Harmodius (see 1.101n). The date and context of this imprisonment are unknown.

[55] Antiphon (not the orator) intended to burn the Piraeus dockyards for Philip at some point between 346 and 343, but had been caught by Demosthenes (Dem. 18.132–134). He was deleted from the citizenship roll and later executed.

[56] Pseudo-Demosthenes (58.37–38) refers to Charinus' exile for treason before 339.

[57] The invocation of a range of gods and heroes lends a pious weight to Dinarchus' case; the "awful goddesses" appear again at 87, also within the context of a trial (see 87 and note); cf. their use at 1.47. Athena is named here in her role of guardian of the city, which is apt since Demosthenes' actions have endangered her city.

[58] There is a short lacuna in the text at this point.

the country, seeing it in danger on behalf of its freedom, its children, its women, its dignity—on behalf of every decent thing. [66] Athenians, when we come out of the court, what shall we say to the people if—as I hope is not the case—you are deceived by this man's sorcery? How will each of you, when you return home, dare to look at your ancestral hearths, if you have acquitted the traitor who first brought into his own home the gold he had received as a bribe and have thus convicted the Council, which is considered the most revered by all men, of reaching false conclusions in its investigation? [67] Athenians, what hopes—think of these yourselves—what hopes shall we have if any danger befalls the city, when we have made it safe to take bribes against the country and have rendered disreputable the Council that has the power to protect the city in these times of crisis? [68] And what if—let us imagine this scenario—Alexander sends an envoy and, in accordance with Demosthenes' decree,[59] demands from us the gold brought into the country by Harpalus and, relying on the existence of the report of the Areopagus, sends us the slaves we recently returned to him, expecting us to find out the truth from them? By the gods, gentlemen, what shall we say?

[69] Will you propose that we go to war, Demosthenes, since you have managed previous wars so well? And if the rest of the Athenians decide to do this, is it fairer to use your gold together with other people's for war, or for everyone else to contribute from their own possessions and to melt down the private ornaments of their wives, the drinking cups, and all the votive offerings to the gods in the country, as you said you would propose, while you yourself contribute fifty drachmas from your houses in Piraeus and in the city?[60] This was what you had contributed at the previous levy; though you now have twenty talents. [70] Or perhaps you will not propose war but will order us to give the gold brought here back to Alexander, according to the decree that you proposed? Then surely the people will have to return it for your sake! But is it then just or right or democratic for

[59] The decree is that of Demosthenes to guard the money (which technically belonged to Alexander) brought into the city by Harpalus (cf. Hyp. 5.9–10).

[60] Aeschines (3.209) and Hyperides (5.17) refer to a house owned by Demosthenes in Piraeus, but one in the city is not attested elsewhere, and the statement at 70 indicates that one did not exist.

those who work to contribute, while you snatch and steal? Or that others make clear the property that they own and pay proportionate contributions, while you, who have taken more than 150 talents from the Persian King and from the money of Alexander,[61] have not made clear what you own in the city but have prepared yourself against the people as if you did not trust your own administration of the state? [71] Is it fitting that while the laws order the orators and the generals,[62] who want to obtain the confidence of the people, to have children in accordance with the laws, to own land within the boundaries, to pledge all the lawful oaths, and in this way to deserve the leadership of the people, you sold your father's land, are passing off children not your own as yours despite the laws that control oaths at trials, and are ordering others to take the field when you yourself deserted the battle line?[63]

[72] Athenians, what do you think is the reason cities sometimes prosper and sometimes fare badly? You will find no reason other than their advisers and leaders. Look at Thebes. It was a city, and it was among the greatest. When was this? Under what leaders and generals? All the older men, from whom I heard the story I will tell you, would agree that it was [73] when Pelopidas, they say, led the Sacred Band, and Epaminondas was general with his colleagues.[64] Then Thebes won the battle of Leuctra, then they invaded the land of the Spartans,

---

[61] On Demosthenes' alleged receipt of Persian gold, see 1.10n.

[62] *Rhētores kai stratēgoi* ("orators and generals") was the common term used by the Athenians for their political leaders (cf. Dem. 18.212).

[63] Cf. 2.17 on the type of questions asked at a *dokimasia. Ath. Pol.* 4.2 tells us that *stratēgoi* and *hipparchoi* were required to have legitimate children and a necessary portion of land, and here we see the elaborate steps taken to make sure that the Athenians' elected officials met various legal requirements. To swear innocence by one's children was a common oath used by those accused of crimes. For Demosthenes' alleged desertion at the battle of Chaeronea, see 1.12n.

[64] Pelopidas and Epaminondas promoted the military supremacy of Thebes from 371 with the Thebans' victory over the Spartans at the battle of Leuctra, until 362, when an Athenian and Spartan force at the battle of Mantinea defeated them. Pelopidas died in battle in 364 against Pherae, and Epaminondas died in 362 at the battle of Mantinea. The Sacred Band was the crack Theban infantry corps, which was annihilated at the battle of Chaeronea; the restored Lion of Chaeronea could well mark the spot where the Sacred Band fell.

which, it was thought, was inviolable,[65] and during that time they performed many great deeds: they founded Messene in the four hundredth year, they made the Arcadians autonomous, and they were highly regarded by all.[66] [74] But when did the opposite apply? When were their achievements meager and unworthy of their spirit? When Timolaus, this man's friend, was bribed and took money from Philip, and Proxenus the traitor was in charge of the mercenaries levied for Amphissa, and Theagenes, a man of misfortune and open to bribery, just like this man, led the phalanx.[67] Then the entire city was destroyed and obliterated together with the rest of Greece because of the three men I mentioned. For it is not false but only too true that the leaders are responsible for all the citizens' fortunes, whether good or the opposite. [75] Think again in the same way about our own city. Our city was great, highly esteemed by the Greeks and worthy of our ancestors, and after those deeds from the past, when Conon,[68] as our elders say, won the naval battle at Cnidus, when Iphicrates destroyed the Spartan company,[69] when Chabrias defeated the Spartan triremes at sea off Naxos,[70] and when Timotheus won the naval battle

---

[65] Epaminondas invaded the Peloponnese after the battle of Leuctra (Diodorus Siculus 15.62.3); he liberated Messenia from Sparta and rebuilt the capital at Messene, which proved economically disastrous for Sparta. The Arcadian League was then able to consolidate its power, and with Theban help it founded a new capital city in South Arcadia named Megalopolis.

[66] The earlier events took place during the course of the Second Messenian War, ca. 630–610; Dinarchus is a hundred years off (cf. Isoc. 6.27, Lyc. 1.62, who are also incorrect).

[67] The three men were Theban commanders. On Timolaus as a traitor, see Dem. 18.48, 295–296. Proxenus, a general in 339/8, secured Amphissa soon after the Theban alliance of that year in order to prevent Philip from threatening Boeotia and Athens. Soon after, it was defeated and Amphissa fell (Aes. 3. 146–147). Theagenes commanded the Theban phalanx at the battle of Chaeronea, hence he was the last commander of the Sacred Band.

[68] On Conon, see 1.14n.

[69] In 390 the Athenian general Iphicrates, while en route to the relief of Corinth, virtually annihilated a Spartan army and was awarded a public portrait in Athens as well as other state honors (Aes. 3.243, Dem. 23.130).

[70] In 376 Chabrias defeated a Spartan fleet off Naxos, which secured Athenian control of the Aegean (Dem. 20.77, Aes. 3.222), and he was also awarded a public portrait (Dem. 13.22–23, 20.84–86, Aes. 3.243).

at Corcyra.[71] [76] At that time, Athenians, at that time the Spartans, who before were famous because of their leaders and had been reared according to their principles, came humbly to our city, beseeching our ancestors for safety. The democracy they had subverted[72] was again made the leading power of Greece, thanks to the advisers we then had, and I think rightly so, for we had such generals as I have just been talking about and had Archinus and Cephalus of Collytus as advisers.[73] For there is only one means of safety for a city or a nation: to obtain brave men and wise advisers as leaders. [77] Athenians, if you recognize and consider these things, then, by Zeus, you should have no more to do with Demosthenes' venality and ill fortune. Do not place your hopes of safety on this man, and do not think you will lack brave men and wise advisers. Take up the anger of your ancestors, and have this robber and traitor, who has been caught in the act, executed and his body cast beyond the borders—this traitor, who does not keep his hands off the money brought into the city, who has brought the city to the most calamitous misfortunes, and who is a plague for Greece.[74] Allow the fortune of the city to change, then look forward to a better lot.

[78] Athenians, listen to that decree proposed by Demosthenes, which this democrat proposed after the battle of Chaeronea when the city was in dire straits,[75] and the oracle that came from Zeus of Do-

---

[71] On Timotheus, see 1.14n.

[72] A reference to the overthrow of democracy by the Thirty in 404, which was supported by Sparta: see 1.25n.

[73] Archinus supported Thrasybulus in the overthrow of the Thirty in 403 (Aes. 2.176, 3.187, 195; cf. Dem. 24.135). On Cephalus, see 1.38n.

[74] Dinarchus' characterization of Demosthenes here echoes Aes. 3.131 and 157 (cf. 253) and was probably a common topos of oratorical invective for use against an opponent.

[75] After the battle of Chaeronea on 2 September 338, Demosthenes and Hyperides proposed a series of emergency defense measures, including the repair of the Piraeus fortifications and the enfranchisement of the *atimoi,* metics, and slaves (Dem. 18.248, Lyc. 1.16, 41, Pseudo-Dem. 26.11), and Demosthenes also secured a commission to acquire grain supplies, which took him away from Athens (Aes. 3.159, 259, Dem. 18.248, Lyc. 1.42). From the disclosure at 1.79–80, the decree appointing Demosthenes grain commissioner (called desertion at 80–82) is the decree read here.

dona.[76] It has been clearly telling you for a long time to be on your guard against your leaders and advisers. First read the oracle.

[ORACLE]

[79] Now read his fine decree.

[DECREE]

A democrat indeed is this one! He arranges for himself, since he is brave and fearless, to remain in arms, but he orders that those citizens he rejects as unfit should go off to their work and do anything else he considers necessary. Read the remainder.

[DECREE]

[80] Gentlemen of the jury, hear this. It says that the chosen embassies shall set out, for when he heard that Philip intended to invade our land after the battle of Chaeronea, he appointed himself an envoy so that he might escape from the city. He snatched up eight talents from the Treasury and left,[77] paying no attention to the current lack of funds, when everyone else was contributing his own resources for your safety. [81] Such is your adviser; and Demosthenes in his lifetime has made only these two journeys abroad: after the battle when he fled from the city, and now to Olympia, since through his presidency of the sacred embassy he wanted to meet up with Nicanor.[78] Is it right when danger threatens to entrust the city to this man, who, when he had to fight with the others against the enemy, deserted the ranks and went home, and, when he needed to be home to face danger with the others, proposed himself as an envoy and left the city in flight?

---

[76] Cf. 1.98, and see too the use of oracles at Dem. 19.297–299 and 18.253.

[77] The context is Demosthenes' mission after the battle of Chaeronea to seek grain (see 1.78 with note). The figure of eight talents here does not occur elsewhere; Aeschines (3.159), referring to the same incident, says that Demosthenes took only a trireme.

[78] This manifestly untrue statement is at odds with 1.12 and 1.13; cf. 1.16 and 1.24. On Demosthenes' "flight" after the battle of Chaeronea, see 1.12n. On Nicanor's mission to Olympia with the Exiles Decree and Demosthenes' diplomatic attempts to forestall its implementation, see the Introduction to Dinarchus, and see also 1.94 and 1.103.

[82] When it was necessary to have envoys for peace, however, he said he would not set foot outside the city, but when it was reported that Alexander was restoring the exiles and Nicanor had come to Olympia, he volunteered himself as *architheōros* to the Council.[79] In a nutshell, this is how he is: in the battle line he is a stay-at-home, among those who remain at home he is an envoy, and among envoys he is a runaway.

Now read the decision over the two citizens and the decree for the investigation into the money,[80] which Demosthenes proposed for the Council of the Areopagus concerning both himself and you, so that by considering both together you will see Demosthenes' madness.

[DECREE]

[83] Did you propose this, Demosthenes? You did propose it—it cannot be denied. Was the Council given power according to your motion? It was. Have these men from the citizenry been put to death? They have been executed. Was your decree valid against them? It is impossible to deny this. Now read again what Demosthenes proposed against Demosthenes.[81] Gentlemen, pay attention.

[DECREE]

[84] The Council has declared against Demosthenes. Is it necessary to say anything more? It has reported him, Athenians! Justice thus dictates that, since he has condemned himself, he be executed straightaway. But now that he has come into your hands, you who have been assembled by the people and have sworn that you will obey the laws and the decrees of the people, what will you do? Will you abandon the reverence towards the gods and the justice recognized by all mankind?

---

[79] This was the head of the Athenian religious delegation; see the Introduction to Dinarchus.

[80] The first decree is that which led to the execution of the father and son who were appointed to guard Harpalus' treasure on the Acropolis (see 1.62n); the second decree refers to Demosthenes' proposal that the Areopagus investigate the whole affair. There is a lacuna in the text at this point.

[81] This is Demosthenes' decree by which he agreed to submit to the death penalty if found guilty of accepting a bribe from Harpalus (see the Introduction to Dinarchus).

[85] No, Athenians, you must not. Others have been executed by Demosthenes' decrees who were no worse than he and have not committed crimes of the same magnitude; it would be an utter disgrace if he with his disdain for you and the laws should walk around the city unpunished, when he has been convicted by his own motion and the decrees that he proposed. Athenians, the Council is the same, the place is the same, and the rights are the same. [86] The same orator was responsible for the adversities that afflicted them and that he himself will experience now. He himself in the Assembly asked this Council to judge his case and made you his witnesses. He made a compact with the people and proposed the decree against himself to be kept by the mother of the gods, who is the guardian of all written agreements in the city.[82] It is not right for you to invalidate these or, when you have sworn by the gods to judge this case, to deliver a vote against the actions of the gods themselves. [87] When Poseidon failed to obtain the vote against Ares in the case of Halirrothius, he accepted the decision.[83] The awful goddesses themselves accepted the verdict of this Council in the case against Orestes, and associated themselves with the truthfulness of this body for the future.[84] What will you do, you who claim to be most pious in everything? Will you invalidate the decision of the Council and follow the baseness of Demosthenes? [88] No, Athenians, if you are wise. For you are judging no small or occasional matter on this day but the safety of the entire city and, in addition to this, bribery, a shameful custom and an unprofitable prac-

[82] Reference to the Metröon (central record office), which housed the state archives, including laws and decrees, all of which were written down in the fourth century and seem to have been freely accessible to the public (Lyc. 1.66, Aes. 3.187). The Mother of the Gods was held to be the protector of the laws, and she had a cult linked to the Boule (see also *Ath. Pol.* 43).

[83] The story is that Poseidon prosecuted Ares for murdering his son Halirrothius, who had raped Ares' daughter Alcippe. Ares was tried before the Areopagus but acquitted (Apollodorus 3.14.2, Pausanias 1.21.4 and 28.5; cf. Dem. 23.66).

[84] The story is dramatized in Aeschylus' play, *Eumenides* (cf. Dem. 13.74). Orestes murdered his mother Clytemnestra and her lover Aegisthus in revenge for their slaying of his father Agamemnon. The "awful goddesses" are the Erinyes of his dead mother, and they pursued him to Athens, where the Areopagus heard his case. He was acquitted thanks to Athena's intervention.

tice to you and the ruin of all men. If you suppress as best you can those who gladly take bribes against you and expel them from the city, then we shall be saved by the grace of the gods. But if you leave it to the orators to sell themselves, then you will watch the city ruined by them.

[89] Demosthenes himself proposed in the Assembly that we should keep the money brought into Attica with Harpalus for Alexander, which clearly shows that this measure was just. Well, my good friend, tell me how we are to guard it, when you have taken twenty talents for your own pocket, someone else has taken fifteen, Demades has six thousand gold staters, and others have the amounts attributed to them?[85] Sixty-four talents have been discovered, for which you must see that the guilt must be placed on these men.[86] **[90]** Which is the better and more just alternative: to keep all the money in the Treasury until the people reach a right decision, or for some of the orators and the generals to seize it as plunder? I myself think that to keep it in the Treasury is accepted as right by everyone and that no one would say it was right for these men to have it.

[91] Gentlemen, this man has made a multitude of differing statements but never the same one. He sees that he has deceived you all along with empty hopes and false claims, and you remember his promises only while they are being made. If the city must reap the rewards of Demosthenes' dishonesty and misfortune so that we are even more possessed by an evil spirit—I'm at a loss to describe it any other way—then we should accept our current circumstances. **[92]** But if we have any feeling for our country and hate criminals and those who take bribes, and want our fortune to change and improve, you must not, Atheni-

---

[85] The "someone else" is probably Philocles, the general who allowed Harpalus to enter Athens in contravention of the directive of the Assembly and was later prosecuted (Din. 3). Demades' bribe would work out to twenty talents, the same as that of Demosthenes, and so we are likely dealing with rhetorical exaggeration. The others are unknown, although Din. 2.1 says that Aristogeiton took twenty minas.

[86] If Harpalus had entered with seven hundred talents, then the Areopagus' six-month investigation had not met with great success for 286 talents remained untraced. More likely is that Harpalus came with 450 talents, and hence 36 were unaccounted for.

ans, be swayed by the entreaties of this wretched magician, and you must not listen to his lamentations and impositions. You have had sufficient experience of him, his speeches, his deeds, and his luck. [93] Athenians, which one of you is so hopeful, which so reckless, which so ignorant of affairs past and present that he expects that the man who has reduced the city from such prosperity to such disrepute, through whatever cause or fortune—and I disregard that—will now save us by serving as adviser and administrator? As well as the other difficulties and dangers that face us, there is the added venality of those in the city itself, and all of us together are disputing a shocking charge, so that all the people should not be thought to have the money that a certain few keep for themselves. [94] I disregard the other fluctuations in his policies and continual ill-judged speeches. At one time he introduced a proposal banning anyone from believing in any god other than the traditional ones and then said that it was necessary for the people not to dispute deifying Alexander.[87] Or when he was about to be tried before you, how he impeached Callimedon for scheming with the exiles at Megara to subvert the democracy and then suddenly rescinded this impeachment.[88] [95] And how he brought forward and primed a false informer at the recent meeting of the Assembly to say there was a plot against the dockyards.[89] He made no proposals about

[87] Alexander's proposed apotheosis in 323 had been resisted by many Greek states, including Athens. When Demosthenes returned from meeting Nicanor at Olympia, he advocated acceptance of it and so was accused of taking a bribe (cf. 1.103 and Hyp. 5.31–32). Dinarchus is misrepresenting Demosthenes' apparent acquiescence to the king's deification; cf. Hyp. 5.31, where Demosthenes is alleged to have said that "Alexander might be the son of Zeus and also Poseidon if he wanted."

[88] The exiles are those gathering at Megara in anticipation of the Exiles Decree (cf. 1.58). Since Athens was resisting their return, it would appear that only a conspiracy would bring this about. Perhaps Polyeuctus too had conspired with the exiles and been caught, hence his citation at 1.58.

[89] At 1.63 Dinarchus cites Antiphon's intention to burn the Piraeus dockyards for Philip (see note). The incident referred to in this chapter cannot be the same, because Antiphon's attempt was between 346 and 343, whereas Dinarchus talks of a recent meeting of the Assembly, and Antiphon was originally acquitted by the people but then condemned by the Areopagus.

these matters but was preparing allegations to use in the present trial. You yourselves are witnesses of all these things. Gentlemen of Athens, this man is a magician and an abomination, unworthy of citizenship by birth or by his administration and actions. **[96]** What triremes have been built by this man for the city, as under Eubulus?[90] What dockyards have been constructed in his administration? When has this man increased the cavalry by a decree or a law? When such opportunities presented themselves after the battle of Chaeronea, what land or sea force did he raise? What ornament to the goddess did he carry up to the Acropolis? What building did Demosthenes construct in your commercial district, or in the city, or anywhere else in the country? No one could show one anywhere! **[97]** If someone has been untrustworthy in matters of war, and worthless in the administration of the city, has paid no attention as his opponents accomplished everything they wished, and has changed his own position and actions in support of the people, will you want to preserve this man? **[98]** Not if you are wise and want what is best for you and the city. You will welcome the good fortune that handed over for punishment those orators whose corruption degraded the city. And you will be on your guard, as the gods have many times warned you in the oracles, against these leaders and advisers. Listen to the oracle itself.[91] Read the oracle.

[ORACLE]

[99] How then, Athenians, shall we have one opinion? How shall we all agree on the interests of the state when the leaders and the demagogues take money and betray the well-being of the country? You and all the people are in danger concerning the very soil of the city, the temples of your fathers, and your children and wives, but these men have reached agreement so that they deliberately vilify and attack each other in the Assembly but in private are united to deceive

---

[90] Eubulus' financial administration of Athens in the mid 350s led to a rapid improvement in the city's prosperity. He was responsible for various economic and military measures, not least being work on the Piraeus dockyards and encouragement to trade. Dinarchus' picture of Demosthenes' failure ignores his payments in the form of liturgies and other public contributions, which would have outweighed any such neglect of the patron goddess, Athena.

[91] See 1.78n.

you, and you are too easily persuaded by their speeches. [100] What is the duty of a democratic orator who hates those who speak and make proposals against the people? What do they say, Demosthenes and Polyeuctus,[92] that your predecessors continued to do even when no danger then threatened the city? Did they not try each other? Or impeach each other? Or bring suit for illegal proposals? You allege that you have the people at heart and that your safety rests upon the vote of these men, but have you done any of these things? [101] Have you censured a decree, Demosthenes, given the many scandalous and illegal ones that Demades proposed?[93] Have you checked any move that he undertook on his own against the well-being of the people? Not a single one. Have you impeached the man who worked against the decrees and the laws of the people? Never. But you permitted him to set up his bronze statue in the Agora and to take his meals in the Prytaneum along with the descendants of Harmodius and Aristogeiton.[94] [102] How, then, did the people experience your benevolence? Where did we see proof of the orators' protecting power? Or will you say that your skills lie in your ability to deceive these men by always saying that "it is not possible for us to leave the country" and "there is no other place of refuge apart from your goodwill"? You should have made it clear that in word and deed you sought to counteract decrees proposed against the people's interests. In this way you would persuade these men that you have no avenue of safety apart from the support of the people. [103] But you fix your hopes on those from abroad and compete in flattery with those who admit that they work for Alexander and have taken bribes from the same sources as you,

---

[92] Polyeuctus is probably Polyeuctus of Sphettus, also accused of taking bribes in the Harpalus affair and apparently acquitted (see the Introduction to Dinarchus).

[93] On Demades, see 1.7n.

[94] Harmodius and Aristogeiton murdered Hipparchus, son of the tyrant Pisistratus, then joint ruler of Athens with his brother Hippias, in 514 (see Thuc. 6.54–59, *Ath. Pol.* 18). Hippias ruled for a further four years until a Spartan force expelled him, but Harmodius and Aristogeiton were still recognized as tyrannicides. They were the first recipients of a public statue, and their descendants received these state awards for life (Is. 5.47, Dem. 19.280 and 20.29); cf. 1.38 and 1.43 with notes.

according to the Council's recent report. And you consulted with Nicanor at Olympia[95] in the presence of all the Greeks and arranged everything as you wanted, but you, a traitor and receiver of bribes, now ask for pity, as though these men will overlook your venality and you will not be punished for the crimes you have been caught committing. [104] In this you are more daring than Demades.[96] He revealed his deranged streak in the Assembly and confessed that he takes bribes and will continue to do so, but he did not dare show his face before these men or presume to contest the Council's report. And yet he did not propose that the Council should have power over him or agree to death if it should be proved that he took money. But you have such enormous faith in your own arguments and such scorn for the simplicity of these men that you think you will convince the jurors that in your case alone the Council has been deceived and that, of those it reported, you alone did not take the gold. Who on earth would be persuaded by that?

[105] Athenians, consider what you are going to do. You have taken over the case from the people who know what happened in order to punish those subject to the reports. Demosthenes is being tried first. We have made our accusation without any concession to anyone in the interests of common justice. [106] Will you overlook all that has taken place and acquit the first man brought before you? Will you, who are sovereign in all things, discard decisions approved by the people, by the Council of the Areopagus, and by all mankind and surrender yourselves to the corruption of these men? [107] Or will you set an example on behalf of the city for all mankind that you detest traitors and those who betray the interests of the people for money? All this is now up to you, the 1,500 jurors who have the safety of the entire city in your hands. Today your vote will bring great security for the city if you are willing to make the right decision; otherwise, if you condone this behavior you will destroy everyone's hopes for the future.

[108] Gentlemen of Athens, if you are sensible, you will not be cowed or abandon the just defense of the city because of Demosthe-

---

[95] On Demosthenes' mission to Olympia about the Exiles Decree, cf. 1.81 and 1.94 with notes.

[96] On Demades, see 1.7n.

nes' pleas for pity. Not one of you forced him to take money that did not belong to him against your interests, when he has far more than he needs thanks to you, nor to defend himself now for the crimes that he admitted when he proposed the death penalty for himself. But the shamelessness and venality inherent in his whole life have brought this upon his own head. [109] Do not feel grieved by his weeping and wailing; you would far more justly feel pity for the land, which this man lays open to danger by doing such things, which beseeches you who are born of it, by your wives and children, to punish the traitor and save it. Your ancestors faced many and glorious dangers on its behalf and handed it over to you free. In it many distinguished examples have been left of the virtue of those who died. [110] Athenians, right-thinking men must look to this land, to the traditional sacrifices celebrated in it, and to the tombs of our ancestors when delivering the vote. And when Demosthenes wants to deceive you and distracts you by lamenting and weeping, think of the city's reputation and the former glory that belonged to it, and judge whether the city deserves more pity because of him, or Demosthenes because of the city. [111] You will find that this man has grown famous from the time he entered political life. After being a speechwriter and a paid advocate for Ctesippus[97] and Phormio[98] and many others, he is now the richest man in the city. From obscurity and with no family tradition of honored forebears, he has become renowned; but the city has fallen into a plight unworthy of itself or of the glory of our ancestors. Therefore disregard his appeals and trickery, and deliver a verdict both proper and just, and give heed to the interests of the country, not those of Demosthenes. For this is the duty of good and noble jurors. [112] And whenever anyone comes forward to speak for Demosthenes, remember that even if he is not a subject of the forthcoming reports, he is ill disposed to the constitution, he does not want those taking bribes against the people to be punished, and he wants the common protection of your persons, for which the Council of the Areopagus has been set up, destroyed and all the rights in the city abolished. But if an orator or a general speaks for him, wanting to weaken the effect of the report they expect

[97] Dem. 20. The outcome is unknown.

[98] Dem. 36. Phormio was acquitted.

will accuse them, you must not listen to their arguments, knowing that a conspiracy arose between all these men over the arrival and escape of Harpalus. [113] Athenians, consider then that all these men come forward against your interests and are common enemies of the laws and of the entire city. Do not listen to them but order them to make their defense speeches in relation to the charges. And do not listen to his ravings: he prides himself on his ability to speak, and since it is clear that he took bribes against you, he has been proved an even greater cheat. No, punish him as you yourselves and the city deserve. Otherwise, by one vote and at one trial you will release all those who have been reported and who will be in the future, and you will bring the corruption of these men onto your own heads and the people. Even if you later indict those who acquitted them, by then this will be absolutely no use to you.

[114] I have done my best with my share of the prosecution, disregarding everything else apart from justice and your interests. I have not deserted the city, nor have I attached greater weight to personal regard than to the vote of the people. I ask you now to share my opinion, and I hand over the water to the other prosecutors.[99]

---

[99] The water is the *klepsydra,* water clock, which timed speeches at trials (*Ath. Pol.* 67.2–5); see Boegehold 1995: 77–78 with plate 13.

2. AGAINST ARISTOGEITON

INTRODUCTION

For the historical background, see the Introduction to Dinarchus. Aristogeiton was a minor orator and perhaps a descendant of the famous sixth-century tyrannicide of the same name, who in 514, along with Harmodius, had been responsible for murdering the tyrant Hipparchus, a son of Pisistratus (see above, 1.101n). Sometime after 338, he was prosecuted for failing to pay his debts; two prosecution speeches from that trial are preserved as Demosthenes 25 and 26, although the common opinion is that Demosthenes did not write them.

In the present trial, Aristogeiton is accused by the Areopagus of taking twenty minas from Harpalus (Din. 2.1); we learn from Demosthenes, *Epistle* 3.37–38 and 42, that he was acquitted. His trial was one of the later ones of those accused in the Harpalus scandal, since we can infer from Dinarchus 3.12 that Aristogeiton followed Philocles (for whose trial Din. 3 was written) and from 3.14 that several others were tried before Philocles. The identity of the speaker is unknown; he may well have been Himeraeus or Menesaechmus, one of whom is likely to have prosecuted Demosthenes. In this speech, Dinarchus uses much the same sort of invective as that against Demosthenes, and again he offers no proof against him.

The end of this speech is lost. Since Dinarchus refers to the prosecution delivering short speeches (7), this speech may not have been much longer than we now have.

2. AGAINST ARISTOGEITON

[1] Athenians, we must expect to hear and see everything in connection with the reports that have been made,[1] but the most amazing fact of all, or so it seems to me, is now before us. Aristogeiton, the most disreputable of all men in the city, indeed in the whole of mankind, has come to challenge the Council of the Areopagus in matters of truth and justice. The Council, which has made its report, is now subject to greater danger than this man who took bribes against you and who for twenty minas sold the right to free speech about justice. [2] It will be nothing new or terrible for this man if he is convicted, for he has previously committed many other crimes that deserve death and has spent more time in prison than out of it. He has also illegally indicted those with full citizen rights while he was a debtor to the state[2] and has committed many other heinous crimes whose details you know better than I. It is a most shameful and shocking thing if the report by the Council against Aristogeiton is considered false, and you think that this man is speaking with more justice than that body. [3] Therefore, Athenians, it seems to me that this man has come to test your attitude, thinking that he is in no danger at this trial. He has often suffered all sorts of terrible things except execution, but this he will suffer on this very day, if God is willing and you are wise. For you must not think, by Heracles, that he will improve if you pity him now or that he will stop taking bribes against you in the future if you acquit him now. It may be possible to nip wickedness quickly in the bud by punishment, but they say it is incurable when it is advanced and has tasted the ordinary penalties. [4] If therefore you want wickedness to grow up inexorably fixed in the city, you must protect Aristogeiton and allow him to do whatever he wishes in the city. But if you hate criminals and accursed men, and can remember with anger what this person has previously done, put him to death. He dared to take money from Harpalus whom he knew was coming to seize your city.

---

[1] These are the reports issued by the Areopagus that accused leading Athenians of complicity in the Harpalus affair; see the Introduction to Dinarchus.

[2] Those in debt to the state lost their political and judicial privileges and became disfranchised until outstanding fines were paid (Dem. 24.123, 58.1, Andoc. 1.74).

Dismiss his excuses and lies, for he puts his faith in these when he comes before you.

[5] Are you aware that despite the problems associated with the arrival of Harpalus, the city has benefited because you were given the chance to learn exactly who received silver and gold and betrayed everything to the enemies of Athens? Athenians, do not be remiss or give up penalizing criminals but banish bribery from the city to the best of your ability. Do not ask to hear arguments from me when you can clearly see that those whom the Council reported have been linked with the crimes. [6] What do you now want to hear against the defendant that you do not already know? Will the report of the Council against Aristogeiton be true and just if we, the ten accusers, use up all the water[3] and declare how terrible it is to acquit those who have been caught in the act[4] of taking bribes against the country? [7] Will the report made by the Areopagites be false and unjust if each of us leaves the rostrum after a short speech, believing that you know as much as we do about where justice lies in these trials? Or, do you not know that taking bribes in order to betray the interests of a city is one of the greatest and most damaging crimes against a city?

[8] Will we hear, by Zeus, that the defendant is a man of moderate temper, who comes from a good family, and has performed many noble deeds for you in private and public life, and that for this reason he deserves to be acquitted? Yet which one of you has not often heard that when Cydimachus, Aristogeiton's father,[5] was condemned to death and fled from the city, his noble son allowed his own father to live without the necessities of life and, when he died, refused him the customary funerary rites, for which he was often indicted? [9] Or, that when he was thrown into prison the first time—you are no doubt

---

[3] The water clock measured the time limits at Athenian trials; see 1.114n.

[4] This phrase has a legal foundation. In some judicial procedures the criminal had to be caught "in the act," but by the fourth century the expression was used with any notorious crime.

[5] In Athenian law, children were to support their parents in old age and to give them a proper burial (*Ath. Pol.* 56.6, Dem. 24.103–107, Is. 1.39 and 8.32). Cydimachus was condemned to death by the Athenians and fled to Eretria (Dem. 25.54, 65, 77), where he died in the 350s, apparently in these miserable circumstances.

aware that this has often happened to him—he dared to act in such a manner there that the prisoners voted not to give him a light or have meals with him or share in the usual sacrifices? Athenians, give thought then to the character of this man, who was thrown into prison because of his wickedness, [10] and while there, among those criminals deliberately isolated from the rest of mankind, he was regarded as so corrupt that even there he was not thought to deserve the same treatment as the others. The story goes that he was caught stealing from them, and that if there were a more shameful place for those who stole in prison, then this creature would have been thrown into it. Who does not know that this evidence—as I've just said—was brought against Aristogeiton when he was selected to be an Overseer of the Exchange, and as a result, he was rejected by those who then decided the appointment to this office?[6] [11] Are you pretending ignorance among yourselves, and, as you are about to vote, do you feel pity for Aristogeiton, who did not weep for his own father when he was reduced to starvation? Do you want to hear yet more facts from us about Aristogeiton's punishment, when you certainly know that his whole life and what he has recently done justly merit the extreme penalty? [12] Athenians, was it not Aristogeiton who wrote down such lies against the priestess of Artemis of Brauron[7] and her family that when you found out the truth from his accusers, you fined him five talents, the same amount as the fine imposed for the crime of illegal proposals? Although he has not yet paid this fine, has he not continued to malign everyone of you he comes across? Has he not continued

---

[6] These officials were appointed by lot (*Ath. Pol.* 51.4); they ensured that two-thirds of all imported grain went to the city of Athens and oversaw matters relating to the market generally (*Ath. Pol.* 51.4, Dem. 35.51, 58.8–9). They were subject to a *dokimasia* (an inquiry to check their qualifications for the post) before entering office (see 17n), as a result of which Aristogeiton's candidature for the office was rejected.

[7] In ca. 332/1 Aristogeiton proposed the execution without trial of Hierocles, son of the priestess of Artemis Brauronia, for sacrilege, accusing him of having in his possession the sacred garments associated with the goddess. Hierocles protested that he had acted on the orders of his mother, and his father successfully challenged Aristogeiton, who was fined five talents.

to speak and propose measures in the Assembly[8] and to treat with contempt all the penalties that are laid down in the laws against wrongdoers? [13] Finally, was not this man indicted by Lycurgus and found guilty?[9] Then, although he was a debtor to the state and unable to speak in public and was handed over to the Eleven[10] in accordance with the laws, was he not seen walking around in front of the law-courts and sitting on the seat of the Prytanes? [14] Gentlemen of Athens, when the laws have many times handed him over to you for punishment, and he has been condemned on information brought against him by citizens, and when neither the Eleven nor prison have been able to guard him, will you want this man as counsellor? The law orders that the herald shall pray with great solemnity and then hand over to you the right to deliberate about state matters. Will you allow this sacrilegious individual, who has been wicked to everyone and especially to his own father, to share in citizenship with you and your families and relatives?

[15] You decided to show no mercy towards Demades[11] and Demosthenes because it was proved that they took bribes against your interests. You punished them, and rightly so, although you knew they had served you well in almost every area of their public duties. Will you acquit this accursed wretch who has never ever done anything good for you but has been the greatest possible source of evil since he entered political life? Who would not condemn you if you accepted this man as counsellor? When a person whose wickedness is familiar and obvious and notorious among all citizens speaks in the Assembly, the spectators will wonder whether you listen to him because you do not have better counsellors or whether you like listening to such people. [16] Athenians, just as the first lawgivers laid down laws con-

---

[8] It was against the law for those in debt to the state to do such things; see 2n.

[9] While Aristogeiton was still in debt to the state, he had illegally attempted to prosecute Ariston of Alopece (Dem. 25.71–73) and so was indicted by Lycurgus and Demosthenes.

[10] The Eleven was a body of eleven magistrates in charge of the prison. They were authorized to arrest people against whom certain formal charges had been made.

[11] On Demades, see 1.7n.

cerning those who addressed your ancestors in the Assembly, so you as listeners should try to make speakers today better. How did the first lawgivers view these men? First, they uttered curses in public against criminals at each meeting of the Assembly, and anyone who took bribes and after that spoke and made proposals affecting public affairs was to be destroyed. Aristogeiton is now one of these. [17] Second, they included indictments for bribery in the laws, and for this crime alone they imposed a fine ten times greater than the damages,[12] thinking that the man willing to take payment for his proposals in the Assembly speaks not in the best interests of the people but for those who paid him. The Council has reported Aristogeiton's guilt. Moreover, they ask those selected to hold public office what sort of person he is, whether he treats his parents well, whether he has been on a military campaign, whether he has an ancestral tomb, and whether he has paid his taxes.[13] [18] Aristogeiton cannot claim any of these qualifications for himself. Instead of looking after his parents, he abused his own father.[14] When all of you were serving in the army he was in prison. And, Athenians, not only can he not point to any memorial to his father but also when his father died in Eretria Aristogeiton did not even give him a proper burial. Although other Athenians are contributing money from their private resources, he has not paid all the money he owes for his public debts. [19] In a nutshell, he has continued to live in contravention of all the laws, and in his case alone the Council of the Areopagus has reported someone whom you had already investigated and knew the facts. You did not learn he is a wicked criminal from the Council—each one of you already knew the full details of his corruption. And so the statement made many times rings true in this context: while you are about to pass judgment on this man, the spectators and everyone else are passing judgment on you.

[20] And so, Athenians, your duty as wise jurors is not to cast your vote against yourselves or all the other Athenians but with one accord

---

[12] The tenfold fine (cf. Hyp. 5.24 and *Ath. Pol.* 54.2) was only one form of punishment; cf. 1.60 with note.

[13] These are the kinds of questions asked at the *dokimasia,* the examination to assess whether candidates for office had the necessary legal qualifications; cf. Dem. 57.66–70, Aes. 1.28, *Ath. Pol.* 55.3.

[14] See 8n.

to sentence him to be handed over to the executioners and receive the death penalty. Do not release him or betray your sacred oath.[15] Remember that the Council convicted him of taking bribes against you, that his father convicted him while alive and when dead of doing him wrong—to use the mildest of terms—and that the people have condemned him and handed him over to you to be punished. [21] He has caused so much damage and has now been caught committing such crimes that it would be shameful for you, his judges, to let him go unpunished. Otherwise, Athenians, how will you vote on the other reports? What excuses will you offer for condemning those you have already tried? How can you have been clearly eager for the Council to report those who took the money, and then let those it reported escape punishment?

[22] Do not think that these trials are private issues involving only those recently reported; they are public issues and involve every other man. A case of bribery or corruption tried by you will have one of two consequences: either men will be encouraged to take money against your interests, since they know they will not meet with justice, or they will be afraid to take bribes since a punishment fitting the crime awaits those who are caught. [23] Are you not aware now that fear of you restrains those who are now ready to take money against your interests, and often makes them refuse bribes, and that the decree of the people authorizing the Council to investigate this money did not get a confession from even those who brought the gold into the country? [24] Athenians, your ancestors passed a truly noble decree about this, setting up a pillar on the Acropolis, when Arthmius the son of Pythonax the Zelite is said to have brought gold from Persia to corrupt the Greeks.[16] Even before anyone accepted it or gave proof of his character, they sentenced the man who brought in the gold to exile and banished him from the whole country. They inscribed this decision,

---

[15] The jurors swore an annual oath when they were first selected for jury service: Dem. 24.149–151.

[16] The decree was set up on a bronze stele on the Acropolis (cf. Dem. 9.41, 19.272). Not long after the formation of the Delian League in 478 Arthmius, son of Pythoanax of Zelea, brought Persian gold into Greece in order to incite a war against Athens (Dem. 9.42–43; cf. Dem. 19.271, Aes. 3.258). He was expelled from Athens and, along with his family, declared an outlaw.

as I said, on a bronze pillar that they set up on the Acropolis as an example to you, their descendants, thinking that someone who took money however he could had in mind not the interests of the city but of those who gave it to him. [25] And in his case alone they inscribed the reason why the people expelled him from the city, expressly stating that Arthmius the son of Pythonax the Zelite was an enemy of the people and its allies, he and his descendants, and that he was exiled from Athens because he brought the gold from Persia into the Peloponnese. And yet if the people considered the gold in the Peloponnese to be a cause of great danger for the Greeks, how can we be indifferent to the bribery in the city itself? Give your attention to this inscription.

[INSCRIPTION]

[26] Athenians, what do you think those men would have done if they discovered a general or an orator from their own citizenry accepting bribes against the best interests of their country, when they had so justly and wisely banished a man who was not Greek in birth or character? For that very reason they faced danger against the barbarian in a manner worthy of their city and ancestors.

3. AGAINST PHILOCLES

INTRODUCTION

For the historical background to this trial, see the Introduction to Dinarchus. Philocles was the general who had been charged by the Assembly with refusing Harpalus entry into Athens when he had first fled from Alexander the Great. Philocles obeyed this directive, but when Harpalus returned to Athens as a suppliant and with a much reduced force, Philocles allowed him into the city. Philocles was allegedly indicted three times (cf. 3.16). In this speech, he seems to be accused of disobeying the Assembly and taking a bribe from Harpalus, which would account for two of the three indictments. It is important to note that the Philocles who held the important position of *kosmētēs* (Guardian of the Ephebes; cf. 15n) in 324/3 was a different person.

It appears that Philocles was condemned (Dem., *Epistle* 3.31). He was guilty of disobeying the Assembly's direct orders; however, Dinarchus cites no evidence of his accepting a bribe from Harpalus. As in the previous two speeches, Dinarchus emphasizes the prestige and reputation of the Areopagus, together with Philocles' apparently unscrupulous character. However, the character denigration in 6 is negated when we are told in 12 that Philocles was elected to several important posts. The identity of the speaker is unknown; again, he may have been either Himeraeus or Menesaechmus, one of whom is likely to have prosecuted Demosthenes.

The conclusion to the speech is missing. As with Dinarchus 2, the present speech may not have been much longer than we now have.

3. AGAINST PHILOCLES

[1] By the gods, what shall we say about men such as these? How will you deal with the wickedness of this man, who was convicted not once but three times by the Council of the Areopagus, as all of you know and heard in the recent Assembly? When he was elected by you as general for Munychia and the dockyards, he lied in front of all the Athenians and other spectators by promising that he would prohibit Harpalus from sailing into Piraeus.[1] [2] He dared to take bribes against all of you, your country, your children, and your wives; he has broken the oath he swore between the holy statue and the table;[2] and has proposed a decree against himself that if he has taken any money brought by Harpalus into the country, he shall be punished by death.[3] [3] Nevertheless, he has dared to come and show himself before you, although you know that he has been proved liable for these charges. Athenians, his case is based not on justice—for how can justice apply to him?—but on daring and shamelessness, which have led him to take bribes in the past, treating you and the city's justice with contempt. He has now come with the defense that he has done none of these things; so thoroughly does he scorn your apathy. [4] The law of the city, which governs us all, says that if anyone breaks an agreement made with another citizen, then this man shall be subject to prosecution as an offender. Shall this man, who has deceived all Athenians, betrayed the trust that he did not merit from you, and ruined everything in the city to the best of his ability, say he has come to present his defense on the charge brought against him? [5] Gentlemen, if I must speak the truth—and I must indeed—I think you are not judging whether the report against Philocles is true or false but must only decide the penalty according to the decree, whether you should fine

[1] Ten generals were elected annually by the people in Assembly, and they played an influential role in Athenian politics. The generalship involved a variety of duties and was divided into a number of areas (*Ath. Pol.* 61.1–2). Cf. 1.71 with note.

[2] We do not know where these were.

[3] Demosthenes and others, including Philocles, had proposed a personal decree agreeing to submit to the death penalty if found guilty by the Areopagus of taking bribes from Harpalus.

the man who has done so much damage to the city or punish him with death, just as he proposed in the decree against himself, and confiscate his property, which was accumulated from these unjust gains.

[6] Do you think that this case of bribery is the first time he has committed a crime or that he has never before taken bribes against you? No; he has been like this for a long time, but you were unaware of it. You have been lucky not to have experienced his venality at more important times—for there is nothing worse than someone's wickedness being unknown. [7] Athenians, will you not all, with one accord, execute the man who brought such shame and injustice on many of our citizens, he who was primarily responsible for the distribution of the gold, thus opening our entire city to blame? Or will you agree to hear him argue—he who has done so much against your interests—that the Council of the Areopagus made a false report, that he himself is just and honorable and incorruptible, and that the Council has produced all this for the sake of favors or illegal gain? [8] Do you understand that with other crimes you must examine the case carefully and calmly in order to discover the truth and then inflict punishment on the criminals, but in clear cases of treason acknowledged by all you must first give reign to anger and the appropriate punishment? [9] Do you not think there is anything of importance in the city that he would not sell if you put him in charge of it, trusting in his loyalty and honesty? Are there any triremes in the dockyards he would not sell?[4] Is there anything he would protect if he thought he could escape notice and take double the gold he has just received? Gentlemen, a man like this would stop at nothing. [10] Whoever considers silver and gold more important than loyalty to you, and treats oaths and respect and justice as less important than taking bribes, will do his utmost to sell Munychia,[5] if he has someone to buy it. He will signal the enemy and reveal your interests, and he will betray your army and fleet.[6]

[11] Athenians, consider that you are about to set the penalty not

---

[4] Cf. 1.96, where Demosthenes is slandered in much the same vein.

[5] Munychia was the fortified citadel of Piraeus and thus crucial to Athenian security.

[6] An allusion to the aftermath of the battle of Marathon in 490, when the victorious Athenian force spotted a signal caused by the sun's rays off a shield from

only for the crimes Philocles committed but also for the others he would have committed had he been able. Give thanks to the gods that you did not suffer far worse at his hands, knowing the sort of person he is, and punish him as befits yourselves and the defendant's wickedness. [12] Athenians, he was appointed to command reputable men in the cavalry three or four times. You elected him general more than ten times, although he was unworthy.[7] He has been honored and admired for his loyalty to you, but he sold and betrayed the dignity of the command you conferred and lowered himself to the same level as Aristogeiton.[8] Instead of a general, he made himself a hireling and a traitor. [13] You are the ones wronged: should you yield and feel pity for this man, who felt no shame in acting against you and the rest? Athenians, those sorts of men could not rightly be pitied by you—not by any means—but rather those whom Philocles would have betrayed if he had had the chance, and among these are the promontory and the harbors and the dockyards, which your ancestors constructed at great cost and left for you. [14] You must remember these things, Athenians, and not be lax about the reports produced by the Council. [Judge this case][9] in the same manner as you judged those before. It is disgraceful not to punish those who have been proved traitors to the city or to let any sinner or criminal survive when the gods have revealed them to you and handed them over for punishment. You see that the entire city has accused Philocles and delivered him first of all to you for punishment.

[15] By Zeus the Protector, I am ashamed that you must be urged on and stirred up by us[10] in order to punish this man now on trial before you. Are you not eyewitnesses of the crimes he committed? The entire city considered it neither safe nor right to entrust its children to

---

the heights of Mount Pentelicus. It was believed that this was a signal to the Persian army that Athens lay undefended. A Persian force was already making its way from Marathon to the city, but it was thwarted (Herod. 6.115–116, 124).

[7] See 1n.

[8] The defendant against whom Din. 2 was delivered.

[9] There is a gap in the Greek text at this point; the words in brackets give the likely sense.

[10] This implies that there was more than one prosecutor in the case against Philocles, although whether he was faced with ten like Demosthenes is unknown.

him and so rejected him as Guardian of the Ephebes.[11] [16] Will you spare someone who has acted like this, you the protectors of the democracy and the laws, to whom fortune of lot has entrusted [the safety][12] of the people through your judgment? You are sovereign in all matters of justice in the city. Will you acquit the man who has taken bribes and been the cause of every depravity? As I said a little while ago, he alone of all those accused has been reported not once but three times and so might already have been justly executed three times according to his own decree.[13] [17] Athenians, what are you waiting for? What worse crimes than those just cited do you want to hear about? Was it not you and your ancestors who took no account of the great deeds of Timotheus[14]—he sailed around the Peloponnese and defeated the Spartans in a naval battle off Corcyra, he was the son of Conon who freed the Greeks, and he took Samos, Methone, Pydna, Potidaea, and twenty other cities as well—you did not let such accomplishments affect the trial then taking place or the oaths by which you cast your votes, but you fined him one hundred talents because Aristophon revealed that he took bribes from the Chians and Rhodians. [18] But this miserable traitor, whom not one man but the entire Council of the Areopagus has revealed, upon investigation, to have taken bribes against you, who has much wealth and no male heirs,[15] and is in need of nothing else that a decent man would require, did not refrain from taking bribes against the country and did not conceal his inherent depravity but completely destroyed his reputation for loyalty towards you. He has aligned himself with men whom he once said he opposed, and his apparent goodness has been proved false.

[19] Athenians, you must all consider these things and bear in mind

---

[11] This was the principal supervisor of the ephebes (*Ath. Pol.* 42.2–3), male citizens aged 18 who underwent a system of military and moral training for two years.

[12] There is another gap in the Greek text here; the words in brackets give the likely sense. Jurymen for each trial were selected by lot from those available.

[13] See 3n.

[14] This chapter is practically a verbatim duplication of 1.14; cf. 1.75. See 1.14n.

[15] This is probably untrue, since at 1.71 Dinarchus paraphrases the law that generals were required to have legitimate male children.

the present circumstances, which cry out for loyalty, not venality. You must hate wrongdoers, you must eradicate such creatures from the city, and you must show all mankind that the majority of the people have not been corrupted by a handful of orators and generals and are not slaves to their reputation. They know that with justice and harmony among ourselves, we shall easily defend ourselves, if the gods are willing, against anyone unjustly attacking us. No city can survive with bribery and treason and other similar evils in it, as are practiced by these men. [20] Therefore, Athenians, you must not accept pleas or feel pity; do not invalidate the guilt that is plainly fixed on the defendants by the facts and the truth,[16] but you must all come to the aid of the country and its laws, which are both on trial now against his venality. [21] Athenians, you are about to vote on behalf of the whole country, its established shrines, your ancestral customs, and the constitution that was handed down by your ancestors. You are voting not just on Philocles, for he sentenced himself to death a long time ago. In asking this of you, I am urging a much more just appeal than those who have committed these acts. Do not forsake the values for which your ancestors faced many dangers, do not reduce the reputation of the city to ignoble shame, do not show goodwill to these men rather than to the laws, the decrees of the people, and the reports of the Areopagus. [22] For well you know, Athenians, well you know, that you are being praised by the whole of mankind for your investigation into this money. Men convicted of taking bribes against their own country are seen as wicked, immoral, and haters of democracy, though they claim to be your friends and to be providing worthy services for the city. They have become renowned because of you.

---

[16] There is a gap in the Greek text at this point.

HYPERIDES

Translated with introduction by Craig R. Cooper

INTRODUCTION TO HYPERIDES

Hyperides, son of Glaucippus, of the deme Collytes was born in the year 389/8.[1] According to tradition, as a young man he studied under Plato and Isocrates, and since such education was expensive, we can assume that he came from a family of considerable means. Hyperides himself is known to have owned at least two or three pieces of property: an estate in Eleusis, a house in Athens, and possibly a house in Piraeus, where he kept one of his many women. He is also known to have leased sacred property at Eleusis and a mine in the mining district of Laurium.

Hyperides, then, had sufficient wealth to rank among the richest families of Athens and to qualify for public services (liturgies) imposed by law on the rich (Fr. 134n). Such duties could include deferring the cost of outfitting a warship (trireme), and it is in this capacity that we first find him performing these public duties. In the spring of 340, Hyperides raised a fleet of forty triremes from private donations, and in 340/39, when Philip was besieging Byzantium, he volunteered as trierarch and served as *chorēgos,* or Chorus producer.[2] These are the only public services that he is known to have performed, and since they all occurred around the same time (340), they may be connected with money he is said to have received from the Persian King, who was alarmed at Macedon's expansion.[3] Two of the activities were di-

[1] Most of our knowledge of the life of Hyperides comes from Pseudo-Plutarch's biography of the orator in the *Moralia* (848d–850b), and from scattered references in the speeches of Aeschines and Demosthenes.

[2] See the Series Introduction, p. xix.

[3] See Davies 1971: 30.

rected against Philip, and as we shall see, Hyperides' rise to prominence and eventual demise would be tied to his opposition to the Macedonians.

Hyperides acquired his considerable wealth from logography and, unlike his more famous contemporary Demosthenes, continued in this line of work long after he began his political career. We know little about his career as a logographer and politician before the 340s, by which time he was a prominent political figure. His earliest known speeches can be dated to the 360s and 350s; they are all of a political nature, and it was his boast (4.28) not to have prosecuted any private citizen, only politicians. In 362, at a relatively young age and perhaps to make a name for himself, he prosecuted Aristophon of Hazenia for making an illegal proposal (Frs. 40–44). Shortly thereafter (360), he charged the Athenian general Autocles with treason over his failed activities in Thrace (Frs. 55–57, Dem. 23.104). The attack was again directed at Aristophon, who, it seems, was behind the expedition in the first place. Hyperides' opposition to Aristophon is curious: we do not know his motives nor with whom he was associated. The next event of political importance in Hyperides' life sees him ranged on the side of Aristophon, the only well-known figure to oppose peace with Philip in 346.

In 343 Hyperides positioned himself clearly within the anti-Macedonian camp, when he prosecuted Philocrates for accepting bribes from Philip (4.29). Philocrates was the driving force behind the peace (Dem. 19.116); his name was attached to the decree that authorized sending envoys to Philip to negotiate terms and to the decree that accepted the terms offered by Philip (Aes. 2.17–19; 3.63, Dem. 19.47–49, 121). Most prominent politicians, including Demosthenes and Aeschines, had spoken in support of peace (Dem. 19.15–16, 144, 307, Aes. 2.75–77, 3.71–72), and in 346 the Athenians were persuaded to sign what became known as the Peace of Philocrates. But between 346 and 343 the mood in Athens changed, largely because of Philip's continued meddling in Greek affairs, and supporters of the peace came under attack. In 343 Aeschines was prosecuted by Demosthenes and, according to tradition, acquitted by only thirty votes.[4] In that same

[4] The speeches in this case are preserved; see Aes. 2 and Dem. 19.

year, and perhaps even before Aeschines came to trial, Hyperides brought an impeachment (*eisangelia*) against Philocrates, who did not await his trial but went into exile (4.29, Dem. 19.116, Aes. 2.6). We may surmise that in 343 began the friendship and association between Hyperides and Demosthenes that would last until 324.

Shortly after the trial of Aeschines, Hyperides was chosen to replace him as Athens' representative in a dispute with Delos (Frs. 67–71; cf. Dem. 18.134). Hyperides won the case, and since he had proven an able spokesman on that occasion, he was again sent to represent Athens in 341, this time as an envoy to Rhodes and Chios to secure an alliance against Philip (Dem. 9.71). In the spring of 340 Philip threatened to invade Euboea; Athens responded by sending a naval expedition on which Hyperides himself personally served. In fact, it was largely through Hyperides' efforts that the Athenians were able to raise the funds needed to equip the forty triremes for the expedition, with Hyperides himself providing two ships. In the next year he was again found in active service as trierarch on his own vessel at the siege of Byzantium.

Philip failed in the siege, and this encouraged the Greeks to confront him more openly. But in 338 Philip defeated the Athenians, Thebans, and their allies (Aes. 3.141–145, Dem. 18.237–238) at Chaeronea. Although Hyperides was not present at the battle, he was active back at home, and after Athens' defeat, he proposed a series of measures to meet the crisis (Frs. 27–39a, Lyc. 1.36–37, 41). He was indicted by Aristogeiton for proposing an illegal measure but defended himself by claiming that Macedonian arms had prevented him from seeing the illegality of his proposal. Soon after the battle, he was sent out to secure support from various smaller Greek cities (Lyc. 1.42) and to this occasion probably belongs his Cythnian speech (Fr. 117).

Philip's treatment of Athens after Chaeronea was moderate, thanks in large part to the efforts of Demades, Phocion, and Aeschines. Accommodation characterized these men, but Hyperides, like his friends Lycurgus and Demosthenes, was far from accommodating. In 338/7 he proposed a crown for Demosthenes (Dem. 18.222) for his efforts after Chaeronea; for this he was indicted by Diondas for making an illegal proposal but was easily acquitted, as Diondas failed to receive even one-fifth of the vote. In 337 Hyperides prosecuted Demades for introducing the outrageous proposal to make the Olynthian Euthycrates an Athenian *proxenos* (or official representative), even though he had betrayed Olynthus to Philip in 348 (Frs. 76–80). Around the same time, Hyperides prosecuted Philippides for his pro-Macedonian measures (Hyp. 2). During this period (338–330) Hyperides was clearly associated with Lycurgus and Demosthenes in exposing anyone suspected of Macedonian sympathies. But he could also act independently, as in his prosecution of Demades, who was Demosthenes' relative and was never prosecuted by Demosthenes himself (Din. 1.101). Moreover, friendship did not prevent Hyperides from writing a speech for Lycophron when the latter was impeached by Lycurgus in 333 (Hyp. 1) or from opposing Lycurgus again with his defense of Euxenippus on a similar impeachment charge (Hyp. 4).

In the summer of 336 Philip was assassinated and succeeded by his son Alexander. In 335 after suppressing a brief revolt by the city of Thebes, Alexander demanded the surrender of several prominent Athenian politicians, whom he regarded as most responsible for the Theban revolt. Some ancient scholars report that Hyperides was among the politicians singled out by Alexander, but others deny this.[5] A heated and bitter debate followed in the Athenian assembly. Phocion advocated giving into Alexander's demands, but Demosthenes and Hyperides urged that they be rejected. In the end, the Assembly voted to send a delegation headed by Demades requesting Alexander to give up his demands; the mission was successful, and Alexander relented.

In the spring of 334 Alexander began the conquest of Persia, an adventure from which he would never return. We then hear little of Hyperides until the notorious Harpalus affair in 324, an event that ended the long friendship between him and Demosthenes. Harpalus was in charge of Alexander's treasury. In 324, to avoid Alexander's anger, he fled with a considerable amount of money to Athens, where he was admitted as a suppliant. Some of that money turned up missing, and a number of politicians fell under suspicion. The Areopagus was entrusted with investigating the scandal, and its report listing

---

[5] Plut., *Demosthenes* 23.4, *Phocion* 9.10, 17.2; Arrian 1.10.4; Diodorus Siculus 17.15. See A. B. Bosworth, *Commentary on Arrian's History of Alexander* (Oxford, 1980): 93–96; C. Cooper, "A Note on Antipater's Demand of Hyperides and Demosthenes," *Ancient History Bulletin* 7.4 (1993): 130–135.

those suspected of taking bribes from Harpalus included Demosthenes. Hyperides, who was the only notable politician not to be implicated, was selected as one of the prosecutors (Hyp. 5). Demosthenes was found guilty and fined fifty talents, but he was allowed to retire into exile. Hyperides' attack was vigorous, and he admits that Demosthenes' corruption had severed their friendship. We do not know, however, whether his participation in the prosecution of his old friend was prompted by public interest or his own self-interest. Hyperides was never officially implicated in the scandal, but rumors circulated nonetheless that he had received his share of the money (see Athenaeus 8.341e–342a).[6]

After Alexander's death in 323, one of his generals, Antipater, was given charge of Greece, and the Athenians prepared once more to throw off Macedonian lordship. Hyperides led the way in promoting war with Macedon, touring the Peloponnese to stir up resistance to Antipater. On his tour he met Demosthenes, and the two were reconciled. Hyperides also played a key role in conducting the Lamian War, which followed. For this he was selected to deliver the funeral oration over those killed in battle (Hyp. 6). But the war ended in disaster in 322, when the Athenians were defeated at Crannon and surrendered to Antipater. The democracy was dissolved, Demosthenes and Hyperides and others were forced to flee Athens, and on the motion of Demades, they were condemned to death. Antipater's men pursued Hyperides to a sanctuary either on Aegina or at Herimone. As he clung to the statue of the god, Hyperides was dragged off to Antipater and put to death. According to one tradition, his tongue was cut out, a fitting end, no doubt, for such an outspoken critic of Macedon; according to another, he bit off his tongue to prevent himself from betraying Athens, a true patriot to the end.

Hyperides was a flamboyant figure, a man of contrasts: in public unwavering in his hostility to Macedon, principled to the point of disregarding friendship for the greater good, but in private overly indulgent. He was a well-known epicure given to fine food and women. There were stories of countless affairs with expensive prostitutes, some

[6] For more on the Harpalus affair, see the speeches of Dinarchus in this volume and the Introduction to Dinarchus.

of whom he even defended in court (Frs. 171–179). His services were open to anyone who would hire him. One comic poet (Timocles) describes him as a river teeming with fish that overwhelms with his rhetoric all that stands in his way, a river that is ready to water the plains of any who will pay him (Athenaeus 8.342a). These same comic poets suggest that he used the profits from his speechwriting to feed his insatiable appetite for sex and food; but, at the same time, they unequivocally admit that he was a skilled orator.

Next to Demosthenes, Hyperides was the most highly regarded orator in antiquity. Indeed, some ancient literary critics considered him far superior. This was particularly true of the "Atticists" (first century BC), rhetoricians who preferred a simple, unadorned Attic prose that avoided any kind of florid language or excessive use of figures of speech, two things for which Demosthenes was criticized. Hyperides, by contrast, was noted for his simplicity and charm, and in these two areas he was often compared to Lysias. But what most critics singled out as a characterizing feature of his style was "acumen," a certain penetration or pointedness to his speaking.

Perhaps the best description of his style can be found in a work of the third century AD entitled *On the Sublime.* Here the author, Longinus, describes Hyperides as a pentathlete who comes in second in each event but wins overall. If Hyperides, he says, were judged by the number of his merits, which are more numerous, and not by greatness, he would surpass Demosthenes. He is simply a more versatile orator. The author goes on to enumerate his many virtues: Hyperides, we are told, imitates all the good features of Demosthenes and has also embraced the charm of Lysias. He talks with simplicity; does not relate everything in a monotonous series as Demosthenes does; and does a good job at presenting character, which he does with a certain sweetness and simplicity. He has an untold store of wit, sophisticated sarcasm, subtle irony, jesting that is neither tasteless nor rude, clever ridicule that is comical and humorous but full of sting. Here we get some sense of how Hyperides achieved that "acumen" for which he was famous. Longinus then goes on to note that Hyperides had a natural talent for exciting pity, narrating myths, and handling topics with great ease. He singles out two examples, the Leto myth in the Delian speech (Frs. 67–71), which was seen by ancient rhetoricians as a model for its treatment of mythology, and the Funeral Oration (Hyp. 6), which Longinus himself regarded as a masterful showpiece. By contrast, he says, Demosthenes has no talent at characterization, is not fluent and facile, and is certainly no show orator. He has none of the virtues of Hyperides. If he tries to be funny or witty, he only ends up turning the laughter on himself. If he tries to be charming, he fails; if he tries to write the little speech *In Defense of Phryne* (Frs. 171–179) or *Against Athenogenes* (Hyp. 3), he would recommend Hyperides all the more to us. It is clear from these last remarks by Longinus that Hyperides excelled all others in the little speech for the courtroom. He is less regarded for his political than for his forensic orations. The speech for Athenogenes is a model of characterization; his defense of Phryne was noted by ancient rhetoricians for its pathos. At the end of speech, so the story goes, in dramatic fashion he paraded Phryne before the courtroom, tore off her upper garments, and broke into such wailing at the sight of her that he succeeded in exciting the jurors' pity and securing her acquittal (Pseudo-Plut., *Moralia* 849e, Athenaeus 13.590d–e). Here is an orator who knew the courtroom well and knew what it took to win a case.

Seventy-seven speeches were transmitted in antiquity under his name, of which fifty-two or fifty-six were regarded as genuine; we know the titles of some seventy-one of these. A single medieval codex of his speeches may have existed into the sixteenth century and was possibly seen by the scholar J. A. Kohlburger (Brassicanus) in 1525 at Buda, when he was viewing the library of King Corvinus. He remarks that "in the library of king Corvinus we saw intact a volume of Hyperides with rich annotations."[7] Unfortunately, the library was destroyed by the Turks in 1526 and with it perished the only manuscript of Hyperides. All that remained of the orator were fragments quoted by other ancient writers, until the late nineteenth century, when a series of papyri dating from the second or third century AD was discovered in Egypt. Six orations have been recovered, contained on four

[7] Preface to Salvianus, *De vero iudicio et providentia Dei,* cited in C. Babington, "Fragments of Hyperides Existing in Hungary in the XVIth Century," *Journal of Classical and Sacred Philology* 1 (1854): 407–408.

rolls of papyri. Of these six, only the speech *On Behalf of Euxenippus* (Hyp. 4) is complete. The Funeral Oration is substantially complete; the remaining four are in a fragmentary condition.

The translations of these speeches follow the most recent edition of Hyperides by Mario Marzi, found in *Oratori Attici Minori* (Torino, 1977). In addition, where the text becomes extremely fragmentary, I have also consulted the edition of G. Colin (Budé, 1946), who is much more adventurous in his conjectures and restorations and tries to reproduce some sense of the missing portions of the text. Because of the fragmentary nature of the surviving speeches, I have done the same, and following Colin's suggestions, I have filled the lacunae, wherever it seemed possible. In some cases we can be fairly certain of the restorations; in others, we can not. Those conjectures, which are marked off by angle brackets and italics, in no way presume to restore the orator's exact words but try only to capture a sense of what may have been said and in so doing provide a continuous narrative. But the reader is advised to approach each conjecture with great caution. The order of the speeches follows the numbering of the Oxford Classical Text, but the section numbers of each speech the Budé edition. These can become quite complicated, since short fragments are normally cited by fragment number (e.g., 2 Fr. 6), while longer fragments are unnumbered but divided into sections (e.g., 2.6). Further complications are that Hyperides 1 has two speeches (1a and 1b), Hyperides 5 has both fragment numbers and section numbers (I use only section numbers), and the fragmentary speeches have consecutive fragment numbers (e.g., Fr. 67).

1. IN DEFENSE OF LYCOPHRON

INTRODUCTION

The papyri that contain the oration *In Defense of Lycophron* supply only the title but no author; but ancient references to and paraphrases of a speech by that title by Hyperides assures us of its authenticity. The preserved fragments each correspond to a new column of the papyrus, from which we can estimate the gaps in the text, which are large indeed. Between some fragments whole columns are missing.

This is the first of at least two defense speeches that were delivered at the trial. A few fragments from a second speech are preserved in another papyrus. Hyperides may have composed this second speech for Lycophron, perhaps to be delivered by Theophilus, who is summoned by Lycophron at the end of his own speech to speak on his behalf (1a.20), and some modern scholars have attributed the preserved fragments to Hyperides. But no such speech is mentioned by ancient writers, and it is possible, as other scholars suggest, that the second defense speech was in fact composed by an entirely different orator for the occasion. The prosecution was assisted by Lycurgus, who is known to have written two speeches against Lycophron. Lycophron was an Athenian citizen and an avid horse breeder, who served for three years as cavalry commander on the island of Lemnos and earned great distinction there. While in Lemnos, he was accused of adultery by Ariston and by Lycurgus, who introduced an *eisangelia* (impeachment) into the Assembly. The matter was referred to the court for trial, and Lycophron returned to Athens and hired Hyperides to compose his defense.

There is no real narrative as such, nor was there a need for one, since the prosecution had already given an account of events, and Lycophron needed only to remind the jurors of certain details and argue from them. As best as we can reconstruct the events, the alleged adultery[1] occurred at least three years before the trial, when Lycophron was still in Athens and before he had set out on his military service. He was accused of seducing the sister of Dioxippus, an Athenian widow betrothed to Charippus. The prosecution alleges that during the wedding procession, Lycophron approached the woman directly and urged her not to consummate her new marriage. As we learn, this was her second marriage, and the adulterous affair had begun while her first husband was still alive. He had died leaving her pregnant, and in his will he appointed Euphemus guardian of the child and the estate, with instructions to provide his widow with a sizable dowry when she remarried. Some of the deceased's relatives, who would stand to inherit in the event of the child's death, disputed the will (1a. Fr. 4) but were prevented from acting by the other relatives. Three years later the child was still alive, and since their chances of inheriting were slipping away, all the relatives joined together to prove that the child was illegitimate. They charged that the real father was Lycophron, who had seduced the mother while her husband was weak and close to dying. If the prosecution could convince the jury of the charge, then the legitimacy of the child would be jeopardized and so would the child's legal claim to the estate, since illegitimate children could not inherit.

The normal procedure in a case of adultery was a *graphē* but Lycurgus used *eisangelia,* apparently arguing that adultery was a threat to citizenship and to the democracy (1a.12, Lyc. Fr. 70). Lycophron counters by challenging the legality of the procedure[2] as well as the truth of the charges against him. The trial itself probably took place in 333.[3] From the first speech, we learn that Lycophron was accused of approaching Dioxippus' sister at her wedding and begging her not to

[1] "Adultery" translates the broader Greek term *moicheia,* which designates sexual activity with any citizen woman who was not one's wife.

[2] Adultery was not traditionally one of the charges covered by the impeachment law but use of this procedure was expanding to cover many more offenses. (See Hyp. 4.1–3; Todd 1993: 114–115.) Lycophron's accusers may have maintained that adultery constitutes a threat to democracy.

[3] An alternative date of 338 is now generally rejected.

consummate her marriage with Charippus (1a.3–4). Lycophron argues that the charge is completely absurd, given that Dioxippus was himself present at the wedding and would have throttled him; he was, after all, the strongest man in Greece (1a.6). This reputation came from his Olympic victory, which we are told (1b. Fr. 13) happened right around the time of the wedding. Dioxippus' victory as pankratiast has been dated to 336, the last Olympic games before Alexander's invasion of Asia. The trial of Lycophron took place three years after the wedding, for Lycophron served as calvary commander on Lemnos for three years before being charged (1a.17). Thus the date of the trial falls in the year 333.

1. IN DEFENSE OF LYCOPHRON: SPEECH A

Fr. 1

< . . . I have come to this court today placing my trust first in the gods in which> each one of you trust, both in private and in public life, then in the law and in the oath[4] by which you are bound to give an impartial hearing to the prosecution and the defense . . .

Fr. 2

<Just as you have allowed my accusers> to conduct the prosecution <as they wanted>, so allow me to deliver my defense, to the best of my ability, in the manner I choose. Don't interrupt me, asking, "Why do you tell us this?" Don't add anything of your own to the prosecution's arguments but rather <listen carefully> to my defense . . . [5]

---

[4] At the beginning of the year, when jurors were selected for jury duty for the upcoming year, they took an oath. In that oath they swore to vote according to the laws and decrees of Athens, and in cases not covered by the law, to vote according to what was most just, without any intimidation or prejudice, with impartiality and without accepting bribes. See Dem. 24.149–151.

[5] Speakers often ask their audience not to interrupt. It is hard to know whether in any given speech this is a real concern or a rhetorical play, but it is likely that such interruptions were not uncommon and the Athenian courtroom could at times be a noisy place, with jurors interjecting their own thoughts and comments.

Fr. 3

. . . The law does not permit volunteers[6] to assist the prosecution against those on trial without granting the same right to assist the defense.[7]

So as not to waste too many words before coming to the issue at hand, I will proceed directly to my defense, praying that the gods will help me and bring me safely through the present trial and asking you, men of the jury, first . . .[8] <or offers to> betray the dockyards or to burn public buildings or seize the Acropolis . . .

Fr. 4

. . . . Euphemus[9] . . . first . . . when the husband died, . . . of Phlya . . . from him . . . they thought it right . . . that the wife . . . he had left his wife pregnant with his child, which was nothing illegal. But if they[10] believed the events were just as Ariston wrote in the

---

[6] A litigant was expected to represent himself in court, but often one or more friends would act as "co-pleaders" (*synēgoroi*). Sometimes the litigant would say only a few words (e.g., Dem. 36) or speak for several minutes before turning the speech over to his co-pleader (e.g., Dem. 59). It was illegal to accept any kind of remuneration for the service (see Dem. 46.26), and at times a litigant would go out of his way to stress his personal relationship with his co-pleader (e.g., Dem. 59.1–15).

[7] Lycophron concludes his proem here with a solemn appeal to the jurors (cf. Dem. 18.8), but before beginning his arguments, he makes a formal protest against the prosecution's illegal use of *eisangelia.* See next note.

[8] It is not certain what exactly the speaker said here but he may have asked the jurors to consider whether there was any basis for a charge of adultery in the impeachment law. To prove there was none, he quoted provisions of the law, including the one against betraying dockyards, burning public buildings, or seizing the Acropolis. For other provisions of the law, some of which Lycophron may have quoted, see 4.7–8, 29.

[9] Euphemus was the man appointed guardian of the child and estate. See the Introduction.

[10] These are the more distant relatives of the deceased who initially opposed the closer relatives when they contested the will. Now they are siding with Ariston, since they will benefit in the event of the child's death or if he is declared illegitimate.

impeachment, they certainly should not have prevented the closest relatives from ejecting Euphemus[11] but allowed them to proceed. But now by acting as they have, their own actions are evidence that the charge against me is false. Besides, isn't it odd that if anything had happened to the child, at birth or later on, they would have stuck to the terms of the will, which <specified that the closest relatives would inherit the estate upon the death of the child.> . . . Euphemus . . . he prevented . . . though he offered . . . witnesses . . .

nor can he deny his own handwriting[12]

[1][13] . . . and he[14] employed Ariston's[15] slaves in his workshops; he himself testified to this in court, when he brought a suit against Archestratides.[16] [2] This is how this fellow Ariston operates. He issues a summons to everyone he meets; those who don't pay him money, he drags into court and prosecutes; those who are willing to pay, he lets off the hook. He gives the money to Theomnestus, who takes it and buys slaves. This gives Ariston the same kind of livelihood as pirates get; for each slave he is paid an obol a day to keep him permanently as a sycophant.[17]

[3] Men of the jury, it is worth examining the matter starting with

---

[11] There is reference here to the formal procedure known as *exagōgē,* whereby someone currently in possession of a piece property prevents another, who has a legal claim to it, from taking possession of that property (see Dem. 30.4, 32.17). *Exagōgē* would then lead to a *dikē exoulēs,* a suit for ejectment, whereby the claimant would try to prove his legal right to the property. See 3.27n.

[12] This is a fragment from a later author (Pollux).

[13] The Arden papyrus begins here.

[14] The subject is probably Theomnestus, who was a relative of the deceased husband by marriage (see 1b. Fr. 5) and may have been responsible for urging the other relatives to take legal action and impeach Lycophron.

[15] Ariston is behind the impeachment of Lycophron. He is not one of the relatives, but, according to the speaker, he makes his living as a sycophant, prosecuting and blackmailing others and has been employed by the relatives. He seems to be a friend and business associate of Theomnestus.

[16] Nothing is known of Archestratides. Hyperides composed a speech (Frs. 49–50) against a man by that name, but whether this is the same person is not known, nor do we know anything about the trial.

[17] A sycophant was a disparaging term describing someone who made a living from prosecuting others. See the Series Introduction.

the charges that my accusers first raised in the Assembly. My relatives informed me by letter of the impeachment and the charges made against me in the Assembly when they introduced the impeachment. Among the charges they mentioned in the letter was a statement by Lycurgus, alleging that he heard from the relatives how at Charippus' wedding to the woman I came up close and encouraged her not to have sex with Charippus but to preserve herself.[18] [4] I will tell you now what I told my friends and relatives as soon as I arrived back: if these accusations are true, I agree that I have committed all the other offenses recorded in the impeachment. But I think it is easy for anyone to see they are false. Is there anyone in the city who is so unthinking to believe these allegations?

[5] First of all, men of the jury, there must have been a coachman and a guide to accompany the carriage in which she rode; then the boys who were leading the procession to accompany her and Dioxippus.[19] He was in the procession because she was a widow and had to be given out in marriage. [6] Was I so senseless that even with so many other men in attendance, including Dioxippus and Euphraeus his wrestling partner, who are acknowledged to be the strongest men in Greece, I had no shame in saying such things about a free woman where everyone could hear and had no fear I might be strangled to death on the spot? Who would have tolerated such remarks about his sister as they accused me of making, without killing whoever said them? [7] To top it all off, is it likely,[20] as I noted a moment ago, that Charippus was so dim-witted, that though the woman, as they claim,

---

[18] Many tales of seduction that we find in comedy or oratory (e.g., Lys. 1.8) began at family gatherings like weddings and funerals, where Athenian women were active participants and allowed to move more freely in public.

[19] This is the bride's brother, who, as her closest relative, would give her in marriage.

[20] Arguments from likelihood (*eikos*), such as this and the arguments in 5–6, were often used to refute hard evidence. They were based on the assumption that individuals acted rationally and predictably. We can assume that the prosecution has introduced witnesses to confirm that Lycophron behaved at the wedding as his accusers claim. Lycophron responds that he would not have put his affair in jeopardy by approaching the woman at the wedding, nor would have Charippus proceeded to marry the woman had the adulterous affair been exposed.

had stated earlier that she was promised to me, and though he heard me encouraging her to abide by the oaths she had sworn, he was still prepared to marry her? Do you even think Orestes the madman or Margites, the greatest fool all, would have done this?[21]

[8] But I think, gentlemen of the jury, that in court prosecutors have many advantages over defendants. Because the trial carries no risk for them, they can easily say whatever lies they want, but those on trial are afraid and forget to say many things, including facts in their favor. [9] Moreover, since the prosecution speak first, they not only mention their legitimate claims in the case, but they invent baseless slanders against the accused and force them to change their defense. Defendants have two options: either they defend themselves against the irrelevant slanders and fail to make an adequate defense on the main issue, or they don't mention the accusations just made and leave the jury with the impression that what was said was true.

[10] What's more, the prosecution create prejudice against those who intend to help the defendants and distort the accused's own defense, just as Ariston here tried to do in his prosecution speech. He does not even allow me to benefit from those who would step forward and join in my defense.[22] Why shouldn't they speak in my defense? Isn't it right for relatives and friends to help those on trial? Is there anything in our city more democratic than those who are good speakers helping citizens who lack that ability when they are in trouble? [11] You Ariston have not only made remarks about my co-pleaders, you also determine my line of defense, telling the jurors what they should listen to, what defense they should instruct me to make and what they should not let me say. How is this fair? You conduct the prosecution as you want, and then you rob me of my defense, knowing full well that I have legitimate responses to your lies.

[12] Now you accuse me in your impeachment of subverting the democracy by breaking the laws, but you yourself overstepped all the laws by bringing an impeachment (*eisangelia*) in a case where the law

---

[21] Orestes killed his mother in retaliation for murdering his father and was driven mad by her avenging spirits, the Erinyes; cf. Din. 1.87n. Margites was the hero of an ancient epic attributed to Homer and came to be regarded as the typical fool.

[22] On the practice of co-pleaders (*synēgoroi*), see above, Fr. 3n.

calls for public indictments (*graphai*) before the Thesmothetae.[23] You did this in the first place so as not to run any risk in the trial[24] and so you could insert tragic verses into the impeachment, just as you have now written, accusing me of causing many women to grow old at home unmarried and many others to live in unlawful wedlock with men they shouldn't.[25] [13] In fact, you cannot name one other woman in the city whom I have wronged in this way, and as for the woman you now accuse, do you think she should live with Charippus, her legitimate husband and one of our own citizens, or should she grow old at home unmarried, though she was married as soon as Euphemus provided a talent of silver for her dowry, clearly not from any ulterior motive but out of the goodness of his heart?[26]

[14] So, gentlemen of the jury, Ariston can tell whatever lies he likes, but I think you should make your decision about me not on the basis of the prosecution's slanders but after reviewing my whole life. For it's impossible, in a democracy such as yours, for anyone within the city, whether a nobody or a notable, to escape detection, but the past is the most reliable witness of any man's character, especially against charges like these. [15] Crimes that can be committed at any time in a man's life should be considered in light of the specific accusation raised against him. But adultery is not something that a man can begin to commit after fifty. Either he has been a seducer for a long

---

[23] There were six Thesmothetae elected each year by lot. Their main duty was to oversee the administrative aspects of the Athenian legal system, fixing the dates for trials and assigning courts to the various magistrates who presided over the trials. But they did have important judicial functions as well. Most public suits (*graphai*) were introduced to the Thesmothetae, who conducted the preliminary hearings and trials for such cases. See *Ath. Pol.* 59.

[24] To prevent frivolous suits, in a *graphē* the prosecutor who did not win one-fifth of the vote was fined 1,000 drachmas. An *eisangelia,* however, carried no such penalty.

[25] Lycophron may be referring to a law requiring a husband to divorce his adulterous wife or lose his civic rights (see Dem. 59.87). But the allusion is very obscure and he may only be paraphrasing the tragic verses out of context.

[26] It is possible that Ariston had accused Euphemus of less pure motives, involving collusion with Lycophron.

time, and let my accusers prove that of me, or the accusation is probably false.

[16] Now then, gentlemen of the jury, I have spent my whole life with you in the city, and during that time never once have I been subject to a single accusation of wrongdoing or accused any other citizen, or been a defendant or prosecutor in any lawsuit, but I have devoted my entire life to breeding horses, with enthusiasm that went well beyond my energy and means.[27] I have been awarded a crown for bravery by all the cavalry and by my fellow officers. [17] You, gentlemen of the jury, elected me first as Phylarch, then as Hipparch at Lemnos.[28] I was the only Hipparch to hold office there for two years, and I stayed on for a third year, not wanting to be rash in demanding pay for the cavalry from citizens who were in financial straits.[29] [18] During that time no one on the island brought a charge against me, either private or public, but I was crowned three times by the people of Hephaestia and other times by the people of Myrine.[30] This should be the proof you need in this trial, that the charges against me are false. It's impossible for a man who is bad in Athens to be good in Lemnos, nor did you hold such a low opinion of me, when

---

[27] Horse breeding was a pursuit reserved for the very rich at Athens (as it still is today), and the ostentation that went along with it was regarded with a certain measure of scorn and suspicion. The cavalry and the rich were sometimes suspected of antidemocratic sentiments.

[28] Ten Phylarchs (tribal leaders) were elected each year, one from each of the ten tribes into which the citizen body of Athens was divided. They commanded the tribal horse regiments and came under the command of the Hipparchs (cavalry commanders). Two Hipparchs were elected each year, one serving in Athens, the other on the island of Lemnos, which was under Athenian control at this time. Military officers were among the few officials in Athens who were elected, not chosen by lot. They could be reelected from year to year. As with all other officials in Athens, Hipparchs were paid; the Hipparchus on Lemnos was paid by the cleruchs on the island (see next note.).

[29] The citizens referred to here are cleruchs (colonists) on Lemnos, who settled there after Athens gained possession of the island in 387. Unlike other colonists, cleruchs retained their Athenian citizenship.

[30] Hephaestia and Myrine were the two main cities on Lemnos.

you dispatched me there and placed in my charge two of your own cities.

[19] And so, gentlemen of the jury, you have heard almost all that I can say in my defense. Since the prosecutor, who is not an inexperienced speaker but is accustomed to frequent appearances in court, has called co-pleaders to help him destroy a citizen unfairly, I beg and plead with you to let me also summon my own co-pleaders to speak at such an important trial and to listen kindly to any relative or friend who can help me. [20] I am one of your fellow citizens, a private man, not accustomed to speaking, on trial and in danger not only of being condemned to death (which is of little importance to men of good sense) but of being banished and refused burial in my homeland, once I am dead. And so, if you give the word, gentlemen of the jury, I will summon someone to help. Come up Theophilus and speak whatever you can on my behalf. The jurors instruct you to do so.

IN DEFENSE OF LYCOPHRON: SPEECH B[31]

Fr. 1

[1] . . . The mere suggestion of Lycophron digging through the wall to have sex with the woman is absolutely incredible. The prosecution has not shown that the accused was at odds with those who previously served him and readily submitted to any order he gave, or that they had a dispute with him and refused their service,[32] forcing Lycophron to dig through the wall, since the servants <inside the house> were no longer <on good terms with him> . . . otherwise he would not have dug through the wall. [2] Why should a man who was not hard pressed but had the opportunity to receive her messages and

---

[31] This is probably part of the speech delivered by Theophilus, but there may have been other speakers. The preserved argument is based on likelihood: if Lycophron was in fact having an affair with the woman, he would have entered the house directly with the help of the servants, not by digging under the wall. We must presume that witnesses testified that they had seen him digging.

[32] In a society where the movement of respectable women was monitored and curtailed, servants and particularly the maids were very important in facilitating an adulterous affair, acting as messengers and arranging clandestine meetings. Often, initial contact began with the maid. See Lys. 1.11–14, 19–20.

to pass on his own and . . . and never once did Ch.[33] refuse him entrance into the house. And in fact, it is next to impossible for her maids to have quarreled with him. Which one would have been so rash as to hide his messages or those she sent to him because of some personal grudge? The danger was obvious. For if . . . which is what these men have proposed. [3] But in fact, they saw that the husband was extremely ill and right before their eyes they had this woman, who was soon to become mistress of the house, as a constant reminder that should anything happen to the husband, they would pay the price for acting against her. So it's not plausible to think that Lycophron dug through the wall. Nor was he in the habit of quarreling with the maids, as the prosecution claims. And why should he? Why should they have quarreled with him, when their mistress was becoming increasingly affectionate toward him. . . .

Fr. 5

. . . And so, what basis of proof does he have to demand that the jury condemn Lycophron. By Zeus, he relies on the testimony of in-laws, Anaschetus, Theomnestus, and Criton.[34] You would do well, gentlemen of the jury, to examine this testimony carefully. For the whole accusation . . .

Fr. 13

. . . <when he was about to give> his sister <in marriage> to Charippus, Dioxippus went off to Olympia where he was to win a crown for the city.[35] Meanwhile Lycophron sent letters that said . . .

---

[33] Only the first letter (*chi*) remains of what was presumably the husband's name, which has been restored as either Charmes or Charisander.

[34] It is not entirely certain whose in-laws these are. Some scholars suggest they are the relatives of the deceased; others think they are the relatives of Ariston, the prosecutor, which is more likely.

[35] Dioxippus won an Olympic victory as a pankratist, perhaps in the year 336. See the Introduction to Hyp. 1.

2. AGAINST PHILIPPIDES

INTRODUCTION

The title and author's name are not preserved in the papyrus, but a speech by Hyperides against Philippides is known from Athenaeus (12.552d), who quotes one line from it (Fr. 15b). The papyrus itself is extremely fragmentary; a few passages remain from the first part of the speech, and only the epilogue is preserved in its entirety. But from it we can reconstruct the charges against Philippides, as they were presented by the prosecution.

He has been indicted for proposing an illegal decree (*graphē paranomōn*).[1] After Athens' defeat at Chaeronea in 338, while peace negotiations were in process under the direction of Demades, Philippides and his supporters proposed in the Assembly a number of decrees honoring certain Macedonians, among them perhaps Alexander (Fr. 8). The process, however, was illegal, since the proposals had not received prior approval from the Council of 500. But despite this, the Presidents,[2] either from collusion or fear, allowed the decrees to be put to a vote, and they were passed. Since it was acknowledged that the Presidents had been intimidated, they were not indicted. The matter might have ended there, had not Philippides sometime later gone one step further and proposed that the Presidents be crowned for carrying out their duties according to the laws. For this proposal he was indicted by his opponents, among them Hyperides, who detested his pro-Macedonian sympathies.

The trial took place after the battle of Chaeronea but before

[1] See 2.4n.

[2] See 2.4n.

Philip's death in 336; a reference to Philip suggests that he was still alive at the time of the trial (2.7n). Hyperides was only one of the prosecutors; if we can believe what he says (2.13n), his speech probably lasted just over thirty minutes in a trial where the prosecution had somewhere over two and a half hours to speak. In the first part of the speech he attacked Philip and Alexander, contrasting them to great figures of the past who had a genuine claim to Athens' gratitude; in the second, the preserved part of the papyrus, he turns his attack on Philippides and his associates, who have a history of disloyalty.

2. AGAINST PHILIPPIDES

Fr. 1

. . . in a free city those who work for the interests of tyrants and plunge the city into slavery . . .

Fr. 6

. . . He[3] was responsible for actions that did honor to our city and to Greece. For this reason he received the greatest honors from both you and all the others. And rightly so. . . .

Fr. 8

. . . we must thank Alexander for all those who died at his hand;[4] but I think . . .

Fr. 10

. . . Further, these men trample on the people in their misfortune, and on this account they deserve your hatred all the more. Just as

---

[3] The reference here is perhaps to Conon, a famous Athenian commander who was often praised for his service in these terms. See Din. 1.14.

[4] There is an allusion here to the battle of Chaeronea, in which the young Alexander commanded the left wing of the Macedonian army. To prove his prowess, he threw himself headlong into the battle and succeeded in rupturing the front line of the allied Greek forces. See Diodorus Siculus 16.86.

human bodies need the most attention when they are sick, so cities in times of misfortune need the greatest care. But these men alone . . .

Fr. 11

. . . democracy. <I will pass over> most of his actions, but I will clearly show the times <he pleaded> Philip's cause and campaigned with him against our country, <which is his most serious offense>. In fact, he did campaign on Philip's side against us and our allies . . . precisely . . .

Fr. 15a

Each one of them <was a traitor>, one in Thebes, another in Tanagra,[5] another in Eleuthera, doing everything in the service of the Macedonians . . .

Fr. 15b

Or do they not pray for the overthrow of all the rest of Greece, since they reap the benefits from the cities that are destroyed? They always want you to live in fear and danger . . .

His appearance is unimpressive because he is so thin.[6]

. . . they make accusations, [1] and make it perfectly clear that whenever they spoke on behalf of the Spartans, it was not because they were their friends but because they hated Athens and wanted to court those who would always use their power against you. But now since that power has passed to Philip, they chose to flatter him. [2] Democrates of Aphidna,[7] who always sits with them and stands in their

---

[5] Tanagra was located in Boeotia about 20 km (about 12 miles) east of Thebes. Eleuthera was on the Attic border, and its territory was a matter of constant dispute between the Athenians and Boeotians.

[6] This unnumbered fragment is from Athenaeus 12.552d, who reports that Philippides' extreme thinness was satirized by comic poets; one poet even coined the expression "to be philippidized" to describe someone who had become thin.

[7] Democrates of Aphidna was a politician who supported the Peace of Philocrates (see Aes. 2.17). In the present trial he served as Philippides' co-pleader (*sy-*

chorus, jokes about the city's misfortunes, and abuses you by day in the Agora, but at night he comes and dines with you. And yet, Democrates, you are the only one who has no right to say anything disparagingly of the people. Why, you may ask? First, because you should have learned from no one else's experience but your own that the people show their gratitude to benefactors; you now receive honors for services that others have rendered. [3] Second, because the people have written a law forbidding anyone from speaking ill of Harmodius and Aristogeiton or singing denigrating songs about them.[8] It is a disgrace to think that when the people felt that not even a drunk should be allowed to speak ill of your ancestors, you should disparage the people when you are sober.

[4] I have a few more words to say, gentlemen of the jury, and then I will make my summation, and step down. You are about to cast your vote in an indictment for proposing an illegal decree (*graphē paranomōn*).[9] The decree under indictment calls for the commendation of the Presidents (*proedroi*).[10] But from laws that were read out in this court, you have heard that Presidents should carry out their duties according to the laws and that these men have violated the laws. [5] The rest is now

---

nēgoros) and seems to have shared his pro-Macedonian sympathies. Like Philippides, he had a reputation for buffoonery and was well known for his wit. (See Arist., *Rhetoric* 3.4.3, Plut., *Moralia* 803d). As a descendant of Aristogeiton, one of the tyrant slayers, he was entitled to free meals in the town hall (Prytaneum). Cf. Din. 1.101.

[8] In 514 Harmodius and Aristogeiton, who were lovers, plotted to assassinate the sons of the tyrant Peisistratus but succeeded only in killing the younger brother Hipparchus. Although they did not actually liberate Athens from tyranny, they were later celebrated as liberators, and their descendants were granted special privileges (see previous note).

[9] The *graphē paranomōn* could be brought by any citizen against the proposer of a decree that contravened the law or had been passed improperly. If the proposal was judged illegal, the decree was annulled, and the person who proposed it was penalized. After one year, the proposer no longer could be penalized (cf. Dem. 20.144), but the decree still could be indicted.

[10] *Proedroi,* nine in number, were members of the Council of 500 and were selected from the nine tribal contingents not "in Prytany" (see the Series Introduction). They served for only one day and directed any meetings of the Council or the Assembly that were called on that day.

up to you. You will show whether you intend to punish those who propose illegal decrees or intend to award Presidents who violate the law with honors reserved for benefactors, even though you have sworn to vote according to the laws. Certainly you cannot be deceived by their argument that the Assembly was forced to vote these commendations, for it cannot be said that we were under any compulsion to crown the Presidents. [6] Besides, the defendant himself has made your decision easy. For he has written down his reasons for crowning the Presidents, namely, that they behaved justly toward the Athenian people and because they carried out their duties according to the law. Have him defend these statements. As for you, Philippides, show us that what you put in the decree about the Presidents is true, and you are acquitted.

[7] But you are a fool if you think that your usual vulgar antics and joking in court will get you acquitted or win a pardon or some undeserved sympathy from the jurors. There's no way. For you have not laid up for yourself any goodwill with the people of Athens but have invested elsewhere, and you thought of flattering only those who strike fear in the people, not those who now have the power to save you. You assumed one person would be immortal,[11] and you condemned to death this ancient city of ours. [8] You did not realize that no dead tyrant has ever come back to life, but many cities that have been utterly destroyed have regained their power. You and your associates have not considered the history of the Thirty and how the city prevailed over the forces that marched against it and those that joined the attack from within;[12] but it was well known that you kept a close watch on the city's fortunes, to see whether an opportunity might arise to say or do anything against the people. Will you now dare to speak about opportunities, when you were only looking for opportunities to harm the city? [9] Have you, Philippides, come to court with your children? Will you bring them forward right now and expect the ju-

---

[11] I.e., Philip, who was still alive at the time of the trial or had just been killed.

[12] In 404 the democracy was dissolved, and in its place was installed a Spartan-backed government of thirty men, whose reign of terror in Athens lasted six months and was finally brought to an end in 403, when exiled democrats under Thrasybulus returned and defeated the forces of the Thirty.

rors' pity? You have no right. When others took pity on the city for its misfortunes, you and your associates exulted.[13] These men chose to save Greece and despite their good intentions suffered an undeserved fate; but you, Philippides, will now receive a well-deserved punishment for unjustly bringing our city to utter shame.

[10] Why should you spare this fellow? Because he is a democrat? But you know that he chose to be the slave of tyrants and thinks he can give the people orders. Because he is a good person? Twice you convicted him of a crime. Yes, but he's useful. But if you make use of a man you have unanimously condemned as a criminal, it will look as if either you make bad judgments or you openly embrace criminals. It's not right for you to take the blame for this man's wrongs, but it is right to punish the criminal. [11] If someone comes forward and says that Philippides has twice before been convicted of illegal proposals, and for this reason suggests you should acquit him, do just the opposite for two reasons. First, because it is your good fortune to find someone who has admittedly proposed illegal measures on trial for a third time. You should not spare such a man as if he were someone good but should remove him as quickly as possible, since he has already twice given you proof of his character. [12] Second, just as you allow those who have been convicted twice of perjury the opportunity not to testify a third time, even when they were present at the events, so that the people are not responsible for disenfranchising anyone but the citizen who does not stop giving false testimony,[14] so too those convicted of illegal proposals can refrain from making any future proposals. But if they do propose something illegal, clearly they are acting for private motives. Such men deserve not pity but punishment.

[13] So as not to speak too long, since I have limited myself to an

---

[13] After Athens' defeat at Chaeronea, Philippides and his associates proposed decrees honoring the victor.

[14] A person convicted three times for false testimony suffered *atimia*, the loss of his citizen rights. Witnesses could not be forced to testify, but a reluctant witness who was present in court could be forced either to testify or to swear under oath that he had no knowledge of the facts. Whether there was a special exemption for people twice convicted of false testimony, as Hyperides implies, is uncertain.

amphora of water,[15] I will have the clerk read out to you the indictment again, and ask you to recall the charges and the laws you heard being read out and to reach a verdict that is both just and to your own benefit.

---

[15] The length of speaking time allotted to a litigant was measured by a water clock. An amphora of water would perhaps provide thirty-six minutes. In public suits of this kind, both the prosecution and defense were each allocated four amphoras of speaking time and a final three for the assessment of the penalty, if the verdict was guilty. Cf. Aes. 3.197–198. On the water clock, see Boegehold 1995: 77–78 with plate 13.

3. AGAINST ATHENOGENES

INTRODUCTION

This speech was noted by ancient critics particularly for its artistic merits, and what remains of it certainly does not disappoint. It shows that gift of characterization, wit, and charm that made Hyperides famous. (See the Introduction to Hyperides.) But the speech that has survived in papyrus was only one of two speeches written for the trial. As in many private suits, the litigants in this case had two opportunities to speak; the first and the more important of the two speeches, and the one that has survived in papyri, was delivered by the plaintiff himself; the second, of which only a few words are known, perhaps by Hyperides.

Everything we know about the case comes from the speech. According to the plaintiff, Epicrates, he was a young farmer who had brought a private suit for damages against Athenogenes, a resident alien (metic) of Egyptian origin. Athenogenes carried on his family's trade in perfumes and owned three shops, one of which was managed by his slave Midas and his two sons. Epicrates took a liking to one of the boys and approached Athenogenes with an offer to set him free. According to Epicrates, Athenogenes first had the boy refuse Epicrates' offer unless he also agreed to buy and set free the boy's brother and father; then Athenogenes enlisted the services of his former mistress Antigone, a famous prostitute (*hetaira*),[1] who used her charms to

[1] A *hetaira* was a higher class of prostitute than a *pornē,* who was commonly a slave working in a brothel. A *hetaira* was normally a free noncitizen, who often established long-term arrangements with her lovers.

persuade Epicrates to accept the boy's request to buy the whole family. According to Epicrates, the whole thing was an elaborate and cleverly staged plot: Athenogenes at first refused any form of compromise, and then Antigone convinced Epicrates that she was on his side and would try to persuade Athenogenes to allow him to purchase the freedom of all three. Epicrates was completely duped; he quickly got together forty minas from friends, and Athenogenes, as a favor to Antigone, or so he claimed, agreed to sell the three slaves outright to Epicrates, who could have unrestricted use of the boy and at a later date choose to set them free. But because he was buying the slaves, Epicrates also assumed responsibility for any debts that they had accumulated. To sweeten the offer, therefore, Athenogenes also threw in the perfume business, which he claimed would easily cover any debts. Anxious to conclude the deal, Epicrates signed a sale's contract without reading it.

Soon after, Epicrates discovered that Midas owed five talents in loans to creditors and to friends. Realizing the seriousness of his predicament, Epicrates gathered his friends and relatives together to examine the document; they discovered that many of the debts had not been recorded in the agreement. They approached Athenogenes in the Agora. A heated exchange followed, but Athenogenes refused to make any concessions and stuck by the contract. Epicrates was forced to sue Athenogenes for damages to cover the debts.

In Athens a sale's agreement could be, but did not have to be, included with the sale.[2] In the present case, Athenogenes included a written agreement to ensure that Epicrates assumed responsibility for any debts previously accumulated by the slaves who ran the perfume shop. Laws existed to protect the buyer against fraud and any misrepresentation by the seller: according to Epicrates, the seller was forbidden from making false statements in the Agora about his merchandise (3.14), and in the case of the sale of a slave, the owner was required by law to inform the buyer of any physical defects the slave might have. If he failed to do so, the buyer could return the slave and demand his money back (3.15). Both these laws are mentioned by Epicrates in support of his case, but they do not directly apply to him; he had willingly

[2] For loans regulating sales, see P. Millet, *Lending and Borrowing in Ancient Athens* (Cambridge, 1991).

agreed to accept any debts incurred by the slaves and had signed an agreement to that effect. The basis of Athenogenes' defense was a law that stated that any agreement made by two parties was binding as long as that agreement was just (3.13n). That the agreement was unjust is precisely what Epicrates had to prove to the jury to secure damages.

The trial took place several years after the battle of Chaeronea in 338, when Athenogenes left Athens for Troezen, where he took up permanent residency, but before 324, the year in which Alexander issued a decree calling for the return of all Greek exiles to their native cities. From the speech (3.31) we learn that many from Troezen were still residing in Athens at the time of the trial. In the same passage we are told that their exile happened more than a hundred and fifty years after the battle of Salamis (480). If this figure is at all reliable, it should mean the trial took place sometime after 330 but before 324. We cannot be more certain than that, nor can we be certain of the verdict. Epicrates' case may not have been the strongest, and in the end, his best strategy was probably to play on the prejudices of the jury, who believed that foreigners like Athenogenes, who prospered in Athens but left the city at a time of crisis, only took advantage of her citizens.

3. AGAINST ATHENOGENES

[1][3] . . . When I told her what had happened, how Athenogenes was hostile to me and was not willing to make any compromise, she said that he was always like this and told me not to worry; she would help me out in everything. [2] She seemed quite earnest when she said this, and she swore the most solemn oath, that she had my best interests at heart and was speaking the whole truth. The result was, to tell you the truth, gentlemen of the jury, that I believed her words. This is how passion, so it seems, unbalances a man's nature, when it enlists a woman's trickery. At any rate, by this deception, she wheedled out of me an additional three hundred drachmas for her kindness, allegedly to buy a girl.[4]

[3] The proem and some of the narrative are lost. But how much of the narrative is uncertain.

[4] The girl was presumably for her brothel.

[3] Perhaps, gentlemen of the jury, it comes as no surprise that I was toyed with in this way by Antigone. The woman, they say, was the most treacherous *hetaira* of her day and now remains in the business as a brothel keeper. . . .[5] She has destroyed the house of . . . of Chollidae, which was as wealthy as any. And yet, if she acted like this on her own, what do you think she has in mind now, in enlisting Athenogenes as her ally, a man who is a speechwriter and marketplace type[6] and worst of all, an Egyptian? [4] Finally, to make a long story short, she sent for me again later and told me that after considerable pleading with Athenogenes, she just barely managed to persuade him to release Midas and his two sons to me for forty minas, and she instructed me to get the money as quickly as possible, before Athenogenes changed his mind. After I gathered it from every source, pestering my friends and depositing the forty minas with the bank, I came to Antigone's house.[7]

[5] She brought Athenogenes and me together, reconciled us, and urged us from this point onward to treat each other well. I agreed to do this, and Athenogenes here replied that I should thank Antigone for what happened. "And now," he said, "for her sake, I will show you right away how well I'll treat you. You are going to put money down for the freedom of Midas and his sons. But I will sell them to you outright,[8] so that no one can bother you or seduce the boy away from you, and so that the slaves don't cause you any trouble, for fear of what may happen to them. [6] Most importantly, as it now stands, they would think that their freedom was the result of my efforts, but if you buy them outright and later, at your own convenience, set them free, they would be doubly grateful to you. However," he said, "you will assume whatever debts they owe,—payment for some perfume to Pan-

[5] A few words are missing that would have described her activities as a brothel keeper.

[6] The Greek term, which was obviously pejorative, refers to someone who frequents the Agora: one who traffics there could be said to be streetwise or business smart.

[7] Epicrates deposited the purchase money with the bank where the transaction would take place. For a similar situation, see Dem. 47.51, 57, 64.

[8] The text actually says, "I will give them for buying and selling," the regular judicial formula for a sales contract.

calus and Procles[9] and any other amount occasionally lent to the perfume shop by a customer. But these are quite small, and far more valuable than these are the wares in the workshop, the perfume, the alabaster and myrrh"—and he mentioned some other names—"which will easily cover all these debts."[10]

[7] Gentlemen of the jury, here was the point of the plot and the elaborate deception. If I paid for their freedom, I would lose only what I gave him and would suffer no serious consequences. But if I bought them outright, and agreed to assume their debts, which I assumed were insignificant, since I had no prior knowledge of them, he intended later to set his creditors and contributors on me,[11] trapping me by the terms of the agreement. And that's precisely what happened. [8] When I agreed to his proposal, he immediately took from his lap a document and began to read the contents of it; it was the agreement with me. Although I listened to what was being read, I was more anxious to complete the business I had come for. He sealed the agreement immediately in the same house, so that none of those who look out for my interests would know the contents, and he added to my name that of Nicon of Cephisia.[12] [9] We went to the perfume shop and deposited the document with Lysicles of Leuconoe.[13] I paid the forty minas and concluded the purchase. Once the transaction was com-

---

[9] The name given below (10) is Polycles.

[10] As a metic, Athenogenes could not own land; the business that he was selling consisted only of slaves, a stall, and ingredients used to make perfume. The value in the business, as in most trades, was in the slaves who had the skills to carry out the operations.

[11] Two terms are used here to describe those who had lent Midas money: creditors who had furnished commercial loans and charged interest, and "contributors of *eranoi*." The second group were friends who provided friendly or interest-free loans that were repaid in installments. See 3.9, 11. The money that Epicrates collected from his friends for the purchase of the slaves (5) consisted of *eranoi*-contributions.

[12] Nicon, an Athenian citizen, must have been a friend of Epicrates, who acted as his surety or security for the purchase. See below, 3.20.

[13] Lysicles was either a citizen of some renown, with whom the original document was deposited for safekeeping, or perhaps the banker with whom Epicrates had already deposited the forty minas (3.5).

plete, I had a visit from the creditors to whom Midas owed money and from his contributors, and we had a talk. Within three months, all the debts had been disclosed; the result was that I owed, as I said a moment ago,[14] nearly five talents, including loans from contributors.

[10] When I realized my predicament, I gathered my friends and relatives together, and we read my copy of the agreement, in which the names of Pancalus and Polycles[15] were expressly mentioned together with the amounts owed them for perfume. These amounts were small, and they could claim that the perfume in the shop covered the money owed. But most of the debts, including the largest ones, were not written in under any names, but, as something insignificant, in a footnote that read "And whatever Midas owes to anyone else." [11] For one of the loans from contributors it was noted that three payments were outstanding. This was written under the name of Dicaeocrates, but the other loans from contributors that were made recently and enabled Midas to acquire everything, these Athenogenes had not written in the agreement but had kept concealed. After some deliberation, we decided to go to him and discuss the matter. We found him near the perfume shops, and we asked him whether he was not ashamed of lying and setting a trap in the agreement by not declaring the debts. He replied that he did not know what debts we meant, and he had no time for us. He had in his possession a document concerning this business of mine. [12] Many men gathered around to listen in on the matter, since our discussion took place in the Agora. Although they really cut into him and insisted that we arrest him as a kidnapper,[16] we didn't think we should do this but instead summoned him before you according to the law. First of all the clerk will read out to you the agreement; for you will learn of this man's plot from the text itself. Read the agreement.[17]

---

[14] This presumably refers to the lost beginning of the speech.

[15] Cf. 3.6n.

[16] Certain types of criminals, including thieves and kidnappers, who were caught in the act could be subject to *apagōgē* or citizen's arrest and hauled before the appropriate magistrates, normally the Eleven; see further below, 3.29n. But it is stretching things to want to apply this procedure to Athenogenes.

[17] At this point, the clerk of the court would step forward and read a copy of the agreement provided by Epicrates; the water clock would be plugged, since the reading of such evidence did not count against the litigant's speaking time.

[AGREEMENT]

[13] Gentlemen of the jury, you have heard all the facts in detail. But Athenogenes will at once tell you that the law declares that any agreements made by two parties are binding. Yes, agreements that are just, my good fellow. But for unjust agreements, the law says the direct opposite; they are not binding.[18] I will make this point clearer from the laws themselves. You have made me so fearful of being brought to ruin by you and your cunning that I have been forced to study and examine the laws night and day to the neglect of all else.[19]

[14] The one law stipulates that no one can make false statements in the Agora, a provision that seems to me to be the finest of all.[20] But you, Athenogenes, lied in the middle of the Agora when you made an agreement against my interests. If you show that you told me about the loans from contributors and the debts or wrote in the contract all the creditors' names that later I learned, then I have no argument with you, but I admit to owing money. [15] Next, there is a second law covering those who have made contracts by mutual

---

[18] Elsewhere (Dem. 42.12, 47.77, 56.2), we learn that the law stated that any agreement freely made before witnesses was binding. It is only here that we are told that such an agreement must be just, that is, fair, and Epicrates infers from this provision that the same law declared unjust agreements, that is, unfair ones, invalid. But another possible interpretation of the law, and perhaps the correct one, is not that the agreement itself had to be just but the thing agreed upon had to be just, that is, lawful and legal. If this is the case, Epicrates is in a difficult situation, since the agreement that he freely entered into was not for illegal ends. Consequently he is forced to cite two other laws, one about making false statements in the Agora and another about disclosing the physical defects of a slave, to prove he was defrauded.

[19] This is a topos. Every litigant was expected to represent himself in court, and part of his task involved locating and examining the laws that were applicable to his case. But Epicrates has hired Hyperides to write his speech, and much of that work would probably have been done by the orator, who was familiar with the law; his comments, then, are purely rhetorical, emphasizing his inexperience in court and his nonlitigious nature. Cf. Dem. 54.17–18.

[20] This first law was enforced by the ten *agoranomoi* (market officials), five appointed for Piraeus and five for the city itself. They oversaw the sale of all goods in the Agora, ensuring that they were in good condition and their quality not misrepresented. See *Ath. Pol.* 51.1.

agreement. It states that when someone sells a slave, he must fully disclose any physical defects the slave may have; and if he does not, the slave can be returned. And yet if it is possible to return a slave, where a seller has failed to reveal the defects caused by chance, how can you not accept responsibility for crimes that you planned yourself? Moreover, the epileptic slave does not cause further loss to the buyer, whereas Midas, whom you sold me, has even cost my friends' money.

[16] Consider, Athenogenes, the law's position not only on slaves but also on free persons. Surely, you and everyone else know that only children born of lawfully married women are legitimate.[21] But clearly the simple act of betrothal by the woman's father or brother did not satisfy the lawgiver, but he expressly wrote in the law "whomever a man lawfully gives in betrothal, children born of her are legitimate," and not, "if someone betroths another woman, falsely alleging that she is his daughter." Rather, he stipulates that lawful betrothals are valid and unlawful ones, invalid.

[17] The law on wills is much like this. For it stipulates that a man can bequeath his property as he sees fit, except when he is adversely affected by old age, sickness, or insanity, or under the influence of a woman, or held in prison or under constraint.[22] But if wills that concern our own personal property are invalid when drawn up illegally, how can terms such as these be valid, when Athenogenes made an agreement that harms my property?[23] [18] If a will is invalid, so it seems, even when a man draws it up under the influence of his own

---

[21] For a marriage to be lawful, the woman had to be Athenian, and her guardian (*kyrios*) had to give her out in marriage by *enguē,* a form of contract; see Dem. 46.18. The word translated here "betrothal" means just that, "to give or promise in marriage by *enguē.*"

[22] For the text of this law, see Dem. 46.14. Cf. also Plut., *Solon* 21.3. The law also includes drugs as grounds for contesting a will, but Epicrates fails to mention this.

[23] In Athenian laws the terms of the law were rarely, if ever defined. This fact allowed considerable scope for interpretation of any particular law or provision of the law by a litigant, who would attempt to persuade the jurors that the lawgiver's intention was this or the law meant that. He could, as here, argue by analogy to another law, how a particular term should be understood. See Todd 1993: 60–62.

wife, must I suffer more, when I was forced by them into making this agreement under the influence of Athenogenes' *hetaira* and when I have the greatest protection afforded by the law? And then, do you insist on sticking to the agreement that you and your *hetaira* tricked me into signing, for which the laws declare you guilty of conspiracy, and do you also expect to profit by it? You were not satisfied with receiving forty minas <for the perfume stall>,[24] but you also <robbed> me <of an additional five> talents, as if I were caught <in a snare by a hunter.>

[19] <Perhaps Athenogenes will say> that he did not know Midas <had so many debts, for the loans were made without his knowledge.> I, who never showed any interest in the business of the Agora, within the space of three months came to know exactly what all the debts and loans from contributors were; but this fellow, who is a third-generation perfume seller, who sits in the Agora every day, who owns three perfume stalls, and who receives accounts every month, he did not know about his debts? In other regards he is no amateur, but with regard to his own slave he was a complete simpleton? He knew about some debts, it seems, but he claims ignorance about any others that he doesn't want to know about. [20] Such an argument on his part, gentlemen of the jury, is not a defense but an admission[25] that I should not have to pay off these debts. For if he says that he didn't know about all the money that was owed, then he surely cannot claim that he fully disclosed his debts. Any debts that I was not informed of by the seller I am not legally bound to pay. I think it is clear to everyone, Athenogenes, that you knew Midas owed this money, particularly because you summoned Nicon as my security. For if <you did not know that the debts were large, my signature on the document would have been sufficient.>[26]

[21] That certainly was not the case. But I want to take issue with

---

[24] There are gaps in the text here, and the restored sense of the missing text is not certain.

[25] There is a play on words here: his argument (*logos*) is not an *apologēma* (defense) but a *homologēma* (admission).

[26] Again, we are faced with gaps in the text. Such gaps are regularly at the bottom of columns, where the papyrus is damaged.

your argument,[27] that <you were ignorant and did not know who invested or exactly how much.> Let's examine it in this way. If through ignorance you failed to disclose fully to me all the debts and I made the agreement thinking the only debts were those you informed me of, who is legally bound to pay them? The subsequent buyer or the former owner of the property, when the money was borrowed? I think it's you. But if we disagree on this point, let the law be our arbitrator, which was made not by lovers or by those plotting to get other people's property but by the greatest democrat of all, Solon.[28] **[22]** Knowing that many sales are made in the city, he passed a law that all agree is just and fair. It states, "Damages and losses caused by slaves are to be paid by the master who owned the slaves at the time they caused them." This is reasonable. For if the slave achieves some success or establishes a business, the benefit goes to the owner. But you ignore the law and speak about contracts being broken. Solon believed that even a decree that was legally proposed should not override the law;[29] but you expect even unjust contracts to override all the laws.

[23] And besides this, gentlemen of the jury, he told my father and my other relatives that he was willing <to give me one of the boys>

---

[27] Epicrates has moved from a hypothetical argument that Athenogenes might make (19–20) to an actual argument that he has apparently already made. It is possible that Epicrates is recalling an argument made by Athenogenes at the arbitration stage. A private suit for damages (*dikē blabēs*), as this one, came before the Forty, who then passed the case on to a public arbitrator, who conducted an initial hearing. The litigants were expected to take the arbitration seriously, arguing their case fully and presenting all the evidence they could. If the arbitrator failed to resolve the matter, he passed the case back to the Forty. All the evidence presented before the arbitrator was sealed in containers, and no new evidence could be entered at the trial. Consequently, each litigant knew what evidence the other would present and in general how the other would argue. See Boegehold 1995: 79–81.

[28] By the fourth century, Solon was regarded as the founder of the Athenian democracy, and orators assigned most laws to him, even if he was not the actual author of all such laws. Cf., e.g., Dem. 18.6, Aes. 3.257. See below, 3.22n.

[29] Only in 403/2, after the restoration of the Athenian democracy, was a clear distinction drawn between laws and decrees; the former were to be permanent and of general application, and the latter, temporary and specific. After that date, no decree could override a law. See And. 1.87, Dem. 23.87.

as a gift and to settle everything satisfactorily and that he had urged me to let him keep Midas instead of buying him, but I was unwilling and wanted to buy them all. I hear that he intends to tell you this, just to appear moderate, as if he were speaking to a bunch of fools who were unaware of his shameless behavior. [24] But you must hear what happened; for it will clearly fit in with the rest of their plot. He sent me the boy I just mentioned,[30] who said that he would not live with me unless I had his father and brother freed. Then when I had agreed to pay the money for the three of them, Athenogenes approached some of my friends and said, "Why does Epicrates want to go to this trouble, when he can take the boy and use him as he wants?" [25][31]<I did not suspect> the trickery he was up to, and his words <gave the impression that he was free> of wrongdoing; yet <none of you should> believe that if <he was pleased to give me> the boy <as a gift and to keep the others,> I would have refused <but had become so demented that I wanted to spend> forty minas and <now risk to lose a further> five talents . . . [26] . . . I am not a perfume seller and do not practice any other trade, but I farm this small piece of land that my father gave me. And then I was rushed into this purchase by these people. Which is more likely, Athenogenes, that I desired your <trade> in which I had no experience or that <you and> your *hetaira* had designs> on my property? Personally, I think all signs point to you.

For this reason, gentlemen of the jury, you can with good reason forgive me for being deceived by Antigone and for being so unlucky to fall in with a man like this, and <you should be angry> with Athenogenes . . .

[27] . . . <Now do you think it's right for me to have all the misfortunes that have come my way because of my simplicity> but for him to have the profits of his fraud? Or for me to be left with the headache of Midas, his daring accomplice, whom he said he was reluctant to set free, and for him to have received money for the boy, much more money than he is worth, although he originally said he

---

[30] That is, the boy whom Athenogenes offered to give him.

[31] The text in 3.25 is extremely fragmentary, and my restorations, which are based on Marzi's text, are largely guesses.

was giving him to me as a gift, so even in the end he is not my own but will be set free by your vote?[32] Yet I myself do not think it's right that <besides all these other troubles> I should also be disenfranchised by Athenogenes.[33] **[28]**[34] The result would be devastating for me, gentlemen of the jury, if <this fellow should get the best of me. For my part,> I went wrong <because of my naïveté, but for his part he has clearly> done me wrong. <Is it not enough for me to be victimized> by his crimes? <Must I also be assessed the additional> penalty <of disenfranchisement? And to think I am a> citizen, <and should be the victim of a metic (resident alien) like this. Don't get me wrong; I do not want to slander a class that has done you tremendous service, but only this villain, Athenogenes.>

[29] <In the past he was never willing> to risk his life <in our time of need, as most loyal> metics <did.> In the war with Philip,

---

[32] Epicrates is rather tendentiously describing the consequences that would follow if he lost his case. Midas and his debt would be his responsibility; the boy, whom Athenogenes said he wanted to give as a gift, would in a sense cost Epicrates five talents and in any case would be free, since it was never Epicrates' intention to buy the boy as a slave.

[33] Two possibilities have been suggested that could lead to Epicrates' disenfranchisement (*atimia*). If he were to lose the case, Epicrates would owe money to the creditors of the perfume shop. To collect their debts, these creditors, could bring a *dikē exoulēs,* a suit to eject Epicrates from the property. Most often this kind of suit was brought by someone seeking to enforce a court verdict in his favor, where the convicted party refused to pay and his opponent was forced to obtain a court ruling to eject him from the property. But it could be brought by anyone with a legal claim to another's property, such as a creditor who was owed money. If the creditors in this case brought a *dikē exoulēs* against Epicrates and he was convicted, in addition to what he owed them, an equal amount would also have to be paid to the state. Epicrates would thus be a state debtor and lose his civic rights. The other possibility is that in a damage suit, as in some other private suits, in the event of losing the case, the plaintiff had to pay the defendant the *epōbelia,* compensation fixed at one-sixth the value of the damages that were being sought. If Epicrates failed to pay Athenogenes this amount, he could be liable to a *dikē exoulēs* and *atimia* as a state debtor.

[34] The next three sections (28–30) of the text are very fragmentary, and some of the restorations are mere guesses.

he left the city just before the battle and did not serve with you at Chaeronea but moved to Troezen, contrary to the law that stipulates that a person who emigrates in time of war is subject to denunciation (*endeixis*)[35] and immediate arrest (*apagōgē*), if he returns.[36] Now he did this, it seems, because he suspected Troezen would survive, but our city he sentenced to death. Moreover, he raised his daughters in prosperity that you provided, but <when misfortune fell> he married them off <elsewhere>, [30] intending all along to come back here and take up his business again when peace was restored. Good <metics have never> done this to you; in times of peace <they have shared in your prosperity and> in times of danger <have fought beside you, as they did> at Plataea,[37] uniting <their own interests with those of Athens>. Athenogenes <has never thought of anything but his own personal interests. . . . Although he benefited from our city, he has deserted it in the face of danger.> . . . after violating the social contract with the city, he insists on his private contract with me, as if anyone would believe that the man who holds his obligations to you in utter contempt would care anything for his obligations to me.

[31] This fellow is so perverse and so utterly true to form that after

---

[35] *Endeixis* and *apagōgē* were two stages of the process of summary arrest, which could be used against individuals who had broken court-imposed bans, whether against someone charged with homicide who had illegally entered a public place, or someone convicted of homicide or punished with exile who had illegally returned to Attica, or even a state debtor caught exercising his civic rights while they were suspended. For *apagōgē,* the citizen would make the arrest himself; in *endeixis,* he would submit in writing to the appropriate magistrate the name of the offender. The citizen was then authorized to make the arrest himself, or the magistrate would do so on his behalf.

[36] The law is read out to the court in 3.33. It appears to apply only to metics who emigrate in time of war and not to Athenian citizens, since Lycurgus (1.53, 144) makes no mention of such a law when prosecuting Leocrates for just that crime.

[37] Apparently this is a reference to the famous battle of Plataea in 479, when the Greeks defeated the Persians and succeeded in driving them from Greece. Nowhere else do we hear of metics fighting there.

he arrived in Troezen and was made a citizen, he offered himself to Mnesias the Argive,[38] who secured his appointment as magistrate and once in office expelled the citizens from the city, something these men can testify to, since they are here in exile.[39] You yourselves, gentlemen of the jury, welcomed them in when they were exiled, made them citizens, and shared with them all your privileges. You remembered, after more than one hundred and fifty years, the kindness that they showed you when facing the barbarian,[40] and you believe that you should rescue from misfortune those who have rendered you service in times of danger. [32] But this polluted creature, who abandoned you and was registered as a citizen at Troezen, did nothing that was worthy of the constitution or the character of that city but treated those who had welcomed him so cruelly that <he was accused soon after> in their own assembly . . . and fearing <dreadful retribution from the Troezenians>, he fled back here again. [33] To prove that I am telling the truth, the clerk will read you first the law that forbids metics from emigrating in time of war, then the testimony of the Troezenians, and besides that the decree passed by the Troezenians to honor your city, which has prompted you in return to welcome them in and to make them citizens. Read them.

[LAW, TESTIMONY, DECREE]

[34][41] Please take the testimony of his father-in-law; <he confirms that Athenogenes received two> inheritances, the estate left <by his father>, and what he got from his brother; and <as soon as he received them, he squandered them> completely, one right after the other <on his *hetaira*> Antigone. <This is sufficient> evidence <to

---

[38] Mnesias is almost certainly the traitor Mnaseas, mentioned by Demosthenes (18.295), along with other traitors in various Greek cities, who promoted Macedonian interests against their own cities.

[39] Since these men were still residing in Athens at the time, the trial took place before 324, the year in which Alexander issued a decree ordering the return of all exiles to their native cities.

[40] In 480 the Persian king Xerxes invaded Attica and destroyed Athens; the Athenians evacuated their women and children to Troezen and faced the enemy in their fleet at Salamis.

[41] Again much of 3.34 is mere guesswork.

prove his prodigal behavior; he has shamelessly squandered his patrimony, which should have been preserved for his family. There is not one of you who does not find such behavior reprehensible. Now you can better appreciate his present conduct towards me.>

[35] <I think you have heard enough about> what he has done, how Athenogenes has plotted against me, and how he has treated you. He is evil in his private life, he has given up hope for the safety of our city, he has abandoned you, he has expelled those with whom he took up residency. You have this man in your grasp; will you not punish him? [36] As for myself, gentlemen of the jury, I beg <and implore you to take pity> on me; understand that in this trial all of you should pity <the plaintiff>, not the <defendant.>[42] In fact, this fellow, if he is convicted, will get nothing he does not <deserve but will suffer> what he should have suffered long ago. As for me, if he is acquitted of the charge I brought, I will be ruined, since I cannot <pay off> even the smallest <portion of these debts>. . . .[43]

---

[42] Normally it was the defendant who pleaded for pity at the trial, but the plaintiff has unexpectedly reversed roles and adopted the standard rhetorical (and largely formulaic) plea by a defendant begging for the court's mercy.

[43] The last few lines of the speech are missing.

4. ON BEHALF OF EUXENIPPUS

INTRODUCTION

This is the only complete speech of Hyperides we have. It is found on the same papyrus that contains the speech of Lycophron, but again the name of the author is not preserved. In fact, no speech by that title under the name of Hyperides has come down to us from antiquity, but there is enough internal evidence to conclude that the speech on Euxenippus was delivered, and thus written, by Hyperides. We learn that the speaker came from the tribe Aegeis (4.12) and that he once prosecuted Aristophon of Hazenia (28) and Philocrates of Hagnus (29). All these facts are known from other sources to be true of Hyperides.

After the battle of Chaeronea in 338, Philip awarded to Athens the town of Oropus, which was on the border between Attica and Boeotia; its territory was divided up among the ten Athenian tribes. A certain hill, which had been awarded to the tribes Hippothoöntis and Acamantis, was regarded by some as sacred to the god Amphiaraus and so unlawfully allocated. To determine whether or not the land actually belonged to the god, the Athenians appointed Euxenippus and two others to sleep in Amphiaraus' temple, where the god would reveal the truth in a dream. Euxenippus had such a dream, which he reported to the Assembly, but it seems that the dream's meaning was not perfectly clear. Polyeuctus proposed a decree that the land be returned to the god and that the other eight tribes compensate Hippothoöntis and Acamantis for their loss. The decree was defeated, and Polyeuctus was convicted in court for proposing an illegal decree but only fined twenty-five drachmas. Not dissuaded, and with the support of Lycurgus who would speak at the trial, he impeached Euxenippus (by *eisangelia*), charging that he had been bribed by the two tribes to report his dream.[1]

The procedure of *eisangelia* was intended for treasonable offenses like subverting the democracy or betraying military forces (4.8–9), but it could be used against someone who had given advice in the Assembly but was suspected of being bribed to give that advice (9). Hyperides argues that this provision of the law should apply only to politicians and not to private individuals like Euxenippus, who have largely stayed out of politics. From Hyperides' reply it seems that Polyeuctus had a rather weak case and was forced to rely heavily on slanderous accusations that had no relevance to the case. A good deal of Hyperides' speech is taken up with addressing allegations of pro-Macedonian sympathies and suggestions that Euxenippus' immense wealth had been acquired through dishonest means, perhaps by abusing the mining regulations. Hyperides was not the first to speak in Euxenippus' defense, and so he limits himself to two points, the legality of the impeachment and the extraneous accusations against Euxenippus. The first speaker would have dealt with other matters.

The date of the trial was perhaps around 330, certainly no earlier than 330, when Olympias acquired Molossia (4.25n) and no later than 324, when Lycurgus died. By that time Hyperides was reconciled with him, and when he defended Lycurgus' children in court, his speech was in part at least an eulogy of Lycurgus' career (Fr. 118). Whatever their differences at the time of the trial of Euxenippus, the tone of his comments about Lycurgus (12) indicates that Hyperides greatly admired the man. He reserves his invective for Polyeuctus.

4. ON BEHALF OF EUXENIPPUS

[1] Gentlemen of the jury, as I was just now saying to those seated next to me, I wonder whether you are not fed up by now with these impeachment trials.[2] In the past you used to impeach men like Timo-

---

[1] Hyperides also opposed Lycurgus at the impeachment trial of Lycophon; see the Introduction to Hyp. 1.

[2] For the procedure of *eisangelia,* see the Introduction to Hyp. 1.

machus, Leosthenes, Callistratus, Philon of Anaea, Theotimus who lost Sestos, and others.[3] Some were accused of betraying ships, others of betraying the city, another of being a politician who did not give the best advice to the people.[4] [2] Not one of these five men awaited trial, nor did many others who were facing impeachment, but on their own they left the city and went into exile. In fact, it was rare to see anyone charged with impeachment come to court, since in those days men were impeached only for very serious and notorious crimes. [3] But today, what's happening in the city is absolutely ridiculous. Diognides and Antidorus, the metic, are accused of hiring out flute girls for more than the price prescribed by the law,[5] Agasicles of Piraeus for being registered in the deme Halimus,[6] and Euxenippus because of the dreams he says

---

[3] All these impeachments occurred around 361/0, and the notoriety that would have come from a series of high-profile trials in a short space of time would have made these names familiar to the jury. Timomachus, who had been sent to deal with the Thracian prince Cotys, was impeached on his return to Athens for his failure, and he was either fined or condemned to death (Dem. 19.180, Aes. 1.56). Leosthenes, who lost five warships in an expedition against Alexander of Pherae, was condemned to death and went into exile (Aes. 2.124). Callistratus, a prominent politician who made his mark as controller of the Athenian treasury, was condemned to death, after Alexander of Pherae attacked Piraeus (cf. Lyc. 1.93). Theotimus was impeached for failing to take Sestos in the region of Thrace. Nothing is known of Philon's trial.

[4] The term that has been translated "politician" is *rhētōr* (lit. speaker). In the fourth century, *rhētōr* referred to anyone who addressed the Assembly, offering advice and proposing decrees, and as such was accountable and could be impeached for his advice. The term, however, was more commonly applied to individuals who regularly spoke in the Assembly and engaged in public suits of a political nature, that is, a politician. Such individuals were a clearly recognized group in Athens. This is the sense that Hyperides wants to impart to the term here, and he contrasts these very public figures with private citizens like Euxenippus, who rarely speak on public matters; only the former and not the latter should be impeached.

[5] Flute girls could not be hired out for more than two drachmas.

[6] That is, as a citizen and not as a metic. According to later sources, Agasicles was a metic who had illegally been registered as a citizen in a different deme (township) from the one in which he had been registered as a metic. Every metic had to have an Athenian sponsor and be registered in the deme of his sponsor.

he saw. Not one of these charges, of course, has anything to do with the impeachment law.

[4] And yet, gentlemen of the jury, in public trials the jurors should not accept the details of the prosecution's case before they have examined the main issue of the trial and the indictment to see whether or not it is within the scope of the law. I do not agree, by Zeus, as Polyeuctus said in his accusation, that defendants should not hold to the letter of the impeachment law,[7] which prescribes that impeachment should be used for politicians (*rhētores*) who have not given the best advice to the people, not just for any Athenian. [5] I want you to keep this law in mind and nothing else. And I do not think we should speak about anything other than how in a democracy the laws will be binding and impeachment charges and other suits will be brought to court in accordance with the law. This is why you enacted separate laws to cover each crime that might occur in the city. [6] If someone commits sacrilege in a religious matter, public indictments for impiety (*asebeia*) can be brought before the King Archon. If someone abuses his parents, the Archon presides over the case. If someone makes an illegal proposal in the Assembly, there is the board of the Thesmothetae. If someone commits a crime deserving immediate arrest (*apagōgē*), the authority of the Eleven takes the case. And in the same way for all other crimes, you have established laws, officials, and courts that are appropriate for each.

[7] So what crimes do you think the impeachment procedure should cover? You have already written down each one in the law so that no one could be in doubt. It says,[8] "If someone subverts the democracy."—Reasonably so, men of the jury. For such a serious charge does not allow any excuse or any oath of postponement[9] but must come to court as quickly as possible.—[8] "Or," it continues, "if he

[7] Polyeuctus seems to have maintained in his speech that the defense should not insist on a narrow interpretation of the law; they should not hold to the letter of the law but rather to the larger spirit of the law.

[8] Hyperides may be quoting selectively to fit his immediate argument. No full text of the law has been preserved, and other offenses not mentioned here may have been included in the law. But Hyperides probably covers the most important provisions.

[9] One party in litigation could seek an adjournment in the case of illness or absence from Attica; his excuse or plea for an adjournment was made under oath;

meets anywhere for the purpose of subverting the democracy, or forms a political club, or if someone betrays a city, or ships, or a land or naval force, or if a politician (*rhētōr*) does not give the best advice to the Athenian people because he has been bribed." The opening provisions of the law you directed against all citizens, since anyone could commit these crimes; but the final provision of the law singles out the politicians, who are responsible for proposing decrees. [9] It would have been sheer madness for you to have written this law in any other way, that is to say, to have politicians enjoy the honors and profits that come with speaking but to have private citizens take on the risks associated with being a politician. Nevertheless, Polyeuctus has the audacity to say, even though he is bringing an impeachment suit, that the defendants should not make use of the impeachment law. [10] All other prosecutors, who think that in their opening speech they need to undermine the defendants' arguments, advise the jurors to refuse to listen to the defendants, when they say something outside the scope of the law, but to challenge their remarks and instruct them to have the law read out. But you, Polyeuctus, think you should do the exact opposite and deprive Euxenippus of his right to have recourse to the law in his defense.

[11] Besides, you insist that no one should help him or speak in his defense, and you urge the jurors to refuse to listen to those who step forward.[10] And yet, of all the many fine institutions that we have in our city, what is finer and more democratic than allowing any citizen who wants to step forward and help a private individual who faces the danger of a trial but cannot defend himself, and so provide the jurors with a fair assessment of the case? [12] You insist you have never followed such a procedure yourself; yet when you were prosecuted by Alexander of Oeon,[11] you asked for ten co-pleaders (*synēgoroi*) from the tribe Aegeis, and in fact I was one of the ones you selected. You also summoned other Athenians into court to help you. But why should I mention other instances? How did you behave at the present

---

the other party could make a counter-oath that his opponent was not prevented from appearing in court. After hearing both sides, a jury would decide whether to grant the adjournment.

[10] This is no doubt an oversimplification of Polyeuctus' argument. He may have warned the jurors against the number of *synēgoroi* Euxenippus would call.

[11] Nothing is known of the person or the trial.

trial? Didn't you make whatever accusation you wanted? Didn't you ask Lycurgus to be part of your prosecution team, who is second to no one in Athens in his ability to speak and has a reputation among speakers for being moderate and fair? [13] If you are permitted, as a defendant, to call co-pleaders, and as a prosecutor to bring forward co-prosecutors, when you not only can speak for yourself but are also quite capable of causing the whole city grief, cannot Euxenippus, who is a private citizen and rather elderly, have the help of his friends and relatives without having you slander them?

[14] By Zeus, the terrible things he has done deserve the death penalty, so you claim in your indictment. Men of the jury, look carefully at it, and examine each and every point. The people (*dēmos*) ordered Euxenippus, along with two others, to lie down in the temple, and he says that he fell asleep and had a dream, which he reported to the people. If you assumed that this was true and that he reported to the people exactly what he saw in his sleep, what crime does he commit in reporting to the Athenians the instructions the god gave him? [15] But if, as you now claim, you thought he lied about the god and sought to curry favor with certain individuals by not telling the people the truth, you should not have proposed a decree opposing the dream but should have made an enquiry at Delphi[12] and learned the truth from the god, just as the previous speaker said.[13] But you did not do this; without any prior consultation (*autotelēs*), you proposed a decree against two tribes, which was not only completely illegal but also in itself contradictory.[14] It was for this reason that you were convicted for illegal proposals, not because of Euxenippus.

[16] Let's examine the matter in this way. The tribes paired off and divided up the mountains in Oropus that were awarded to them by the

---

[12] Delphi was the site of a famous oracle to the god Apollo. Both individuals and cities consulted the oracle for advice.

[13] At least one other co-pleader has spoken before Hyperides on Euxenippus' behalf.

[14] The normal procedure for getting a decree introduced in the Assembly required the Council of 500 to vet the proposal first before it ever reached the Assembly for discussion and voting. Hyperides may be suggesting that Polyeuctus had circumvented the normal procedure; at least this is one interpretation of *autotelēs,* but if he had done this, there would surely have been challenges, and Hyperides would have mentioned these.

people.[15] This mountain range was allotted to Acamantis and Hippothoöntis. You proposed that these tribes return the mountain and the proceeds of the sale of its produce to Amphiaraus,[16] on the grounds that the fifty boundary officials had already chosen it and marked it off for the god, and the two tribes had no right to keep it. [17] A little further in the same decree you proposed that the other eight tribes provide compensation to the two so they would not suffer any loss. And yet, if you were robbing the tribes of the mountain that really was theirs, we have every right to be angry with you. On the other hand, if they had no right to have it but it was the god's, why did you propose that the other tribes reimburse them? They should have been content to return what belonged to the god and not have to pay an additional fine.

[18] When these proposals were examined in court, it was found that they were improperly proposed, and the jurors condemned you. If you had been acquitted of the indictment, Euxenippus would not have been lying about the god, but since you happen to have been convicted, why should he be ruined? Should this man who lay down in the temple on the order of the people be denied burial in Attica, when you were fined only twenty-five drachmas for proposing such a decree?

[19] Yes he should, you say, for he did something terrible, when he allowed Olympias to dedicate the cup to the statue of Health.[17] You assume, by introducing her name in court for your own benefit and by falsely accusing Euxenippus of flattery, you will arouse the hatred and anger of the jurors against him. My good friend, you should not

---

[15] Oropus was on the northeastern border of Attica and Boeotia, and its possession was often a matter of dispute between the Athenians and Boeotians. See the Introduction.

[16] Amphiaraus was a legendary figure who took part in the famous campaign of the Seven against Thebes. At the battle he was swallowed up in a cleft in the ground created by Zeus' thunderbolt. On that spot arose an oracular shrine to the hero, who later achieved the status of a god; it is believed by some, however, that Amphiaraus began as a chthonic deity before becoming a hero. At some point his cult was brought from Thebes to Oropus.

[17] Olympias was the wife of Philip and mother of Alexander the Great. We know nothing else about this affair.

try to harm any citizen by bringing up Olympias' and Alexander's names; [20] but when they give the Athenian people unjust and inappropriate commands, then you should stand up, speak against them on the city's behalf, plead her cause with their envoys, go to the Hellenic Congress and help your country.[18] But you never once stood up there or said anything about them; only here do you express your hatred of Olympias, just to ruin Euxenippus, claiming that he flatters her and the Macedonians. [21] If you can show that he has ever been to Macedonia, or has received any Macedonian into his home, or is friends with or meets with any one from there, or has even mentioned these matters in a shop or in the Agora or anywhere else, and has not conducted his affairs quietly and modestly just like any other citizen, the jurors can do with him what they like. [22] If your accusations were true, you would not be the only one who knew it, but the rest of the city would too. Such is the case with all those who speak and act on behalf of the Macedonians; not only they themselves know, but all other Athenians, even the little school children, know which politicians receive money from the Macedonians and who the others are that entertain Macedonian visitors, receive them into their homes, and go to meet them in the streets when they arrive. Nowhere will you see Euxenippus numbered among any of these men. [23] But you do not accuse or prosecute any of those whom everyone else knows do these things; instead, you accuse Euxenippus of flattery, though his whole life refutes the charge. If you had any sense, you would not have blamed Euxenippus for the cup's dedication or have said anything else on that matter, since this is out of place here. Why you may ask? Well, listen, men of the jury, to the account I am about to give.

[24] Olympias has made complaints about the Dodona affair,[19] unfair ones at that, as I have already proven twice to her envoys in the Assembly in your presence and in the presence of the other Athenians, showing that the complaints she brought against our city were inap-

---

[18] The Hellenic Congress was created by Philip after the battle of Chaeronea (338). See Diodorus Siculus 16.89.

[19] Dodona, located in Epirus in northwestern Greece, had a famous oracle of Zeus.

propriate. For Zeus of Dodona commanded you by his oracle to embellish the statue of Dione.[20] [25] You had the face and all the other parts near it sculptured in the finest manner possible, and provided the goddess with very expensive decorations, and dispatched state envoys with an expensive sacrifice; in this way you embellished the statue of Dione and did credit to yourselves and the goddess. You received complaints about these activities from Olympias in the letters in which she claimed that the region of Molossia where the temple stands belonged to her, and consequently we had no right to meddle with anything there.[21] [26] Now if you vote that what was done with regard to the cup is a crime, in a sense we will be condemning ourselves and admitting that what we did there in Dodona was wrong. But if we just disregard what has happened, we will deprive Olympias of the opportunity of making her theatrical complaints. For I suppose, if Olympias can decorate the temples of Athens, surely we cannot be prevented from decorating those at Dodona, especially when the god commanded it.

[27] It seems to me, Polyeuctus, that there is nothing you would exclude as grounds for an accusation. And yet, since you have chosen to enter politics, and, by Zeus, you are certainly good at it, you should not prosecute private citizens or go after them like some young kid, but you should prosecute a politician if he commits a crime, or impeach a general if he does not do what he should. These are the men who have the power to harm the city, if they so choose, not Euxenippus or any of these jurors. [28] It's not that I am advising you to act in this way, having conducted my own political career differently, but I have never in my life prosecuted a private citizen, and in fact I have helped several individuals as much as I could. Tell me, whom have I prosecuted or brought to trial? Aristophon of Hazenia, who had become extremely powerful politically—he was acquitted in this court by just two votes.[22] [29] Then there was Diopeithes of Sphettus, re-

---

[20] Dione was Zeus' consort and was worshipped in his temple at Dodona.

[21] Olympias gained control of the region in 330 when her brother, also named Alexander, was assassinated.

[22] Aristophon was active in politics from 403/2 to the 340s but most influential in the period from 363 to 350. In 363/2 he was prosecuted by Hyperides for pro-

putedly the most dangerous man in the city;[23] and Philocrates of Hagnus whose political conduct had been insolent and wanton.[24] I impeached this fellow for the services he rendered to Philip against the city, and I secured his conviction in court; and I drew up an impeachment that was just and based on the law, namely, that "he was a politician who was not giving the best advice to the Athenian people because he took money and gifts from those who were acting against the interests of the people." [30] And I was still not content to enter the impeachment in just these terms, but I added below: "The following advice he gave was not in the best interests of the people because he was bribed"; then I wrote under it his decree. And then once more I added, "The following advice he gave was not in the best interests of the people because he was bribed," and I added the decree. I wrote this statement five or six times, because I thought I should be strictly legal in the way I presented the trial and my accusation. But you were not able to include in your impeachment the advice you claim Euxenippus gave that was not in the best interests of the people. Rather, you accuse a private citizen as if he were classified as a politician.

[31] After a few brief words about his plea, you come up with other accusations and slanderous remarks against him, claiming that he gave his daughter in marriage to Philocles,[25] adopted Demotion's way of living,[26] and other accusations like these. Your intent is that if the defense ignore the impeachment charge and address the accusations that are irrelevant to the matter at hand, the jurors will object and ask, "Why are you telling us this?" But if they do not mention these accusations, their case will be weakened, for not answering them leaves

posing an illegal decree involving his settlement of Ceos. This was not the first time he escaped conviction; he boasted that he had been prosecuted seventy-five times under the *graphē paranomōn* without ever being convicted.

[23] We know almost nothing about Diopeithes, who seems to have been a man of little political importance, or about this trial.

[24] Philocrates was an important figure who had proposed peace with Philip in 346. Hyperides impeached him in 343 (see the Introduction to Hyperides).

[25] Nothing is known of Philocles.

[26] This may be the Demotion satirized in comedy for his prodigal behavior. See Athenaeus 6.243b.

the accused open to the jurors' anger. [32] And the most dreadful thing you said in your speech, and you thought your motive for saying it went unnoticed but it did not, was when you often slipped in that Euxenippus was rich, and again after an interval, that he had amassed vast wealth by unlawful means. It surely has nothing to do with this case whether he has great wealth or little; it is just malicious talk and unfairly assumes that the jurors might base their verdict on anything other than the issue at hand and whether the man on trial has done you wrong or not.

[33] It seems to me, Polyeuctus, that you and those who think like you do not realize that in the world there exists no democracy or monarchy or nation more magnanimous than the Athenian people; they do not desert their fellow citizens when they are falsely accused by others, whether alone or together with others, but they help them out. [34] In the first place, when Tisis of Agryle submitted an inventory (*apographē*)[27] against the property of Euthycrates, which was worth more than sixty talents, on the grounds that it was public property, and again afterwards when he promised to enter an inventory against Philip's and Nausicles' property, alleging that they had made their money from unregistered mines, these jurors, far from accepting such an allegation or coveting other people's property, immediately disenfranchised the man who undertook these false accusations by not giving him one-fifth of the vote.[28] [35] But if you like, the verdict just recently reached by the jurors within the past month certainly deserves your approval. When Lysander reported (*phasis*)[29] that the

---

[27] An *apographē* was the procedure used against state debtors who were withholding payment from the state, though they possessed the means. It could be initiated by any citizen who would submit an inventory of the debtor's property to the Eleven and prosecute him in court. If he was convicted, his property was confiscated and sold, with two-thirds of the proceeds going to the prosecutor. See Todd 1993: 118–119.

[28] The prosecutor in a public suit who failed to receive one-fifth of the vote was fined one thousand drachmas and as a state debtor, lost his civic rights until he paid the fine.

[29] A *phasis* was a public suit that could be initiated by any citizen. The procedure was used against those running contraband or violating other trade regulations, against those committing certain types of religious offenses, and against

mine of Epicrates of Pallene had been excavated within the limits of another's concession,[30] a mine that had been worked for three years and in which nearly all the richest men of Athens had some share, Lysander promised to collect three hundred talents for the city, for that was the amount they had taken out of the mine. [36] Even still the jurors didn't pay attention to the prosecution's promises but followed the demands of justice; they determined that the mine was within its own boundaries and with that same vote firmly secured their property and guaranteed the remaining period for working the mine.[31] As a result, new cuttings, which previously had been avoided through fear, are now under way, and the city's revenues from the mines are again increasing, revenues that some politicians jeopardized by deceiving the people and imposing taxes on the miners. [37] Gentlemen of the jury, a good citizen is not one who provides a little revenue but in the long run does more harm to the public treasury, nor one who provides immediate income from an illegitimate source but destroys the city's legitimate source of revenue; rather, he is one who is also concerned about the city's long-term profits, the unity of its citizens, and your reputation. Some do not care about these things. They rob the contractors of their source of income and claim that they are securing revenue, but they are really placing the city in financial difficulty. For when earnings and savings come with fear, who will want to take the risk?

[38] Perhaps it is difficult to prevent these men from doing this. But you, men of the jury, just as you have saved many other citizens

---

those breaking certain mining regulations, such as working an unregistered mine or mining beyond the prescribed boundaries of a mine. The successful prosecutor in a *phasis* received half the fine imposed by the court on the offender. See Todd 1993: 119.

[30] The expression "within the limits" appears in Dem. 37.36, where the sense is clearly extending one's mining beyond one's own concession into the concession of another.

[31] Mining leases were typically three years in length for active mines and seven years for abandoned or new mines. Since Epicrates' mine had already been worked for three years before Lysander initiated his suit, and the court guaranteed the remaining term of the lease, we must assume that the mine was either a newly developed work or one that had been abandoned and reopened by Epicrates.

who were unjustly brought to trial, so come to Euxenippus' rescue. Do not abandon him over a trivial matter in an impeachment case like this; not only is he not subject to impeachment but the impeachment itself was introduced contrary to the laws, and besides it has been in a sense invalidated by the prosecutor himself.[32] [39] Polyeuctus has impeached Euxenippus for not giving the best advice to the Athenian people because he has taken money and gifts from those acting against the interests of the Athenian people. If he accused Euxenippus of receiving gifts from and cooperating with men outside the city, it would be possible for Polyeuctus to claim that since these men cannot be punished, those in the city who were working for them should be brought to justice. But, in fact, he claims it was from Athenians that he received the bribes. Well, then, you have men in the city who are acting against the interests of the people, and you don't punish them but harass Euxenippus?

[40] I still have a few words to say about the vote you are about to cast, and then I will step down. Men of jury, when you are about to vote, have the clerk read out the impeachment, the impeachment law, and the jurors' oath;[33] set aside all our arguments, and on the basis of the impeachment and the law, consider what you think is just and true to your oath, and vote accordingly.

[41] As for you, Euxenippus, I have helped as much as I can. It remains for you to ask the jury to allow you to call your friends and bring forward your children.

---

[32] Because Polyeuctus failed to include in his impeachment the advice Euxenippus offered the people. See 4.30.

[33] On the juror's oath, see 1a Fr. 1n.

5. AGAINST DEMOSTHENES

INTRODUCTION

This speech was preserved on the same papyrus on which we find the first four fragments of *In Defense of Lycophron.* Although the speech itself is very fragmentary, substantial portions remain from the proem (1–7),[1] the prothesis (7–8), the narrative (8–14), and the peroration (37–38). The argument (15–36) that comprises over half of the speech is by far the most fragmentary, but enough of the text is preserved to get a clear sense of how Hyperides argued.

In 323 Hyperides was one of the ten prosecutors appointed to prosecute Demosthenes and a number of other prominent Athenians for accepting bribes from Harpalus, a Macedonian noble and childhood friend of Alexander the Great.[2] Demosthenes was the first to be tried, and because of the importance of the case, a jury of fifteen hundred was selected. The first prosecutor to speak was Stratocles, followed by the client of Dinarchus who gave the speech preserved as Dinarchus 1 (translated earlier in this volume), and then perhaps Hyperides, who repeats some of the ground covered by the previous speakers. At times his attack displays a degree of bitterness at one who betrayed his loyalty to his country and to his friend (20–21). In the end, Demosthenes was convicted and fined fifty talents. Unable to pay, he was imprisoned but allowed to escape to Aegina. He was recalled after the death

---

[1] The section numbers in the speech roughly correspond to the column numbers of the papyrus.

[2] See the Introduction to Hyperides, and for a more detailed account of the Harpalus affair, see the Introduction to Dinarchus and Worthington 1992.

of Alexander, by which time Hyperides and Demosthenes had been reconciled.

5. AGAINST DEMOSTHENES

Fr. 1

[1] Gentlemen of the jury, as I was saying a moment ago to those seated next to me,[3] it would surprise me if Demosthenes is the only man in the city not bound by the laws that uphold the validity of any agreement made by a person against his own interests, or by the people's decrees that you have sworn to follow when casting your vote; these decrees were not proposed by any of his enemies but by Demosthenes himself, and they were approved by the people on his own motion, almost as if he was bent on destroying himself. . . .[4] [2] And yet, gentlemen of the jury, I think it is simple for us to render a just verdict against Demosthenes. As in private suits many things are decided by challenges,[5] so too has this case been decided. Look at it this way, gentlemen of the jury. The people accused you, Demosthenes, of accepting twenty talents against the interests of the state and the laws. You denied it and wrote up a challenge that you submitted before the people in the form of a decree, entrusting the matter on which you stood accused to the Council of the Areopagus. . . .[6]

---

[3] These are the same opening words as in 4.1.

[4] Three lines are missing here.

[5] The challenge or *proklēsis* was a formal request by one litigant of the other to let a slave be interrogated under torture, to let an oath be sworn, or to admit a piece of evidence, whether an object or a person. The refusal or the acceptance of the challenge was entered as evidence in court. If the challenge was accepted, it could resolve the case.

[6] The Areopagus was composed of ex-archons, who held membership for life. It tried cases of intentional homicide and certain cases of impiety. But in 343 on the motion of Demosthenes (Din. 1.62), the Areopagus was given the power to investigate those suspected of serious violations of the law. The procedure usually began with a decree in the Assembly authorizing the Areopagus to begin an investigation of a suspected crime, usually treason. After their investigation, the Areopagus would make a report (*apophasis*) to the Assembly, which decided whether or not to act on the Council's findings. Hyperides is arguing that as the originator

Fr. 2

[3] . . . and you slander the Council, by publishing challenges and asking in the challenges, how you came by the gold, who gave it to you, and where you were paid off. Perhaps you will end by asking what use you put it to once you got it, as if you were demanding a banker's account from the Council. [4] I would like to learn just the opposite from you, why the Areopagus informed <the people> that you had unlawfully <accepted> the gold. . . .

[7]<*Without a doubt, you are going to maintain that the Areopagus has special authority to carry out its investigations without any supervision;*

Fr. 3

[5] *that the proceedings are fully under its control, and that any citizen in these circumstances is justified in fearing that guarantees*> of justice <have not been included> in its reports (*apophaseis*). This is not the case, but it will be clearer than anything that they have handled the matter in a most democratic fashion; they reported the criminals, and they did this not by their own choice but under repeated pressure from the people. They did not punish the guilty on their own but left it to you jurors, who have the final authority.

[6] Not only does Demosthenes think he should deceive you at his own trial by slandering the report (*apophasis*), but he also wants to detract from all the other trials in the city. You must keep this in mind when you now make your deliberations, and do not be deceived by this man's argument. These reports on the Harpalus money have all been drawn up in the same manner by the Council; they are exactly the same for all the accused; the Council has not attached to a single one its reason for the report but wrote summarily how much gold each man received, and noted that this was the amount he had to pay. [7] Is Demosthenes to have more weight with you than the report against him? If you reject the report, then no one has taken money, and all the others are ac-

---

of the process, Demosthenes has in effect challenged the Areopagus to find him guilty, and they have accepted the challenge (cf. 5.29).

[7] Restorations marked in italics and angle brackets are only hypothetical reconstructions of what may have been said by Hyperides.

quitted, since I don't suppose this decision will be valid only for Demosthenes and not for the others. You are not deciding about twenty talents but about four hundred, not about one crime but about them all. Your madness, Demosthenes, has put you ahead of all criminals in the danger you face and your shameless behavior.

That the Council to which you entrusted yourself has condemned you is, I think, sufficient proof to the jury that you took the gold. [8] I will now produce the evidence relating to the gold you previously took and, as I already said, will make clear your reasons for taking it and your motives for disgracing the whole city.

Gentlemen of the jury, when Harpalus arrived in Attica and the envoys from Philoxenus[8] demanding his surrender were at once introduced to the Assembly, Demosthenes came forward and gave a long talk claiming that it was not good for the city to surrender Harpalus to Philoxenus' envoys, nor should they leave Alexander with any cause for complaint against the people on that man's account. [9] The safest thing for the city to do, he said, was to guard both the man and his money, take all the money Harpalus had with him when he entered Attica up to the Acropolis the next day, and have Harpalus declare right away how much there was. His motive, it seems, was not to learn how much money there was but to figure out how much commission he would get. Sitting, where he usually does, down under the cut,[9] he told Mnesitheus the dancer to ask Harpalus how much money was to be taken up to the Acropolis. He replied that there were seven hundred talents[10] . . . [10] Although Demosthenes told you himself in the Assembly that's how much money there was, yet when only three hundred and fifty talents instead of the seven hundred were brought to the Acropolis, he did not utter a single word, for he had received his twenty talents. < . . . So Demosthenes,> after stating in the Assembly that there were seven hundred talents, now you report half; <you did not bother to think> that <if the exact amount that was reported publicly> was not brought to the Acropolis, <then someone must

---

[8] One of Alexander's generals and governor of Cilicia in Asia Minor.

[9] This was perhaps a niche cut into the base of the Pnyx, where the Assembly met.

[10] Twelve lines are missing here.

have been bribed; *certainly you did not; you were preoccupied with your own commission; don't tell us you received nothing, when others were paid handsomely.* [11] Otherwise, the jurors> would not be deciding on these matters . . . nor would Harpalus have bought <the help that he received>, nor would the city be faced with accusations and slanders. But all these things, Demosthenes, <*were of no concern to you; nothing would stand in your way; you might*> disgrace <*the city but you would get your*> gold. For . . . five thousand staters.[11] [12] It was you who proposed the decree to post the guard on Harpalus' person, and when the guard failed in its duties, you did not correct the situation, and when it was disbanded you did not prosecute those responsible. No doubt you managed this crisis free of charge? Now Harpalus paid off the lesser politicians (*rhētores*)[12] who have nothing to offer but a bunch of clatter and shouting; did he overlook you, who are in charge of all our political affairs? Can anyone believe this?

Such, gentlemen of the jury, is the extent of Demosthenes' contempt for the matter, or, if I must be frank, for you and for the laws, [13] that at the very outset, so it seems, he admitted to taking the money but claimed to have used it for your benefit, borrowing it for the Theoric Fund.[13] Cnosion[14] and his other friends went around saying that Demosthenes' accusers would force him to disclose facts he wanted to keep secret and to admit that he had borrowed the money on your behalf to meet government expenses. When those of you who heard this became even more incensed at the aspersions he cast on your democracy, since he was not satisfied with taking bribes on his own, but thought he should infect the people with his shame, [14] <*he began to change tactics and tried to raise suspicions about the impartiality of the*

---

[11] A stater was probably worth about 25 drachmas, so that 5,000 staters would be about 20 talents. Din. 1.89 reports that Demades received 6,000 staters.

[12] On the term *rhētōr,* see 4.1n.

[13] The Theoric Fund was probably established in the fifth century by Pericles to subsidize the poor for their cost of attending the theater. In the fourth century under the direction of Eubulus, the fund achieved healthy surpluses that were used for a variety of projects unrelated to its original purpose.

[14] Cnosion was a young man with whom Demosthenes seems to have had a close friendship, for which he was slandered by his political enemies. See Aes. 2.149.

Areopagus>, accusing the Council of wanting to destroy him as a favor to Alexander; as if all of you did not know that no one destroys a man like this, who can be bought, but they go after the man who cannot be persuaded or corrupted by money and use any means to get rid of him.

Perhaps there is a chance, Demosthenes, that you cannot be moved by prayers or persuaded to take bribes [15] or that someone may think that only unimportant matters are affected by the corruption of these men. It is no secret that <all> who plot against Greek power secure the smaller cities by force of arms but the larger ones by buying off the men of influence in them. Nor is it a secret that Philip became so powerful from the very beginning by sending money to the Peloponnese, Thessaly, and the rest of Greece and by corrupting those with power and rank in the cities . . . [15]

Fr. 4

[16] . . . [17] <*To enhance your own reputation as our political leader*> you tell some wild stories. Don't you realize it is obvious to everyone that you were clearly speaking in Alexander's interest, though you claimed to be speaking for the people? I think even before now everyone knew that that is how you acted with the Thebans and all the others: you kept for yourself the money sent from Asia for their cause and spent much of it for your own personal use.[16] Now you engage in mercantile trade and make loans on cargo; you have bought

---

[15] The last five lines of column XV and almost all of column XVI are lost. In this gap Hyperides may have described how Alexander continued to increase Macedonian power over Greece by following his father's example of intimidation and corruption. What has happened in other cities, he may have suggested, has happened in Athens; Demosthenes, like other political leaders, has been corrupted, and his leadership has proven to be a disaster to Athens. Hyperides then goes on to cite the two examples found in columns XVII and XVIII that show how Demosthenes has been working in Alexander's interest, the example of Thebes and the Harpalus affair.

[16] In 335 Thebes revolted and called on the Peloponnese and Athens for help. At Demosthenes' prompting, the Athenians voted to send help but never acted on their promise, and Thebes was destroyed by Alexander. Demosthenes was later accused by his enemies of having received three hundred talents of gold from the Persian king to finance the insurrection. See Din. 1.10, 18–22, Aes. 3.239–240.

a house <that serves as a safe harbor where you can slip away at the crucial moment,> so you do not live in Piraeus, but you anchor there away from the city.[17] A true leader of people should save <his city, not desert it.>

[18] <When Harpalus recently> descended on Greece <so suddenly> that no one anticipated it, and he found affairs in the Peloponnese and in the rest of Greece in a state because of Nicanor's arrival with orders from Alexander on the exiles and <sanctions against> the Achaean, Arcadian, and Boeotian leagues,[18] <*there was a golden opportunity for you to enlist the aid of the satraps of Asia, but you let it slip.*> [19] You accomplished this with your decree, when you arrested Harpalus, and you caused all the Greeks to send envoys to Alexander, since they had no other option. As for the satraps,[19] who would have willingly joined forces with us, bringing all the money and troops that each one had, you not only prevented them all from revolting by arresting Harpalus, but you caused each one of them <to vie with the other in showing their loyalty to Alexander and hatred of Athens. *Perhaps you once preached patriotism in your attacks on Philip. You made us believe that you had a single purpose, a constant policy, that you acted for the public good. But oh how things have changed; you are now Alexander's supporter and have agents in contact with the Macedonians.*>

Fr. 5

[20] < . . . Aristion the Samian> was sent <to Hephaestion> by Demosthenes;[20] Callias, the Chalcidian, the brother of Taurosthenes to

---

[17] This house in Piraeus is also mentioned by Dinarchus (1.69) and described in the exact terms by Aeschines (3.209).

[18] Nicanor was the son-in-law of Aristotle and served with Alexander in Asia. He was sent by Alexander in 324 to proclaim that all exiles could return to their native cities. See Din. 1.82.

[19] Satraps were the governors of the provinces of the Persian empire.

[20] Aristion and Hephaestion are restorations, based on information in a late source (Harpocration) that Aristion was mentioned in the speech and was sent by Demosthenes to Hephaestion. Elsewhere (Aes. 3.162), Aristion is described as an intimate friend of Demosthenes. Hephaestion was a close friend and companion of Alexander.

Olympias.[21] Demosthenes proposed that these men should be made Athenian citizens, and now he uses them as his special agents. And it's no wonder. Since he cannot stick to the same convictions, I suppose it is reasonable for him to have friends from Euripus.[22]

So do you dare <to speak> to me of our friendship, <*which you betrayed?*> **[21]** You yourself destroyed it when you accepted bribes against your country and changed sides. You made yourself a laughingstock and disgraced those who had previously supported your policy. When we could have had the highest renown among the people and been honored for the rest of our lives, you overturned everything. And you are not ashamed, even now at your age,[23] to be tried for bribery by mere boys. It should have been the exact opposite: you should have taught the younger politicians; you should have criticized and punished them for anything that they did too recklessly. **[22]** But now we see the opposite: the young are teaching decency to men over sixty.

For this reason, gentlemen of the jury, you have a right to be angry at Demosthenes; though he has gained a modest reputation and great wealth with your help, as he approaches old age, he has shown no concern for his country. You used to feel a certain shame before the Greeks who were watching,[24] when you were condemning certain individuals, especially if it meant you had in your grasp popular leaders, generals, and guardians of public affairs . . . **[23]** <*But since you have*

---

[21] Callias and his brother Taurosthenes played a prominent role in the political affairs of Chalcis and the island of Euboea. In 343 Callias sought Macedonian help to create an independent Euboean league but failed in his venture and so transferred his allegiance to Athens. Sometime later, both he and his brother were awarded Athenian citizenship with the support of Demosthenes, who was accused of accepting a bribe. See Din. 1.44, Aes. 3.85–100.

[22] Euripus is the narrow strait between Euboea and Boeotia, and it was known for its rapidly shifting currents. Aeschines (3.90) makes the same comparison for Callias.

[23] Demosthenes was sixty or sixty-one at the time.

[24] When the Athenian Assembly met, the Pnyx was fenced off with barriers (Dem. 59.90) to prevent foreigners from entering the auditorium, but they could watch the proceedings from the escarpment that bounded the auditorium on the south.

condemned, though with some reluctance, such distinguished men as Timotheus for taking money, when it was proven they had done wrong, you cannot but condemn Demosthenes on the same grounds. His position in politics has made the crime all the worse.>

Fr. 6

[24] It is not so serious a crime to take money as is it to take it from an illicit source, and private individuals who took the gold are not as guilty as the politicians and generals. Why? Because Harpalus gave the gold to private individuals to safeguard, but the generals and politicians took it for political reasons. The laws set a simple fine for those committing misdemeanors, but for those accepting bribes they prescribe a fine ten times the amount taken; and under the law, the death penalty can be assigned to these men alone. In this way you have laid down more severe penalties for them.

[25] As I said in the Assembly, gentlemen of the jury, you readily allow the generals and politicians to make large profits, not because the laws grant them this right but because of your indulgence and generosity allow it. But you make sure of this one thing, that what they take is for your benefit and not to your detriment. Both Demosthenes and Demades have received, I believe, more than sixty talents from actual decrees passed in the city and from proxenies,[25] in addition to the King's gold and money from Alexander. If all these sources were not enough for them but they now have taken bribes that threaten the very life of the city, how can you not be justified in punishing them?

[26] If one of you private citizens makes a mistake while holding some office, through ignorance or inexperience, he will be sunk in court under their eloquence, and either put to death or banished from the country. Will these men, then, receive no punishment at all, when

---

[25] A *proxenos* was a citizen of one city appointed by another to act as a liaison for any of its citizens when they came to visit the *proxenos'* country. By the fourth century it had become an honorary title often bestowed by Athens on foreign dignitaries in recognition of some service. Such honors were decreed in the Assembly, and Hyperides suggests that Demosthenes and Demades, who sponsored many of these decrees, received kickbacks from the foreign dignitaries who were so honored.

they have done such tremendous harm to the city? Conon of Paeania[26] took money from the Theoric Fund for his son who was abroad, and when these men prosecuted him in court, he had to pay a talent for taking five drachmas, even though he begged for mercy. Aristomachus, who became head of the Academy,[27] removed a shovel from the palaestra to his own garden nearby and used it and <with these politicians against him, had to pay severely for his misdemeanor.> . . . [27] . . . [28]

Fr. 7

[28] . . . Nonetheless, in the period that followed,[29] the people did not prevent us from approaching them and discussing matters with them; to the contrary, they even used us as their advisers and advocates. <At that time, Lycurgus was their preferred leader,> and in the following month, the people elected him treasurer over all their finances,[30] believing we owed him a debt of gratitude, and rightly so. [29] Besides, we later faced many court challenges over that policy and over the war itself, and never once did these men[31] vote against us, but they got us safely through it all, a very obvious and certain sign of the people's favor. <And although you had the arrogance, Demosthenes, to propose the death penalty for yourself, if the Council reported that you had received anything from Harpalus, when they made the report, and it turned out that you had been convicted> automatically by the terms of your own decree, <these men did not take into account what

---

[26] This may be the banker mentioned by Dinarchus (1.43) who had been granted Athenian citizenship by a decree of Demosthenes.

[27] The Academy was a gymnasium on the outskirts of Athens dedicated to the hero Academus; it became home to the school of Plato. Nothing is known of the incident involving Aristomachus.

[28] Except for a few letters, almost all of column XXVII is missing.

[29] That is, the period following Chaeronea, when a number of political trials took place (see Dem. 18.249). In fact, Hyperides himself was prosecuted in 337 by Aristogeiton for an illegal decree that would have authorized freeing slaves and granting citizenship to metics. See the Introduction to Hyperides.

[30] Lycurgus succeeded in substantially improving the financial condition of Athens; see the Introduction to Lycurgus in this volume.

[31] That is, the jurors.

happened to them but allowed you a regular trial.> [30] The people have always treated <us politicians in this way>: although stripped of their own crown by fortune, they have not stripped us of the one they awarded.

When the people have behaved towards us in this way, shouldn't we render all the service that is rightfully due them and, if need be, die for them? I think so. But you <acted> against the interests of the people, <and you do not realize there are men who want to repay> the kindnesses <they have been shown,> and who want to do their own country and not someone else's a good turn. [31] By contrast, you have continued <to be disloyal and> to display the power of your eloquence <to deceive the people.> Now when you thought the Areopagus would report those who had the gold, you became belligerent and started raising a ruckus in the city to hinder the investigation. But when the Council delayed its report, claiming it had not yet uncovered the truth, then you conceded in the Assembly that Alexander was the son of Zeus and Poseidon, if he wanted to be, [32] and when <Nicanor> arrived . . . <*then we saw clearly the man who had always advanced his own interests over that of the city. It was he who*> wanted to set up <in the Agora> a statue of King Alexander, the invincible god, . . . and when Olympias sent her message <*one could again see clearly where his loyalties lay* . . . > announce to the Assembly . . .

Fr. 8

[33] . . . [34] <*The people offered to acquit those who had received money from Harpalus of all*> charges[32] and made a proclamation to that effect. But instead of returning what they took and being acquitted, they proposed penalties and inquiries directed against themselves. What are we do with men who began by committing a crime and taking bribes but refused to return the gold when granted an amnesty? Are we to allow them to go unpunished?

It would be a disgrace, men of the jury, to risk the safety of the city over charges against individuals. You cannot acquit these men unless you are willing to assume responsibility for their crimes [35] . . . <*This*

[32] That is, if they confessed.

is no ordinary lawsuit that involves the fate of only an individual; it affects the whole city. Now if the Macedonians had recovered all the money brought here by Harpalus, this would have gone a long way to restoring your fortunes. But now you have heard rumors of war, and by next spring you could, because of the crime of these men, see> Alexander <attacking> Attica <*and the city brought to complete ruin.*>[33] For this reason, gentlemen of the jury, do not place their greed before your own safety; do not make war for sordid gain [36] but for more honorable achievements and improved fortunes. . . .

Fr. 9

[37] . . . <*Through the course of our history, we have undertaken fierce battles against the Persians, Sparta and Philip, and*> we have concluded peace with them on honorable terms. . . . <*That we should act in the same way today*> is my advice. <*We should not protect men who are clearly guilty by the terms of their own decree and should have long since been punished.*>

<*You have been informed of Demosthenes' offenses, the gravity of the situation and the grave consequences that could follow for Athens. It is now time for you to do your duty.*> [38] <The people have laid down exactly what> they expect of each one of us; they have assigned to us, their chosen prosecutors, the task of prosecuting in court those who have taken money and accepted bribes against the interests of the country and of convicting them. The task of reporting the names of those who took money, they have given to the Council of the Areopagus, which revealed them to the people. But the task of <punishing the guilty they have assigned to you. . . . This is your duty, and if you condemn these men, you will only be sanctioning the investigation> of the Areopagus. [39] But if the vote does not conform with the laws and with justice, this acquittal, men of the jury, will remain as your legacy and no one else's. For this reason, you must all <fulfill the duty the people have assigned you with all justice>, looking to the safety of the city and all the other prosperity that exists in this country for

---

[33] Athens remained relatively independent until 322, when the Macedonian general Antipater imposed on the city constitutional change and a garrison.

you, collectively and individually. You must remember the tombs of your ancestors and punish the wrongdoers in the interests of the whole city. Do not give into their seductive arguments and <allow entreaties to save> [40] those who took bribes against their country and the laws.

Do not pay attention to Hagnonides' tears;[34] remember that only the man who has accidentally made a mistake <deserves to be pitied, *and only after you have examined the facts, do you, in certain cases at least, take into account the extenuating circumstances and regard them, as it were as*> an allowance <from you.> But this fellow should have no more right to weep and wail than pirates who wail away when put on the wheel, when they did not have to embark on the ship in the first place. The same is true of Demosthenes; what good reason will he have to weep, when he did not have to take <money from Harpalus?>

Citations from Later Authors[35]

Not even within the terms of a *paragraphē.* (Harpocration)

But you call to your aid the young men whom you used to insult and abuse by calling them winos. (Priscianus 18.235)

Anyone who drank a little too much would distress you. (Athenaeus 10.424d)

Coward. (Photius 116.22)

---

[34] From this remark it would seem that Hagnonides assisted Demosthenes at his trial, but there is evidence that he was also implicated in the Harpalus affair, prosecuted by Dinarchus (Din. Fr. 9) but acquitted. See Worthington 1992: 12, 54, 56, 279.

[35] These fragments are assigned to this speech by later authors; they must have appeared somewhere in the missing portions of the text.

6. THE FUNERAL ORATION

INTRODUCTION

In 322 Hyperides was selected to deliver the funeral oration over the Athenian dead in the Lamian War. He was the natural choice: Demosthenes was still in exile; Demades, who had earlier been convicted of accepting bribes from Harpalus and later fined for proposing the deification of Alexander, was disenfranchised; and Phocion, who still advocated peace, had no credibility. Hyperides thus emerged not only as the leading politician in Athens but as a forceful advocate of resistance; he was also behind the choice of Leosthenes to lead that resistance against Macedon.

Leosthenes, who had served in Alexander's army in Asia as one of the commanders of the Greek mercenaries, organized the return of these mercenaries to Taenarum when they were disbanded. There he waited for his moment, which came with the death of Alexander in 323. With eight thousand mercenaries, financed by Harpalus' silver, he headed north and occupied Thermopylae, the pass into central Greece. Initially he met with success. He defeated the Macedonians in Boeotia, and when Antipater moved south into Thessaly, he scored a second victory and succeeded in shutting up Antipater in the mountain stronghold of Lamia, just north of Thermopylae. But the siege dragged on through the winter, and during the operations, Leosthenes was killed. His successor Antiphilus was forced to lift the siege, but in the battle that followed, the Greeks were again victorious, and Antipater withdrew to Macedonia to await the help of his fellow Macedonian commander Craterus. Once he arrived, Antipater again descended in Thessaly, and in August of 322 at Crannon, he defeated the Greeks in the field. So ended the Athenian and Greek hopes of freedom.

In the spring of 322, before the defeat at Crannon, the Athenians honored those who had died at Lamia with a public funeral. It was a long-standing tradition (see Thuc. 2.34.1), unique to Athens (Dem. 20.141), that a citizen of distinction would deliver an oration over the dead who had fallen in battle during the previous year. As a conventional form, the funeral oration had a set structure that included praise, consolation, and exhortation. The tribute to the dead often became a tribute to the glorious deeds of Athens' past, and in other examples of the genre (e.g., Lys. 2), the speaker would pass quickly over the actual events that occasioned his speech and dwell at length on Athens' heroic past or the glory of the city; such is the case in the best known example of the genre, Pericles' funeral oration (Thuc. 2.35–46).

Hyperides departs significantly from convention; though he praises the city (3–5) and consoles the living (41–43), he concentrates almost exclusively on recent events and in particular on Leosthenes. He will not recount in detail Athens' past accomplishments but will reserve his words for Leosthenes and his companions (6). Whatever mythological events (Troy) or Athenian heroes of the past (Miltiades, Themistocles, Harmodius and Aristogeiton) he does mention, redound not to the praise of Athens but to the praise of Leosthenes. These heroes will greet him with awe in Hades, a general who not only matched but even outdid their heroic exploits. The attention that Hyperides pays to Leosthenes and the others who died at Lamia adds a certain immediacy and sincerity to his words that cannot be found in other orations of this type (Kennedy 1963: 165). The sincerity was no doubt genuine; he was praising a friend and fellow compatriot who died in a cause he deeply believed in. It is no surprise that Hyperides' funeral oration was highly regarded in antiquity.

BIBLIOGRAPHY

Loraux, Nicole, 1986: *The Invention of Athens: The Funeral Oration in the Classical City.* Cambridge.

6. THE FUNERAL ORATION

[1] The words to be delivered over this grave, declaring the bravery of the general Leosthenes and the other men who have died with him in the war, have as witness time itself, which preserves a record of their

deeds to their glory. For no man we know or <have heard about> in all of history has ever seen resolve more noble than this or men more courageous than those who have died or deeds more magnificent. [2] For this reason, what I fear most today is that my speech will fail to measure up to their deeds. However, I do take heart again in this thought, that what I leave out you who hear me will supply, for my words will not be addressed to a random crowd but to men who witnessed their deeds.

[3] Our city deserves praise for the policy it chose, a policy that matched and even surpassed the proud and noble deeds it accomplished in the past; those who have died also deserve praise for their bravery in battle, bravery that did not disgrace the valor of their ancestors; and finally the general Leosthenes deserves praise on both counts, for he led the city to adopt the policy and was appointed commander of our citizens for the expedition.

[4] As for our city, I will not recount in detail every previous benefit that it has bestowed on all of Greece; I do not have enough time. This is not the appropriate moment to make a long speech, and it would not be easy for one man to go through and remember so many great deeds. But I will not hesitate to summarize its main accomplishments. [5] As the sun covers the whole of the inhabited earth, dividing the seasons appropriately, setting everything in harmonious order and looking after men who are wise and good, providing for their birth and upbringing, for the fruits of their labor and for all the other necessities of life, so too does our city never fail to punish the wicked, help the just, <dispense> equality to all in place of injustice, and at its own personal <risk> and expense ensure the <common security> of Greece.

[6] As I said before, I will leave untold the collective deeds of our city and direct my words to the feats of Leosthenes and his companions. So, where should I begin, and what should I mention first? Should I trace the ancestry of each man? I suspect that would be foolish. [7] If one is praising different men who have come together from many different places to live in one city, each contributing his own lineage, one has to trace the separate ancestry of each man. But if he is speaking of Athenians who are indigenous to the land and share a common ancestry of unsurpassed nobility, it is superfluous, I think, to praise the ancestry of each man. [8] Well, should I mention their education and

how as children they were reared and educated with strict discipline,[1] as some usually do? But I think you all know that we educate our children in order to make them brave men, and it is obvious that men who showed exceptional courage in the war were well educated as children. [9] So I think, the simplest thing is to recount their courage in battle and show how many benefits they have bestowed on their country and the rest of Greece. I will begin first with the general, as I should.

[10] Leosthenes saw that all of Greece was on its knees and seemed to be cowering, corrupted by men who were bribed by Philip and Alexander to work against their own countries. He realized that our city needed a man, just as Greece needed a city, that could assume leadership, so he gave himself to his country and his city to Greece for the sake of freedom. [11] He raised a mercenary force, took command of the Athenian army, and in a battle in Boeotia defeated those who from the beginning opposed Greek freedom, the Boeotians, the Macedonians, the Euboeans, and their allies. [12] From there he reached Thermopylae[2] and occupied the pass through which the barbarians once marched to attack the Greeks. He checked Antipater's advance into Greece and, surprising him in that area, defeated him in battle, forced him to take refuge in Lamia,[3] and began a siege of the city. [13] He made allies of the Thessalians, the Phocians, the Aetolians, and all the others in the region. Philip and Alexander prided themselves in commanding men who were unwilling to serve; Leosthenes took command of the same men, who were ready and willing. He managed to accomplished the goals he set for himself, but he could not overcome fate. [14] It is right to express our gratitude to Leosthenes first and foremost for the deeds he achieved in his lifetime but also for the battle that was fought after his death and for all the

---

[1] The term here is *sōphrosunē,* which carried the idea of both discipline, essential for a good soldier, and moderation, essential for a good citizen.

[2] Thermopylae ("the Gates") was the pass from Thessaly into Locris north of Boeotia. It was here in 480 that the Spartans under the command of Leonidas bravely but futilely resisted the Persian advance led by Xerxes. See Herod. 7.201–222.

[3] Lamia lay in Thessaly, some twenty kilometers (about twelve miles) north of Thermopylae.

other benefits the Greeks derived from that campaign. For it is on the foundations laid by Leosthenes that men today build their future successes.

[15] Let no one think I am not saying anything about the other citizens and praising only Leosthenes. In fact, to praise Leosthenes for these battles is also to pay tribute to the rest of the citizens. A general may be responsible for a well-devised strategy, but victory in battle depends on those willing to risk their lives. So when I praise the victory we won, I am praising both Leosthenes' leadership and the bravery of the others at the same time. [16] For who would not have good reason to praise those citizens who died in this war, who gave their lives for the sake of Greek freedom, and who believed that the clearest proof of their desire to preserve freedom for Greece was to die fighting on its behalf?

[17] An important event that contributed to their eagerness to fight for Greece was the battle that took place earlier in Boeotia. They saw that the city of Thebes had been wretchedly destroyed into oblivion, the acropolis garrisoned by Macedonians, the inhabitants reduced to slavery, and their land parceled out to others.[4] These terrible sights that they saw with their own eyes gave them an undaunted courage to face danger readily. [18] But the battle that took place near Thermopylae and Lamia has proven no less glorious for them than when they fought in Boeotia, not only because they defeated Antipater and his allies in battle but also because the battle was located there. For all the Greeks who gather twice a year for the Amphictyonic Council[5] will see the deeds they accomplished, and as soon as they gather at that spot, they will recall their courage. [19] Never did men fight for a more noble prize against stronger enemies with fewer allies. They believed there was strength in courage and superiority in bravery, not in a large number of bodies. They secured freedom for all Greece to share in,

---

[4] Thebes was destroyed by Alexander in 335.

[5] The various ethnic groups of Greece (Ionians, Dorians, Phocians, etc.) sent representatives to the Amphictyonic Council, which was in charge of the oracle at Delphi, the Pythian games, the finances of the sanctuary, and the maintenance of the temple. Once a year it met at Anthela near Thermopylae; the other time, in Delphi, which was some thirty kilometers (about eighteen miles) south of Thermopylae.

but the glory of their deeds is a crown they won for our country alone.

[20] Now then, it is worth considering, what do we think would have happened, if these men had not fought as duty required? Would not the whole inhabited world be subject to a single master? And would not Greece be forced to regard his capricious behavior as law? In short, Macedonian arrogance and not the power of justice would prevail among all people; no woman, no girl, no child would be safe from the endless violations forced on each and every one of them. [21] That is clear from what we have been forced to endure up to now: sacrifices are made to men, and while statues, altars, and temples to the gods are neglected, those to men are carefully cultivated.[6] We ourselves are forced to honor their slaves as heroes.[7] [22] When respect for the gods has been destroyed by Macedonian arrogance, what can we expect would have happened to human respect? Would it not have been utterly destroyed? The more frightening we think the consequences would have been, the greater, we must realize, is the praise those who have died deserve.

[23] No campaign displayed the courage of its soldiers more than this last one. Daily they were forced to prepare for battle, to fight more engagements on a single campaign than the blows all other soldiers have endured in the past, to withstand with such resolve the extremes of winter and the lack of daily necessities that were so great and so severe that it is difficult to describe in words. [24] Such were the hardships that Leosthenes urged his fellow citizens to endure without flinching, and they themselves readily offered to fight alongside such a great general. Should we not consider it their good fortune that they displayed their courage rather than their bad fortune that they lost their lives? For the price of their mortal bodies they gained immortal glory, and by their personal courage they secured universal freedom

[6] Alexander had demanded divine honors for himself. See 5.31 and Din. 1.94.

[7] Hephaestion, a Macedonian noble who had been Alexander's closest friend, suddenly died in 324. Alexander staged an extravagant funeral in honor of his friend and decreed at the end that all should worship him as a god. Apparently, heroic cults were established by his command both in the East and in Athens. See Diodorus Siculus 17.115.6.

for the Greeks. [25] There cannot be complete happiness without independence. For men to be happy they must be ruled by the voice of law, not the threats of a man; free men must not be frightened by accusation, only by proof of guilt; and the safety of our citizens must not depend on men who flatter their masters and slander our citizens but on our confidence in the law. [26] To defend all of this, these men endured toil upon toil; and by facing dangers daily, they removed for all time the fears that gripped our citizens and the Greeks. They gave their lives so others could live well.

[27] Thanks to them, their fathers are honored, their mothers are admired by the citizens, their sisters have found and will find legitimate marriages worthy of them, and their children will find that their courage provides access to the goodwill of the people. Indeed, they have not really died, for it is not right to call it "death" when they have given their lives for such a noble cause but have just exchanged this life for an eternal post. [28] If death, which is so distressing to others, has been the source of great benefits for them, it is surely right to consider them fortunate, for they have not left life, but rather they have been born again, in a birth more noble than the first. [29] Then, they were just senseless children, but now, they have been born as courageous men. Then, it was only after the long passage of time and in the face of many dangers that they revealed their courage, but now, owing to this new birth, they can quickly become well known to all and renown for their bravery.

[30] Is there any time that is not right to remember their valor? Is there any place where we will not see them receive the highest honor and praise? What about when the city prospers? Will the benefits we received because of these men bring praise and renown to anyone else but them? What about in times of personal successes? Only their courage will allow us to enjoy our successes securely. [31] What generation will not regard them as most blessed? Our elders? Certainly, for they will realize that the rest of their lives will be happy and free of fear because of these men. Their peers? Certainly, since their death has instilled a noble desire to emulate men who achieved through their own courage a fame that is by far the most distinguished. [32] The younger men and the boys? Surely they will envy their death and be eager to imitate them. If they have left these men their courage as an example for their own lives, must we not acknowledge that they have

achieved immortal fame? [33] What <poets and philosophers will lack words or songs to celebrate their deeds to> the Greeks? Who will not praise this expedition even more than the one that conquered the Phrygians?[8] Where in Greece will they ever stop commemorating their exploits in word and song for future generations? [34] On two counts they should praise Leosthenes and those who died in the war. If men take pleasure in recalling such displays of courage, what could bring more pleasure to the Greeks than praising those who won them their freedom from the Macedonians? If, on the other hand, the aim of such recollections is profit, what speech could profit the hearts of its listeners more than the praise of courage and courageous men?

[35] That they should be honored by us and by all others is perfectly clear from what I have said. But it is also worth considering who will be in Hades to greet the leader of these men? Can you not imagine that we would see the so-called demigods, those who sailed to Troy, greeting Leosthenes and looking on him with wonder? Though he performed the same kind of deeds as they, he far surpassed them; for with the help of all Greece they took one city, while he with only his country to help[9] humbled completely the power that controlled Europe and Asia. [36] They fought for one violated woman, but he, with the help of these men now buried by his side, prevented the violation that threatened all Greek women. [37] There were also those born after the famous heroes of Troy whose exploits matched their courage: I mean Miltiades and Themistocles[10] and their companions, and others who liberated Greece, and brought honor to their country and glory to their lives. [38] Leosthenes so surpassed these in courage and foresight that he actually prevented the invasion of a barbarian force, whereas they only defended against it. They saw the enemy fighting in their country, whereas he defeated the enemy in its own territory.

---

[8] That is, the expedition to Troy celebrated by Homer.

[9] Hyperides fails to mention the foreign mercenaries Leosthenes had in his army (see 6.11).

[10] Miltiades was the Athenian general credited with defeating the Persian army at Marathon in 490. In 480 Themistocles, by threatening to withdraw the Athenian fleet, convinced the other Greek commanders to stand and face the Persian navy in the narrows of Salamis; the Greek victory that followed led to Xerxes' withdrawal from Greece. See Herod. 6.108–117, 8.70–97.

[39] I think even these men who demonstrated to the people most clearly their friendship for one another, I mean Harmodius and Aristogeiton,[11] would agree that none are so nearly at the same level as Leosthenes and his companions in arms; nor is there anyone with whom they would rather associate in Hades than with these men. Quite rightly. For the exploits of these men were not inferior to theirs, but if we need say it, even greater. They deposed the tyrants in their own country, whereas these men deposed the tyrants of all Greece.

[40] How noble and incredible was the courage shown by these men here; how glorious and magnificent the choice they made; how surpassing the valor and bravery in the face of dangers that they displayed for the collective freedom of the Greeks . . . [12]

[41] Perhaps it is difficult to console those who are overwhelmed by such grief as this. Sorrows are not soothed by words and law, but each one's nature and feelings of affection for the deceased set the limit to his grief. Nonetheless we must take heart, restrict our grief to what is acceptable, and remember not only the death of those who are gone but also the example of courage they have left us. [42] Though their suffering deserves mourning, their exploits deserve great praise. Though they will not reach old age in their mortal lives, still they have won a fame that is ageless and are counted blessed in every way. For those who have died childless, the praises of the Greeks will be their immortal children. For those who left behind children, the goodwill of their country will become their children's guardian. [43] Moreover, if death is like not existing, they are free from sickness and grief and everything else that besets human life. But if we are conscious in Hades and come under the care of some deity, as we believe, it is probable that those who defended the honors of the gods that were threatened with destruction will receive the fullest care and attention from the deity[13] . . .

---

[11] See 2.3n.

[12] The papyrus ends here. The epilogue (41–43) given below is preserved only by the late author Stobaeus.

[13] There is a clear echo of Plato's *Apology* 40c–41d here.

FRAGMENTS[1]

5–6. AGAINST ARISTAGORA FOR FAILING TO OBTAIN A SPONSOR (TWO SPEECHES)

Aristagora is likely the same woman who, according to tradition, was a mistress of Hyperides (Pseudo-Plut., *Moralia* 849d). If this is true, it is strange to find him prosecuting her in court, though it is possible that Hyperides did not deliver the speech himself but composed it for a client. Aristagora, who was a *hetaira* (see the Introduction to Hyp. 3), was charged with not obtaining a sponsor or patron (*prostatēs*). Every metic (resident alien) was legally required to have an Athenian sponsor and register in his deme. Failure to do so could leave the metic open to an indictment (*graphē aprostasiou*) and enslavement upon conviction. The date and circumstances of the trial are not known, but what is known is that Aristagora had been tried once before on a similar charge (Athenaeus 13.587c), and we can infer from Fragment 20 that she was acquitted at the first trial.

13. So that Laïs whose beauty is said to have surpassed that of any woman who ever lived, and Ocimon and Metaneira. . . .[2]

---

[1] The fragments from various lost speeches of Hyperides were preserved by later writers, many of whom were either lexicographers (*Suda*, Harpocration) or concerned with rhetoric, or scholiastic commentary. The majority consist of one or two words or a short phrase. The longer fragments and some of the shorter ones are translated here.

[2] All three women were famous *hetairai*. Metaneira may be the same woman who was involved with the orator Lysias; see Dem. 59.21–22.

16. To use a *diamartyria.*[3]

20. It is appropriate to cite at the present trial the law regarding bribery by foreigners. Since it states that anyone can bring a fresh indictment against those acquitted on charges of usurping citizenship, if they think they were unjustly acquitted the first time, can there be any doubt about the justice of the case against Aristagora?

21. So you must instruct those who give such testimony and produce witnesses not to waste time deceiving you, if they do not have anything more just to say. Make them produce the law that instructs metics not to have a sponsor.[4]

24. And again in the same way you summoned the so-called Anchovy sisters.[5]

7. AGAINST ARISTOGEITON

After the battle of Chaeronea (338), when Athens faced the possible threat of invasion by Philip, Hyperides proposed a decree to meet the emergency. Measures included evacuating all women and children to Piraeus, arming the Council of 500, restoring all exiles and disenfranchised citizens, granting citizenship to all metics, and freeing and arming slaves for Athens' defense (see Lyc. 1.36–37, 41, Pseudo-Plut., *Moralia* 849a). Although the Assembly approved the decree, it was never put into effect, since Philip, largely through the efforts of Demades (see below Frs. 76–80), proved conciliatory towards Athens. Sometime later, Hyperides was indicted by Aristogeiton for proposing an illegal decree (*graphē paranomōn*) but was acquitted.

27. Why do you keep asking me in these words about my duty? "Did you propose in the decree to grant freedom to slaves?" I did, to prevent free men from experiencing servitude. "Did you propose to restore exiles?" I did, to prevent anyone else from suffering exile.

---

[3] A *diamartyria* was a formal statement of fact made by a witness at the preliminary hearing, with the object of preventing the case from going forward. If the testimony of the witness was not challenged, the case was thrown out.

[4] It is possible that Hyperides is addressing the *diamartyria* that was entered by the defense (Fr. 16).

[5] A famous pair of *hetairai* who were so nicknamed because they were thin and had pale skin and big eyes.

"Now then, did you not read the laws that prohibited this?" I couldn't, because Macedonian arms stood in the way and obstructed their words.[6]

28. I did not propose the decree; the battle of Chaeronea did.

29. That first more than one hundred and fifty thousand slaves from the mining works and the rest of the countryside, then state debtors, the disenfranchised, those voted out of citizenship and the metics. . . .

30. You cannot even learn from the proverb: let sleeping dogs lie.[7]

31. They said that they heard in Oenoë that a battle had taken place.

39. The city was apprehensive at this news.

39a. Another time is appropriate for debate and advice; but when an armed enemy is present, he must be resisted not with words but with arms.

8. AGAINST ARISTOPHON FOR AN ILLEGAL PROPOSAL

In 363/2 Aristophon of Hazenia, a prominent political figure of long standing, was sent as general to the island of Ceos, and in the wake of his success there, he proposed a decree to settle the affairs of the island. In 362, at the relatively young age of 28, Hyperides prosecuted Aristophon for proposing an illegal decree, charging that his settlement was harsh and motivated out of pure greed. Hyperides seems to have conducted a vigorous attack against the wily old politician,[8] for Aristophon was acquitted by only two votes (see 4.28), a remarkable accomplishment for what may have been Hyperides' political debut. The fragments suggest a speech full of abuse and invective, a strategy that nearly paid off.

40. Ardettos.[9]

---

[6] This fragment and Fr. 39a are preserved only as Latin translations of Hyperides.

[7] Lit. "don't stir up an evil that's happily resting."

[8] It was Aristophon's boast that he had been acquitted seventy-five times on charges of making an illegal proposal.

[9] The hill where jurors (dikasts) annually swore the dikastic oath. Our source (Scholiast Aes. 1.64) states that Hyperides had nicknamed Aristophon Ardettos

41. For he knows that he's been given license to do and propose virtually anything he likes.

44. When you try to deceive the opinion of others, you deceive only yourself. In fact, you are not convincing when you call yourself wise instead of crafty, brave instead of reckless, careful of your patrimony instead of miserly, stern instead of spiteful. There is no vice that you can boast of simply by praising it as a virtue.[10]

9. IN DEFENSE OF HARPALUS

Presumably this speech was composed for Harpalus' defense, but its authenticity was doubted in antiquity. For the Harpalus affair, see Hyperides 5 and the Introduction to Dinarchus in this volume.

45. Leaping out of the partridge coops.

10. AGAINST ARCHESTRATIDES

In the speech for Lycophron (1a.1), we learn that Archestratides was entangled in litigation with Theomnestus, but whether this is the same man as here is not known. Nothing is known about the date or circumstances of the present trial, except that it seems to have involved sacrilege.

49. The sacred victims.

50. Those who dance the Ithyphalloi[11] in the orchestra.

11. AGAINST AUTOCLES FOR TREASON

Shortly after the acquittal of Aristophon (Frs. 40–44), Hyperides indicted the general Autocles for treason over his failed activities in Thrace (Dem. 23.104). The attack was, in fact, directed at Aristophon,

---

because he had so often perjured himself on the spot, that is to say, Aristophon had broken the terms of that oath in various trials where he had served as juror.

[10] This is another Latin translation.

[11] They were participants in the phallic procession in honor of Dionysus. The procession ended in the orchestra of the theater, where the Ithyphalloi turned to the audience and exhorted them to make way for the god. They were elaborately dressed, wearing masks and brightly colored tunics. See Athenaeus 14.662b.

who in 362/1 persuaded the Athenians to pass a decree dispatching an expedition to the Hellespont under Autocles' command. Since the one-year time limit for indicting the proposer of the decree had passed, Hyperides went after his associate; he had Autocles removed from office (Dem. 50.12) and at the trial was supported by Apollodorus (Dem. 36.53), who had served as trierarch on the campaign. The outcome of the trial is not known. See Trevett 1992: 129–133.

55. Our ancestors punished even Socrates for his words.

57. Deeds of action are the concern of young men.[12]

13. THE DELIAN SPEECH

In 343 Aeschines was brought to trial by Demosthenes for his conduct on the embassy to Philip that led to the Peace of Philocrates. He was acquitted, but shortly after the trial, Hyperides was chosen in his place to represent Athens in a dispute with Delos over control of the temple of Apollo on Delos, which was under Athenian administration. In 346 Philip had been admitted to the Amphictyonic Council, a religious synod that oversaw the affairs of Delphi, and the Delians submitted their grievance before the Council expecting the support of Philip. The Areopagus appointed Hyperides to plead the Athenian case (see Dem. 18.134). He apparently won the case, and Athens remained in control of the temple.

67. We are told that Leto, when she was pregnant with Zeus' children, was driven by Hera across the entire earth and sea. Finally, wearied and distressed, she came to our land and loosened her girdle on the spot now called Zoster.[13] Then she crossed over to Delos, where she gave birth to twins, the gods Artemis and Apollo.

68. Here they sacrifice daily to Apollo and serve him a portion of it as a meal.

69. And in common the Greeks mix the Panionian bowl.[14]

---

[12] This is the first part of a proverb quoted by Hyperides from Hesiod; it continues: "advice of the middle aged, prayers of old men."

[13] A cape on the west coast of Attica where Leto had rested before continuing her flight to Delos.

[14] This is a reference to the festival celebrated in honor of Apollo on Delos by all (*pan*) Ionians.

70. [1] Some rich Aeolians arrived in Delos with a large quantity of gold. They were traveling from their country to see Greece. These men were found dead, cast up on the shores of Rheneia.[15] Once news of incident spread, the Delians accused the Rheneians of the crime and indicted their city for impiety. The Rheneans were angered at this action and indicted the Delians on the same charge. [2] When the hearing (*diadikasia*)[16] was held to determine which of the two had done the deed, the Rheneans asked the Delians what reason the men would have had for coming to Rhenea, where there were no harbors, no market, and no other attraction. Everyone goes to Delos, they argued, even they themselves spend a good deal of time on Delos. [3] When the Delians replied that the men crossed over to Rhenea to buy sacrificial victims, the Rheneans asked, "If they came to buy victims, as you claim, why then did they not bring their slaves who attend on them to bring back the victims, but they left them with you on Delos and crossed over alone? Besides, though it is thirty stades[17] from the landing point to the city of Rhenea and the road over which they had to travel to make the purchase is rough, they crossed over without sandals on, even though in the temple on Delos they walked around with sandals on?"

71. At present we pay no one tribute, but once we had the right to receive it.

14. AGAINST DEMADES FOR ILLEGAL PROPOSALS

Demades' crucial role in negotiating peace with Philip after the battle of Chaeronea (338) (see Dem. 18.285) enhanced his reputation, which he exploited to political ends when he proposed making the Olynthian Euthycrates an Athenian *proxenos,*[18] even though he had betrayed the city to Philip in 348. For Hyperides, this amounted to blatant Philipizing, and in 337 he indicted Demades for proposing an illegal decree. Although Demades' support of Euthycrates clearly revealed his pro-Macedonian sympathies, he may have been motivated

[15] A small island close to Delos.

[16] A trial where there is no actual plaintiff or defendant, but two or more litigants with equal claims.

[17] That is just over five kilometers (three miles).

[18] See above, 5.25n.

by other reasons. Hyperides claims elsewhere (5.25) that Demades made considerable money from proposing such decrees and grants of *proxenia,* and Demades did have a reputation for venality. Whatever the reason, Hyperides' attack was vicious, and his speech, we are told, was full of abuse.

76. The points Demades has advanced do not contain the real reasons for the grant of *proxenia.* If Euthycrates must become your *proxenos,* let me submit in writing the reasons why he will receive this honor. "It has been resolved that he be *proxenos* because he speaks and acts in the interest of Philip, because when he was cavalry commander he betrayed the Olynthian cavalry to Philip, because by this action he caused the destruction of the Chalcidians, because after the capture of Olynthus he assessed the value of the prisoners, because he opposed the city over the matter of the Delian temple, because, after the city's defeat at Chaeronea, he did not bury any of the dead or ransom any of the captives."

76b. If Demades wished to tell the truth about Euthycrates, he should have proposed a decree like this that gave the reason why he made Euthycrates *proxenos.* I will write up a decree in Demades' name, listing what he has done and read it out. Demades, son of Demeas, of the deme Paeania proposed: "Since Euthycrates betrayed his country Olynthus and was responsible for the destruction of forty Chalcidian cities . . ."

77. We made Alcimachus and Antipater Athenians and *proxenoi.*

78. They have won neither a city nor citizenship.

79. In his case the garbage dumps would be a much more suitable place for the inscribed stone than our temples.

80. Politicians are like snakes in that all snakes are detestable; but whereas some snakes like adders are harmful to men, others like brown snakes eat the adders.

21. AGAINST DOROTHEUS

This speech is attributed to Hyperides or Philinus. The date and circumstances of the trial are not known, but according to one source, Dorotheus was indicted for *hybris,* an extreme form of violence that aimed at humiliating the victim. The term *hybris* could cover a wide range of behaviors that did not always involve physical assault. But the language of the law clearly indicates that acts of violence, especially sexual offenses, were the primary concern of the law. Such violence could be prosecuted through a public suit (*graphē hybreōs*), but the victim may have needed to prove the intent of the aggressor, which was often difficult to do, and consequently would opt to sue for simple battery (*dikē aikeias*). See below, Fragments 120–121.

97. I am told Autocles[19] the politician got into an argument with Hipponicus, son of Callias, over a piece of land, and when they started insulting each other, he slapped Hipponicus in the face. . . . Hipponicus, then, was only slapped in the mouth by Autocles, but these men dragged me by the hair and hit me with their fists.

98. To punch . . . to be punched . . . to spit in the face.

99. Like the cheapest slave.

24. AGAINST THE THASIANS

This speech may have been delivered at the arbitration of a dispute between Thasos and Maronea over possession of Stryme, a colony of Thasos (Dem. 12.17, 50.20–22). Both Maronea and Stryme stood on the coast of Thrace to the east of the island of Thasos. The Athenians were involved in naval operations in the region (362/1) and got entangled in the dispute, when they were convoying grain ships for both Maronea and Thasos; at one point the Athenians almost faced a naval engagement with Maronite ships off Stryme. In the end, they prevailed upon the two cities to submit their dispute to arbitration, and Hyperides was present, representing Athenian interests. The actual date of the arbitration is unknown, and some have connected it with Hyperides' diplomatic activities against Philip in 341.

107. And immediately to enjoy the produce of a fertile and expansive country.

30. THE CYTHNIAN SPEECH

After Chaeronea (338), when Athens feared an attack from Philip, Hyperides was sent out to secure support from various smaller cities in the Peloponnese and the Cyclades (see Lyc. 1.42). This speech may

[19] Perhaps the same man of Frs. 55–57.

belong to that occasion and was delivered on Cythnos, a small island south of Attica.

117. Rash men do everything without reflection; but courageous men confront the dangers that assail them with calm reflection.

31. IN DEFENSE OF THE CHILDREN OF LYCURGUS

After his death (324), Lycurgus was accused by Menesaechmus of leaving a deficit in the treasury. Lycurgus' children now became liable for their father's debt, consequently were indicted by Thrasycles presumably by an *apographē,* and imprisoned by the Eleven. Hyperides spoke in their defense; through his efforts and the intervention of Demosthenes, who wrote a letter on their behalf from exile (Dem., *Epistle* 3), Lycurgus' children were released.

118. What will those who pass his grave say? "This man lived a sober life; when he was appointed to administer the finances, he found resources to build the theater, the Odeion, and the dockyards and to construct triremes and harbors. Our city dishonored the man and imprisoned his children.

33. AGAINST MANTITHEUS FOR ASSAULT

The date and circumstances of the trial are not known, but our sources indicate that Mantitheus was sued for battery (*dikē aikeias*), even though Hyperides cites the law of *hybris* as evidence that even slaves were protected from such violence (Fr. 120).

120. They established the law to protect not only free men but also slaves, for if anyone violates the person of the slave, an indictment can be brought against those guilty of violence (*hybris*).[20]

121. Bringing Glycera daughter of Thalassis[21] in a carriage.

42. AGAINST PASICLES

The trial arose out of an *antidosis* over the performance of a trierarchy. The trierarchy, which involved the upkeep of a warship (tri-

---

[20] For *hybris,* see above, *Against Dorotheus* (Frs. 97–99).

[21] Glycera was a famous *hetaira.* Thalassis also sounds like the name of a *hetaira.*

reme) for a year, was one of many state services (liturgies) imposed on the rich by Athens. The citizen selected to perform the service could protest to the magistrate assigning the duty (in this case, the ten generals) that another citizen was financially better able to carry the burden; he would challenge that person either to undertake the service or to exchange properties (*antidosis*). If that person refused, a trial would follow to decide which of the two should undertake the liturgy.

The circumstances of this trial are unknown, but it must have occurred after 340. Before that time, 1,200 of the richest citizens liable for the trierarchy would undertake the service in small groups of five or six men and sometimes as many as sixteen (Dem. 18.104), and each member of the group regardless of his wealth shared the cost equally. The system proved a financial hardship for poorer members who shouldered a disproportionately higher burden than the very rich. Under a law proposed by Demosthenes in 340, the cost of furnishing the ships would be based on a person's wealth. Consequently, a very rich person might have to pay for two ships. See Hansen 1991: 112–115.

134. While the very rich were trierarchs sharing the duty with five or six others and defrauding the city by spending moderate sums of money, these men kept quiet. But when Demosthenes saw this and brought in a law that the Three Hundred[22] serve as trierarchs, the trierarchy has become a burden, and now Phormio[23] sneaks away.

43. AGAINST PASICLES ON AN ANTIDOSIS

This title, which is known to the rhetorician Pollux, may refer to the same speech as 42.

137. The big house called Chabrias' and the alley next to it.

44. AGAINST PATROCLES FOR PROCURING

The authenticity of this speech was questioned in antiquity. It was written for the prosecution of Patrocles, who was indicted (*graphē*) on

---

[22] These were the very rich who were subject to the *eisphora* or property tax, which was levied occasionally in times of need. The same group sustained the heaviest burden of the trierarchy.

[23] Presumably the freedman of the very rich banker Pasion, who took over operation of the bank when Pasion died. See Dem. 36.

a charge of procuring (*proagōgeia*) sexual services, most likely, of a freeborn boy. The penalty was death (Aes. 1.14, 184). Male or female prostitution was not illegal in Athens, and, in the case of the latter, sex with a freeborn woman who worked the streets or in a brothel was not considered seduction (*moicheia*). See Dem. 59.67 and MacDowell 1978: 125.

139. The nine archons were feasting in the stoa, having partitioned off a part of it with a curtain.[24]

139a. Let him buy a male who has never been a slave or a barbarian.

141. Nannion[25]

142. Nemeas[26]

143. Common (*pandēmos*) Aphrodite[27]

144. A stuffed couch to prevent the girl from becoming disheartened.

60. IN DEFENSE OF PHRYNE

Phryne was the most famous *hetaira* of her time. The story is that she was indicted for impiety (*asebeia*) on the charges of reveling shamelessly in the Lyceum, introducing a new divinity, and forming illicit *thiasoi* (cult gatherings) of men and women. The precise date of her trial is unknown, but it may be connected with events following Chaeronea, when Aristogeiton indicted Hyperides for proposing an

---

[24] Boards of magistrates regularly took communal meals together. The nine archons met in the Thesmotheteum (*Ath. Pol.* 3.5), which has been identified with the South Stoa in the Agora. See H. A. Thompson and R. E. Wycherley, *The Athenian Agora: The Agora of Athens: The History, Shape, and Uses of an Ancient City Center* (Princeton: 1972), 77–78.

[25] The name of a famous *hetaira,* who was satirized in comedy. See Athenaeus 13.587a.

[26] The name of a flute girl.

[27] That is, the physical and baser form of love between men and women or with prostitutes and not the spiritual and more intelligent form of love of the Heavenly Aphrodite, associated with a male homosexual relationship (Plato, *Symposium* 180d). Allegedly, Solon was the first to erect a temple to Aphrodite Pandemos from the income of brothels he had established in Athens (Athenaeus 13.569d).

illegal decree (see Frs. 27–39a). The prosecution of Phryne was likely politically motivated. According to one tradition, Hyperides was one of her lovers, and Aristogeiton is known to have delivered a speech against Phryne (Athenaeus 13.591e). He may have been one of the accusers at this trial, in which Phryne was defended by Hyperides; but the prosecution was led by Euthias, who had hired Anaximenes of Lampsacus, the fourth-century rhetorician, to write his speech. The defense delivered by Hyperides was regarded in antiquity as an exceptional piece of oratory and was greatly admired by rhetoricians and literary critics alike. But, according to ancient critics, Phryne would have been condemned, despite Hyperides' brilliance, had he not in a dramatic stroke brought her before the court and bared her breasts before the jurors. Her beauty, we are told, saved her.[28]

171. I have been intimate (with her).

172. It's not the same thing for one man to try to save her by every possible means and for the other to do everything to destroy her.

173. Why is she to blame if a stone hangs over Tantalus' head?[29]

179. Ask him (Euthias) for anything,[30] and you will find yourself setting fire to the dockyards or destroying the laws.[31]

61–62. IN DEFENSE OF CHAEREPHILUS ON THE SALT FISH (TWO SPEECHES)

In the late 330s Chaerephilus, a wealthy importer of salt fish, along with his three sons, had been granted Athenian citizenship on the motion of Demosthenes (Din. 1.43). The grant was notorious enough to be satirized in comedy (Athenaeus 3.119f), but whether the present

---

[28] On the biographical fiction of this episode, see C. Cooper, "Hyperides and the Trial of Phryne," *Phoenix* 49 (1995): 303–318.

[29] The stone hanging over his head was part of the punishment Zeus devised for Tantalus in the Underworld. It is mentioned by many early poets but not by Homer (*Od.* 11.582–592), who describes Tantalus' other famous punishments of having food and drink just out of reach.

[30] That is, for her money. In later sources (Alciphron), Euthias is made out to be the jilted lover, who has bitterly retaliated by making serious but unfounded accusations against Phryne in court.

[31] For this last fragment, which is not found in Marzi, I use the Oxford Classical Text.

case has any connection with it, as some scholars have thought, is unknown. We do know, however, that Chaerephilus was accused of breaking the laws connected with his business, and apparently he was not the only one charged. His trial began as an impeachment process, either as an *eisangelia* or an *apophasis* from the Areopagus to the Assembly; either procedure would have resulted in a preliminary vote of condemnation by the Assembly (*katacheirotonia*). He was defended by Hyperides in two speeches. See E. Carawan, "Apophasis and Eisangelia: The Role of the Areopagus in Athenian Political Trials," *Greek, Roman, and Byzantine Studies* 26 (1985): 115–140, especially 137–138, and Hansen 1975: 44–45.

181. Letting go of the cables, he chases the sail.[32]

182. And when the Pnyx[33] found out as much.

184. After this they later came to load on board the salt fish.

186. Wharf . . . Market (*deigma*)[34]

187. Condemnation by the vote (*katacheirotonia*).

187a.[35] As to what the Council (of the Areopagus) reported to the people from its investigation, nowhere did it demonstrate to the people wrongdoing on the part of Chaerephilus, and though, it says, the secretary read out the names disclosed from the interrogations of slaves (*basanoi*), not one of those tortured accused him of any wrongdoing. As a result, at least from the charges written in the decree,[36] he is not even liable for trial. Why, then, has this case arisen?

63. AGAINST CHARES FOR GUARDIANSHIP

Chares is being sued by his wife's son over his mismanagement of her estate (*dikē epitropēs*). Under Athenian law, when a man died leaving only a daughter to inherit, she became an heiress (*epiklēros*) and was claimed in marriage by her father's closest male relative, who

---

[32] A proverb spoken of those who neglected important matters to waste time on trivial things.

[33] The escarpment where the Assembly met.

[34] Two locations in the harbor of Piraeus.

[35] This fragment is not found in Marzi but comes from Oxyrhynchus Papyri 34 (1968) 2686.

[36] Presumably the decree that authorized the Areopagus to conduct its investigation.

would manage the estate until her sons came of age. They then would take control of the estate as the rightful heirs.

192. When I was registered[37] and given control of what was left to my mother, according to the law that stipulates that the sons are to be in charge (*kyrioi*)[38] of the heiress (*epiklēros*) and all the property, two years after they come of age.

FRAGMENTS FROM UNIDENTIFIED SPEECHES

195. What is obscure, teachers must examine in light of evidence and probabilities.

196. There is no sign of a person's intelligence on his face.

197. The name, Freer (Eleutherius), has been given to Zeus, gentlemen of the jury, because the freedmen (*exeleutheroi*) built the stoa near him.[39]

200. He hung him from the pillar and thrashed him to the point that even now his skin is still covered in welts.[40]

202. Since I had fallen ill and this indictment was postponed under sworn oath,[41] the trial was delayed.

204. At the very onset of crimes one should block their paths. Once evil has taken root and grown old, like a congenital illness, it is difficult to heal.[42]

205. If a woman ventures outside her house, she should have reached an age that those who meet her will ask not whose wife she is but whose mother.[43]

206. A woman should do herself up however she wants for her husband, but if she does so when she goes out, one needs to fear

---

[37] In his father's deme.

[38] The *kyrios* was head of the household and had control over all property and all members within that household.

[39] This fragment has been assigned by scholars to *Against Aristagora for Failing to Obtain a Sponsor* (Frs. 13–24).

[40] This fragment could belong to either *Against Dorotheus* (Frs. 97–99) or *Against Mantitheus for Assault* (Frs. 120–121).

[41] On the oath of postponement, see Hyp. 4.7n.

[42] For a similar thought, see Din. 2.3.

[43] This fragment has been assigned to *Against Aristagora for Failing to Obtain a Sponsor* (Frs. 13–24).

that it is no longer for her husband that she's doing it but for other men.

208. The good man should reveal how he thinks by his words and how he acts by his deeds.

210. There are two motives that keep men away from crimes, fear and shame.

213.[44] We are willing to let the jurors assume that no one was more closely related to the deceased than you. We agree that you had done him some kindnesses. No one denies that you had served some time together in the military. But why do you contest the will in which my client's name is mentioned?

214. Living in a democratic state where justice prevails through the laws is not at all like coming under the power of one tyrant, where an individual's caprice is supreme. We must either put our trust in the laws and remember freedom or surrender to the power of one man and daily ponder our servitude.

215. What if we conducted this case with nature as our judge, which distinguished man and woman by assigning to each their own tasks and duties, and what if I showed that this man misused his own body like a woman? Would not nature be extremely surprised, if someone failed to consider it the most gratifying gift to be born a man but perverted nature's generosity by hurrying to change into a woman?[45]

216. The miser and the profligate have one and same fault. Both don't know how to use money, and for both it is a source of disgrace. For that reason, both are rewarded with a similar punishment, because they equally don't deserve to have it.

217. Are you forcing me to reveal the reason you committed wrong? It's of no use. I will not say. But time itself will reveal it.

218. But now, gentlemen of the jury, I say nothing of the complete justice and legality, as I have shown, of my case. I allow you to decide what you think is most fair. For I have no fear that even if you have to do something new, you will gladly concede what I ask because of my service to public morality.

---

[44] Fragments 213–218 are Latin translations of Hyperides.

[45] This fragment comes from a speech delivered at the trial of a citizen indicted for male prostitution (*graphē hetaireseos*). It was illegal for any citizen to exercise his civic rights, such as speaking in the Assembly, once he had prostituted himself. See Aes. 1.21–32. Such behavior reduced the man to the level of a woman.

LYCURGUS

Translated with introduction by Edward M. Harris

INTRODUCTION TO LYCURGUS

Lycurgus, the son of Lycophron, was one of the most influential Athenian politicians in the period between the Athenian defeat at Chaeronea in 338 and the death of Alexander the Great in 323.[1] Despite his importance, relatively little is known about his life. He was born sometime in the 390s into the distinguished genos of the Eteobutadai,[2] and his family held the priesthood of Poseidon and traced its origins back to Erechtheus, one of the legendary kings of Athens.[3] His ancestors may have included the Lycurgus who controlled the plain of Attica in the mid-sixth century and opposed Peisistratus[4] and the general Lycurgus who led a disastrous expedition against the Thracian city of Eion in 476.[5] His grandfather Lycurgus was active enough in politics in the late fifth century to draw the attention of Aristophanes (*Birds* 1296) and to win the honor of burial in the Ceramicus.[6] His

---

[1] The main ancient source for the life of Lycurgus is the biography found in Pseudo-Plut., *Lives of the Ten Orators* (*Moralia*) 841a–844a, with the decree at 851e–852e. Our knowledge of Athens in the time of Lycurgus has benefited from the discovery of several inscriptions, many of which are collected in the valuable work of C. Schwenk, *Athens in the Age of Alexander the Great: The Dated Laws and Decrees of the Lykourgan Era 338–322 B.C.* (Chicago, 1985) (cited below as Schwenk).

[2] Pseudo-Plut., *Moralia* 841b. The Eteobutadai held the priesthood of Athena Polias (Aes. 2.147).

[3] Pseudo-Plut., *Moralia* 843e.

[4] Herod. 1.59.3, Plut., *Solon* 29, *Ath. Pol.* 13.4.

[5] Scholion on Aes. 2.31.

[6] Pseudo-Plut., *Moralia* 843e, 852a. His relative Lycomedes was also granted this honor.

prominence under the democracy may have been responsible for his execution by the Thirty.[7]

Nothing is known about Lycurgus' political career until he convicted the general Lysicles for losing the battle of Chaeronea (Diodorus Siculus 16.18).[8] His hostility to Macedon drew the suspicion of Alexander the Great. After destroying the city of Thebes in 335, Alexander demanded that the Athenians surrender Lycurgus, Demosthenes, and several other opponents of Macedon. Phocion argued that these men should sacrifice themselves for their country, but Demades persuaded Alexander to allow the Athenians to punish them in their own courts if they had done anything wrong.[9] Alexander's attempt to punish Lycurgus only enhanced his reputation in Athens; in the following years, Lycurgus became the most powerful politician in Athens.

Lycurgus exerted his influence through his control of Athenian finances during a period of twelve years, probably from 336 to 324.[10] According to our sources, he increased public revenues to 1,200 talents a year and brought in either 14,000 talents or about 18,000 talents during his administration.[11] The increase may have been in part due to Lycurgus' measures to promote trade. In one of his decrees, he persuaded the Assembly to grant privileges to merchants from the city of Citium on Cyprus and in another to send the Athenian fleet to suppress piracy and protect trade routes in the Adriatic.[12] He was also active in the courts; his successful prosecution of Diphilus brought the treasury 160 talents.[13]

---

[7] Pseudo-Plut., *Moralia* 841b.

[8] Lycurgus may have accompanied Demosthenes on an embassy to the Peloponnese in 343, but this is not certain. See Dem. 9.72 with Pseudo-Plut., *Moralia* 841e.

[9] Arrian, *Anabasis* 1.10; Plut., *Dem.* 23.4, *Phocion* 17.2.

[10] Pseudo-Plut., *Moralia* 841b; 852b; Diodorus Siculus 16.88.1, with the discussion of Faraguna 1992: 197–205.

[11] For the total of 1,200 talents a year: Pseudo-Plut., *Moralia* 842f. Total revenues of 14,000 or 18,650: Pseudo-Plut., *Moralia* 841b. For the figure of 18,900 talents, see Pseudo-Plut., *Moralia* 852b.

[12] Privileges to merchants of Citium: *IG* II² 337. Mission against pirates: *IG* II² 1623, lines 276–285. Lycurgus later proposed a decree of honors for the general Diotimus, who led this mission (Pseudo-Plut., *Moralia* 844a with Schwenk no. 25).

[13] Pseudo-Plut., *Moralia* 843d.

Lycurgus' adept financial administration enabled the Athenians to embark on their most ambitious building program since Pericles. Under his direction, work was completed on the Panathenaic stadium, the theater of Dionysus was rebuilt and extended, and a gymnasium was added to Lyceum and a palaestra.[14] Lycurgus also kept the Athenian armed forces strong: he maintained four hundred triremes ready for battle[15] and may have played a role in the reorganization of the Ephebeia, the two-year program of military training for Athenian youth, that took place in this period.[16]

One of Lycurgus' main interests was religion.[17] In a decree passed in his honor after his death, the politician Stratocles credited him with preparing adornment for the goddess Athena, solid gold Victory statues, and gold ornaments for a hundred basket carriers in the Panatheniac procession.[18] In 334 he passed a major law about religious cults.[19] The law survives only in fragments but appears to contains provisions for the cults of numerous deities, including Zeus the Savior, Athena, Amphiareus, Asclepius, Artemis of Brauron, Demeter, and Kore. In 329/28 he was elected one of the administrators of the new games for the hero Amphiareus and received a vote of honors and a gold crown for his work in that office.[20] A decree of 329/8 shows him taking an active role in new construction in the sanctuary of the Eleusinian Mysteries.[21] Lycurgus was also responsible for measures about the Festival of Jars and the dramatic festival of the Dionysia.[22] During his administration there was also a reform of the Lesser Panathenaea.[23]

Lycurgus left between thirteen and fifteen speeches, but only his

---

[14] Pseudo-Plut., *Moralia* 841d, 852c.

[15] Pseudo-Plut., *Moralia* 852c with *IG* II^2 1627, lines 266–269.

[16] On the reform of the Ephebeia, see Faraguna 1992: 274–280.

[17] There is a valuable summary of Lycurgus' religious administration in R. Parker, *Athenian Religion: A History* (Oxford, 1996), 242–255.

[18] Pseudo-Plut., *Moralia* 852b

[19] Schwenk no. 21.

[20] *IG* VII, 4254 (= Schwenk no. 50), lines 23–24.

[21] *IG* II^2 1672, lines 302–303.

[22] Pseudo-Plut., *Moralia* 841f.

[23] *IG* II^2 334 with Schwenk no. 17.

speech *Against Leocrates* has survived intact.[24] Many of his speeches reflect his religious interests,[25] while others concern his administration or prosecutions of politicians and generals. Lycurgus' oratory possesses a certain solemn dignity, but as an artist he does not rank with Demosthenes and Lysias. At its best, his style conveys deep sincerity and a strong religious conviction; at his worst, Lycurgus is repetitive and bombastic. Aside from a few attempts at sarcasm, there is little variation in tone. The literary critic Dionysius (*Letter to Ammaeus* 1.2) found him lacking in wit and charm but judged his style forceful; the notable features of his style are his tendency to emphasize the importance of his subject (*auxētikos*), his elevated tone (*diermenos*), and his dignified manner (*semnos*). Hermogenes (*On the Types of Oratory* 416 Spengel) was less favorable: he considered Lycurgus' style harsh, vehement, and careless. One critic said he wrote his speeches with a pen dipped not in ink but in death.[26] Lycurgus is also notable for his use of exempla from myth and history, though he is more interested in moral edification than in historical accuracy.

The best modern account of Lycurgus and his administration is Faraguna 1992. Useful summaries of the Lycurgan period in Athens in English can be found in Bosworth 1988: 204–215 and C. Habicht, *Athens from Alexander to Antony* (Cambridge, MA, 1997), 6–35.

The following translation is based on the Greek text of E. Malcovati, *Licurgo. Orazione contro Leocrate e frammenti* (Rome 1966).

---

[24] The fragments of his speeches can be found in N. C. Conomis, *Lycurgi Oratio in Leocratem cum Ceterarum Lycurgi Orationum Fragmentis* (Leipzig 1970).

[25] Pseudo-Plut., *Moralia* 843d; "On the Priestess" (VI, 1–22 Conomis), "On the Priesthood" (VII, 1–6 Conomis), "On the Oracles" (XIII, 1 Conomis).

[26] Pseudo-Plut., *Moralia* 841e.

1. AGAINST LEOCRATES

INTRODUCTION

The facts of the case appear to be simple and straightforward. After their defeat at Chaeronea in late 338, the Athenians were terrified that Philip would soon invade Attica and passed several emergency measures (16; cf. 36, 39–42). During the crisis, Leocrates sailed to Rhodes (16–19; cf. 14–15), then later to Megara, where he lived as a metic (resident alien) for about six years (21). While in Megara, he sold his property in Attica and used the money to invest in the grain trade (21–27). Lycurgus presents documents and witnesses to support his account, and the basic facts appear to have been beyond dispute. In 331 Leocrates returned to Athens, where Lycurgus immediately charged him with treason (*prodosia*).[1]

Lycurgus uses the procedure of *eisangelia* to indict Leocrates (5). In this procedure, the prosecutor makes his accusation first in the Assembly or Council, then brings the case before one of the popular courts for trial.[2] The law concerning *eisangelia* provided that the procedure

[1] The trial must be dated to early 331, because Lycurgus says it took place seven years after Leocrates left Athens (45), and Leocrates remained abroad for six entire years (58). On the basis of similarities between this speech and Demosthenes' *On the Crown*, E. M. Burke ("Contra Leocratem and De Corona: Political Collaboration?" *Phoenix* 31 [1977]: 330–340) claims that Lycurgus brought his case against Leocrates in collaboration with Demosthenes as part of a plan to attack politicians sympathetic to Macedon. But there is no evidence that points to any close ties between the two politicians. For criticism of Burke's arguments, see E. M. Harris 1995: 173–174.

[2] For a study of the procedure, see Hansen 1975.

could be used to prosecute serious crimes against the community, including conspiracy to overthrow the democracy and treason endangering the city's defenses.[3] Lycurgus charges that Leocrates' departure from Athens amounted to treason (*prodosia*), but it is clear from his arguments that he was attempting to stretch the meaning of "treason" to cover an action the Athenians did not normally associate with the term (8–9). The law on *eisangelia* specifically mentioned and was normally applied to acts like betraying ships and strategic positions to hostile forces or deserting to the enemy. All Leocrates did, however, was to leave Athens during an emergency.

Leocrates and his supporters appear to have argued that merely leaving Athens was not equivalent to treason (68). Leocrates lacked the intent to commit treason, since his motive for sailing to Rhodes was to pursue trade, not to harm Athenian interests (55).[4] Lycurgus also expected them to point out that Leocrates held no official position that made him responsible for any part of the city's defenses (59) and that the absence of one man had not posed any serious threat to its security (63). Lycurgus responds to these objections by drawing attention to the circumstances surrounding Leocrates' departure, which indicated that the goal of his voyage to Rhodes was betrayal, not trade. Even though Leocrates held no official position, Lycurgus claims Leocrates had a duty not to desert Athens in an emergency. If everyone had acted like Leocrates, Attica would have turned into a wasteland (59–62). To support his view of the duties of citizenship, Lycurgus quotes from the Ephebic Oath (76–77) and contrasts Leocrates' actions with the loyalty of his fellow citizens (43). This gives Lycurgus the opportunity to present a lengthy civics lesson about the importance of patriotism and respect for one's parents and ancestors. To

[3] The main source for the law about *eisangelia* is Hyperides 4.7–8 (translated in this volume).

[4] Lycurgus claims that in Rhodes Leocrates spread news about Athens that discouraged merchants from sailing there (18–19), but he provides no witnesses who were in Rhodes at the time. His only evidence for the charge is the allegation made by Phyrcinus in the Assembly that Leocrates' report damaged Athenian trade. Leocrates might have claimed that he sailed to Rhodes to purchase wheat and bring it back to Athens, then changed his plans when he heard that Philip made peace with the Athenians.

illustrate his points, he retells stories from the distant past about King Codrus (84–88), Praxithea's sacrifice of her daughter (98–101), Tyrtaeus (105–107), and the Persian Wars (68–73, 104, 108–109). He links their actions with the sacrifice of the Athenians who died at Chaeronea to defend Greek freedom (46–51) and contrasts their valor with the cowardice of the traitor Leocrates. To convince the court to condemn Leocrates, he reminds them of the way their ancestors dealt harshly with traitors (111–127) and how the Spartans punished Pausanias (128–129). The weakness of Lycurgus' case is that the law does not state that citizens were obliged to contribute to the city's defense even if they were not explicitly ordered to do so.

Lycurgus' appeals to patriotism as well as his personal prestige almost succeeded in winning the case; Aeschines (3.252) says that Leocrates escaped conviction by a single vote. Yet despite Lycurgus' best efforts, a narrow majority of the court rejected his attempt to extend the definition of treason to cover all acts detrimental to Athenian security and prosperity.

AGAINST LEOCRATES

[1] I will make the beginning of this prosecution of Leocrates, which I have brought on your behalf and for the sake of the gods, both righteous and just. This is my prayer to Athena and the other gods and heroes whose statues stand throughout the city and countryside: if the indictment (*eisangelia*) I have brought against Leocrates is just and if I have brought this man to court because he has betrayed the temples, shrines, and precincts of the gods as well as the honors granted by the laws and the sacrificial rites handed down by your ancestors, [2] then on this day may you gods make me equal to the task of prosecuting Leocrates' crimes for the good of the people and the city. You are about to make a decision affecting your fathers, children, and wives, your fatherland and holy rites, and you have the man who betrayed them all subject to your vote: may the gods make you, both now and in the future, implacable judges to all men who commit such great offenses against the laws. But if the man I have brought to trial has neither betrayed his country nor abandoned the city and its holy rites, I ask that both the gods and you judges save him from danger.

[3] Our city benefits by having men in it who bring lawbreakers to

justice,[5] and I wish, gentlemen, that I could have counted on gratitude from the many for doing this. But it has now come to the point where the man who puts himself in danger[6] and risks being hated for pursuing the public good does not earn a reputation for being a patriot but for being a troublemaker; this is not right nor good for the city. Three things are most responsible for guarding and protecting the democracy and the city's prosperity: [4] first, the system of laws; second, the vote of the judges; and third, the trial, which brings crimes under their control. It is the function of the law to indicate what must not be done, the task of the accuser to denounce those who are subject to the penalties set forth in the laws, and the duty of the judge to punish those whom both of these bring to his attention. Neither the law nor the judges' vote therefore has any force without a prosecutor to bring wrongdoers before them.

[5] When I saw that Leocrates had run away from the dangers threatening the country, abandoned his fellow citizens, betrayed all your forces, and was thus subject to all the penalties the law provides, I initiated this prosecution. I decided to bring this case not for any personal feud nor out of personal ambition or any other such motive but because I thought it shameful to allow this man to burst into the Agora and share in our public sacrifices when he is a disgrace to his country and to all of you. [6] It is the duty of the just citizen therefore not to bring to public trial for the sake of private quarrels people who have done the city no wrong but to regard those who have broken the law as his own enemies and to view crimes that affect the commonwealth as providing public grounds for his enmity against them.

[7] Everyone must accordingly treat trials that affect the public interest as very important, especially this one in which you are going to cast your vote. When you judge charges brought against illegal de-

---

[5] Athens relied for the most part on volunteer prosecutors to bring actions against criminals.

[6] The prosecutor who failed to win one-fifth of the votes had to pay a fine of one thousand drachmas and lost his right to bring public charges. This discouraged prosecutors from using public procedures to pursue private feuds. On this topic, see E. M. Harris, "The Penalty for Frivolous Prosecutions in Athenian Law," *Dike* 2 (1999): 123–142.

crees,[7] you correct this one abuse alone, and you put a stop to this single action to the extent that the decree would have harmed the city. But this contest that has now started does not affect some small class of men in the city nor for a short time. This trial concerns the entire city and will be famous for all time in the eternal memories of our descendants. [8] The crime that has been committed is so dreadful and so enormous that it is impossible for a prosecutor to find an appropriate charge or for the law to provide adequate punishment for his misdeeds. What penalty should there be for the man who deserted his country, failed to protect his ancestral shrines, abandoned the graves of his ancestors, and left the entire land in the hands of the enemy? The greatest and most severe of all punishments, death, which is the mandatory punishment in the laws, does not measure up to Leocrates' crimes. [9] The penalty for such an offense was omitted from our laws not through any oversight of the lawgiver but because no such crime occurred in earlier times, and no one at the time expected it would happen in the future.[8] As a result, gentlemen, you must above all act not only as judges for this crime but also as legislators. In cases where a law has indicated what crimes are subject to punishment, it is easy to use this as a guide and hand out punishments for those who have broken the law. In cases where a law has not specified each particular crime, however, but designates several with one name and where someone has committed greater crimes than all of them and is thus subject to all the law's penalties, your decision must serve as a precedent to be left behind for future generations.[9] [10] So, be aware, gentlemen, that your vote for conviction not only will punish this man today but will inspire all our younger men to lead a life of virtue. There are two main factors in the education of young men, the punishment imposed on those who do wrong and the

---

[7] When someone proposed a decree in the Assembly that violated the law, it was possible to bring an action called a *graphē paranomōn* against the proposer. The Assembly could not pass the decree until after the proposer was acquitted of the charge.

[8] A similar argument is found at Lys. 31.27.

[9] Such a case could have served only as an informal precedent, since the Athenian legal system, unlike Common Law, had no means of enforcing such precedents.

rewards given to men of virtue. With an example of each before them, fear leads them to avoid the one, and desire for fame inspires them to pursue the other. For this reason, gentlemen, you must pay close attention to this trial and place justice ahead of all other considerations.

[11] The charge I am about to bring is just and contains no lies or irrelevant material. Most of the men who come before you act in the strangest way: they either give you advice about public business or make charges and accusations about everything except the issue about which you are going to cast your vote. Neither of these—giving an opinion about matters you are not discussing and finding an accusation to make about crimes no one is on trial for—is hard to do. [12] But prosecutors have no right to ask you to vote for justice when they themselves bring charges that are without justice. You are the ones, gentlemen, who are responsible for this situation. You have allowed those who come into court to do this, although you have in front of you the splendid example of the Areopagus Council.[10] This court is so superior to all other courts that even the men convicted by it agree that its verdicts are just. [13] It is their example you should follow and not give in to those who do not keep to the relevant issues. This way, defendants will not be tried on the basis of slander, prosecutors will not bring baseless charges, and you will cast a vote completely true to your oath.[11] For if men are not correctly instructed about a case, they will not be able to make a correct decision.

[14] You must also keep in mind, gentlemen, that this man's case is different from that of other private individuals. If you were trying a man with no reputation in Greece, your verdict, whether good or bad,

---

[10] The Areopagus tried cases of intentional homicide and a few other religious crimes and was the most respected court in Athens. It consisted of men who had served as archons. Since its members served for life and were subject to strict discipline, they were more professional than the other courts in Athens. The Areopagus received summary powers during the crisis after Chaeronea, which prompted some to call it "oligarchic." See Dinarchus 1.62. Lycurgus alludes to this criticism in 52.

[11] The six thousand judges who were selected each year swore an oath to render their verdicts in accordance with the laws and decrees of the Athenian people, to refuse gifts, and to disregard irrelevant arguments.

would matter to you alone. But whatever you decide about this man will be the talk of all the Greeks, for they know that his actions are totally unlike those of your ancestors. This man has quite a reputation for that trip he took to Rhodes and the damaging news about you he told the people of Rhodes and the merchants who were staying there. [15] These men then sailed around the entire world on business telling people the tales about your city they heard from Leocrates. This means you need to take the task of making the right decision about him very seriously. You are well aware, Athenians, that you are far superior to others when it comes to piety toward the gods, respect for your parents, and patriotic devotion to your country; but should this man escape punishment at your hands, you would appear to care nothing for these qualities.

[16] I ask you, Athenians, to hear my accusation through to the end and not to be angry if I begin with the disasters that struck the city at that time. You should save your anger for those responsible who have forced me to remind you about them. After the battle at Chaeronea was over,[12] all of you ran to meet in the Assembly, and the people voted to bring the women and children in from the countryside behind the walls and to have the generals assign for guard duty any Athenians and the rest of those resident in Athens in whatever way they saw fit. [17] Paying no attention at all to these decisions, Leocrates gathered up his possessions and put them in a dinghy along with his slaves (his ship was already anchored off shore). Late in the afternoon he went out with his mistress Eirenis through the gate to the middle of the Akte peninsula.[13] From there he sailed out to his ship and fled away, feeling no pity for the city's harbors from where he set out to sea, nor shame before the walls of his native land, which he did everything in his power to leave defenseless. He felt no fear as he saw in the distance the Acropolis, and the temple of Zeus the Savior and that of Athena the Savior, which he was betraying[14]—but soon he will call on them to save him from danger!

[18] After landing and arriving in Rhodes, he reported that the city

[12] The battle of Chaeronea took place in early September of 338.

[13] Akte was a peninsula that separated the port of Piraeus from the port of Zea.

[14] There were temples of Zeus the Savior and Athena the Savior in Piraeus.

he left was in enemy hands with Piraeus under siege (as if he were announcing some good news about a great success for his country!) and that he was the only one to reach safety. He showed no shame in calling the city's disaster his own good fortune! The Rhodians placed so much trust in his report that they manned their triremes and forced cargo ships into port. The merchants and ship captains, who were ready to sail here, unloaded their grain and the rest of their cargoes all because of this man. [19] To show you I am telling the truth, the clerk will read to you everyone's testimony, first that of his neighbors and those who live in that area who know he fled in wartime and sailed away from Athens, then the statements of the people who were in Rhodes when Leocrates gave his report, and after this the testimony of Phyrcinus, who, as many of you know, accused him in the Assembly of greatly reducing the revenues from the 2 percent tax when he owned a share of it.[15] [20] But before the witnesses come forward, I wish to say a few brief words to you. You are well aware of the tricks defendants use and the pleas of those who beg to have them acquitted. But on the other hand you know exactly how money and personal favors have persuaded many witnesses either to forget or not to come forward or to find some pretext to avoid giving testimony.[16] Insist therefore that these witnesses come forward and not hold back; demand that they do not place personal favors ahead of their respect for you and the city but that they either repay their country with truth and justice and not desert their post in imitation of Leocrates or perform the rites and refuse on oath to testify in accordance with the law. If they do neither of these, we will issue them a summons so they do their duty to you, to the laws, and to the democracy. Read the testimony.

---

[15] This tax was a duty levied on all exports and imports into Athens. Private individuals bid for the right to collect the tax, and the successful bidder made a down payment and then regular payments to the Council.

[16] If a witness refused to testify, a litigant could issue him a summons. The witness then had either to swear that he did not know or was not present or to pay a fine of a thousand drachmas. For the procedure of *klēteusis,* see C. Carey, "The Witness's Exomosia in the Athenian Courts," *Classical Quarterly* 45 (1995): 114–119.

[TESTIMONY]

[21] After this, gentlemen, some time went by, and ships began arriving in Rhodes from Athens. When it became obvious that nothing drastic had happened to the city, Leocrates got scared and sailed away from Rhodes and arrived in Megara. He lived in Megara for more than five years under the protection of a Megarian patron.[17] He felt no shame at all being just across the border from Athens but remained as a resident alien in the land of the people who live next to the country that raised him. [22] As a result, he condemned himself to permanent exile and sent for Amyntas, the man who married his elder sister, and one of his friends, Antigenes of Xypete. He asked his brother-in-law to buy from him his slaves and house and to pay him a talent, instructing him to use this sum to pay off his debts and friendly loans, then return the remainder to him.[18] [23] Amyntas conducted all this business and sold the slaves for 35 minas to Timochares of Acharnai, who was married to Leocrates' younger sister. Timochares had no money to give him, so he drew up a contract, deposited it with Lysicles, and paid Amyntas interest of one mina.[19] The clerk will read you the testimony of these two men so that you know the actual truth and do not think this is just some story. If Amyntas were still alive, I would produce him as a witness. As it is, I am calling on the men who know what happened. Read the testimony that Amyntas bought the slaves and the house from Leocrates in Megara.

[TESTIMONY]

[24] Listen also to how Philomelus of Cholargeus and Menelaus, who once went on an embassy to the King,[20] received forty minas from Amyntas.

---

[17] Those who lived in foreign cities as metics (resident aliens) were required to have a patron to represent them in legal proceedings and other matters.

[18] The *eranos* or "friendly loan" was raised from a group of friends, who did not charge interest.

[19] The normal rate of interest was 1% a month or 12% a year. Interest of one mina a month on a loan of thirty-six minas was unusually high, over 34% a year.

[20] When the orators refer to "the King," they mean the King of Persia.

[TESTIMONY]

Submit also for me the statement of Timochares, who bought the slaves from Amyntas for thirty-five minas, as well as their contract.

[TESTIMONY, CONTRACT]

[25] Gentlemen, you have heard the witnesses. For what I am now about to tell you, Leocrates deserves both your anger and your hatred. It was not enough for him just to save his own skin and his own property; he also sent for his ancestral sacred images, which his forefathers had set up and then handed down to him in accord with your laws and traditional customs, and he transported them out of our country. He was not deterred by their name "ancestral" when he left his ancestral country[21] and took them with him into exile, asking them to abandon their temples and their country where they had dwelled and then set them up in a foreign and alien land as outsiders in the land of the Megarians and strangers to the traditional customs of that city.

[26] Your forefathers called their country Athens after the goddess Athena [who had received this land as her allotment][22] so that by honoring the goddess for whom the city was named they would not abandon it. Leocrates showed no concern for our laws, our traditions, or our shrines. In fact, he put the help you receive from the gods up for export. Nor was it enough for him to commit so many great crimes against the city. While living in Megara, he invested the money he took away from you and used it to ship grain from Cleopatra in Epeirus[23] to Leucas[24] and from there to Corinth.[25] [27] And yet for these

---

[21] Lycurgus' choice of words suggests a connection between ancestral sacred images (*patrōa*) and his country (*patris*).

[22] Some editors think this phrase is not part of the original text but an explanatory gloss added by a later scholar.

[23] Epeirus was a kingdom in northwestern Greece ruled by King Alexander the Molossian. At the time he was campaigning in Italy to help Tarentum against the Lucanians, and his wife Cleopatra, the sister of Alexander the Great, was acting as regent.

[24] Leucas is an island off the western coast of Greece.

[25] Corinth was one of the largest commercial cities in Greece. It was situated near the Isthmus and could take advantage of trade moving between the Aegean and western Greece.

crimes, gentlemen, your laws provide the most extreme penalties if any Athenian transports grain to any other place than to you.[26] He betrayed your country during war, he traded in grain in defiance of the laws, he paid no heed to your sacred rites, your country, and your laws. Now that you have him in the power of your vote, will you not put him to death and make him an example for others? If not, you will be the most easygoing people in the world, feeling hardly a trace of anger even when terrible crimes are committed. [28] Look at how fairly I am going about examining these issues. In my opinion you should not rely on conjecture when judging such crimes but should cast your vote only when you know the truth. Witnesses should give their testimony not before but after their reliability has been proven. For this reason, I have drawn up a written challenge about all these issues, asking him to question his own slaves under torture.[27] It is worth hearing the challenge.[28] Read this for me.

[CHALLENGE]

[29] You hear the challenge, gentlemen. At one stroke Leocrates both refused the challenge and testified against himself, proving he is a traitor to this country—the man who does not let us find out the truth from those who know the facts has admitted the charges against him are true. Who among you does not know that the fairest and most democratic way of resolving a dispute between opponents, when male or female slaves know the necessary facts, is to put them to the test and torture them, that is, to put your confidence in deeds, not words,

---

[26] It was illegal for Athenian citizens to transport grain to any other port than Athens or to lend money to merchants for the purpose of bringing grain to other ports.

[27] In theory, the interrogation of slaves under torture (*basanos*) was the only means of introducing the testimony of slaves in court. The interrogation is regularly proposed in a challenge, issued by one litigant to the other. We know of no cases, however, where a challenge actually resulted in an interrogation. In practice, the challenge is rejected by the other litigant, providing the challenger with the rhetorical opportunity (as here) to tell the court what the slaves would have said had they been interrogated (see M. Gagarin, "The Torture of Slaves in Athenian Law," *Classical Philology* 91 [1996]: 1–18).

[28] The text of the passage is corrupt. I have adopted the restoration proposed by Malcovati.

especially when the issue is about important public matters that concern the state and affect its interests?

[30] You see how I have avoided conducting my case against Leocrates unfairly: I went so far as to be willing to take the risk of having the test of his guilt depend on the testimony of his own male and female slaves. But this man did not consent to my offer because of his guilty conscience and refused it. And yet Leocrates' male and female slaves would have been quicker to deny any of the actual facts than to invent lies incriminating their master. [31] Aside from this, Leocrates will soon shout out that he is a private citizen and a victim trapped by the clever skills of a politician and an unscrupulous prosecutor. But all of you realize, I think, that it is typical of clever men who try to bring baseless charges to anticipate this objection and look for topics where they can confuse and distract their opponents. But men who bring honest charges and show precisely how defendants are subject to the herald's curse clearly act very differently, just as we have. [32] Consider it this way in your own minds. What people are in no position to use their cleverness and verbal tricks to deceive you? The male and female slaves, if they had been tortured, would have naturally told the whole truth about all his crimes. But Leocrates refused to hand them over although they belonged to him and no one else. [33] On the other hand, whom do you think it is possible to captivate with words and use tears to seduce their impressionable character into pity? The judges. Leocrates, the man who betrayed his city, came here terrified by nothing so much as the possibility that the people who would prove his guilt would come from the same house as the man who would be proven guilty. What need was there for excuses, arguments, or pleas? Justice is a simple matter, truth is even easier, and the way to test them is quick.

[34] If he admits that the charges in the indictment are righteous and true, why does he not deserve the penalty provided by the laws? If he says they are not true, why has he not turned over his male and female slaves? When one is on trial for treason, the proper thing to do is to hand over your slaves for torture and to avoid none of the most accurate means for determining the truth. [35] But he did neither of these things. Instead, after testifying against himself and proving that he is a traitor to his country, its holy rites, and its laws, he will ask you to ignore his confession and his own testimony when you cast your vote. This man has turned down my fair proposal and rejected in

many other ways the possibility of defending himself—how then is it right that you allow him to deceive you about the crimes he has admitted?

[36] I think you have learned enough about the challenge and the crime he has confessed to. Now I want to remind you about the nature of the situation and the enormity of the dangers the city faced when Leocrates betrayed it. Clerk, take for me the decree of Hyperides[29] and read it out.

[DECREE]

[37] You hear the decree, gentlemen: it is resolved that the Council of 500 take up arms and go down to Piraeus to make plans about protecting the city and should be prepared to do whatever it thinks is in the people's best interests. Indeed, gentlemen, if those who were exempt from military duty so that they could make decisions about public business were going around like soldiers, do you think the fears that gripped the city were trivial and insignificant? [38] In this crisis Leocrates here ran off like a fugitive and left the city. He took all his available property abroad and sent for his ancestral cult images. Such was his treason that as far as his decision was concerned, our temples were deserted and the guard posts on the walls empty and both city and countryside were abandoned.

[39] And yet at that time who would not have taken pity on the city, not just a citizen but even a foreigner who had merely visited here in the past? Who could have hated our people and despised Athens so much that he could have let himself desert his post? When the news of the defeat and disaster reached the people, the city was anxious about recent events, and the people placed their hope for safety in men over fifty.[30] [40] You could see free women cowering in fear at their doors, trying to find out if their husband, or father, or brothers

[29] For Hyperides, see Part II of this volume. After the defeat at Chaeronea, Hyperides proposed to free all slaves in Attica and to restore rights to those who had been disenfranchised. The decree was attacked as illegal in court and ultimately rescinded.

[30] All Athenian citizens above a certain property qualification were technically liable for military service up to age fifty-nine, but men above forty-five were only called up in serious emergencies.

were still alive, a sight humiliating both for them and for the city.[31] You could see men far past their prime and physically weak, who were legally exempt from military duty, wandering around the whole city, men weak with age with their cloaks pinned double.[32] [41] In the middle of these many disasters for the city and terrible misfortunes for all its citizens, anyone would have shared their pain and would have wept to see the people who prided themselves on their freedom and racial purity voting to grant slaves their freedom, give citizenship to foreigners, and restore privileges to the disenfranchised. [42] The city's fortunes were turned upside down: in the past we fought for the freedom of the rest of Greece; now we would have been glad to risk our lives for the secure defense of our own safety. In the past we ruled much of the territory of the barbarians; now we were struggling against Macedon to protect our own land. The Athenian people, whom in the past the Spartans, the Peloponnesians, and the Greeks living in Asia called on for help, were now begging for troops to be sent from Andros, Ceos, Troezen, and Epidauros.[33]

[43] So therefore, gentlemen, if someone in the midst of such terrors, such great dangers, and so enormous a public humiliation deserted the city and did not take up arms to defend his country or report to the generals for duty but instead fled and betrayed the security of the people, what patriotic judge willing to do his sacred duty would vote to acquit him? What public leader would respond to an appeal for help from a man who betrayed his city, especially one who did not have the courage to share in our sorrow for the country's misfortunes and contributed nothing to protect the city and its people at a time when the countryside was sacrificing its trees, the dead their tombs, and the temples their sacred weapons? [44] And yet in those days every part of the population threw itself into the task of saving the city. Some men took on the job preparing the fortifications, others the task of digging ditches, still others to making palisades. Everyone

[31] This passage appears to imply that respectable women would not be seen alone in public.

[32] Normally, men wore a cloak over one shoulder that reached below their knees. Here, the old men have folded their cloaks double and pinned them so as to give them greater maneuverability for fighting.

[33] Andros and Ceos were islands in the Aegean east of Attica. Troezen and Epidauros were small cities in the northeastern Peloponnese, not far from Attica.

in the city was hard at work. For none of these tasks did Leocrates report himself for duty. [45] You should keep these things in mind and sentence this man to death, for he did not even deign to contribute anything, not even to join in the funeral procession for those who gave their lives at Chaeronea to protect the people's safety and freedom. If Leocrates had had his way, these men would remain unburied today. And now seven years later he shows no shame as he passes by their graves and calls their country his fatherland!

[46] There are a few more things, gentlemen, I wish to say about these men. Please listen to what I have to say and do not consider such arguments out of place at a public trial.[34] When you praise good men, you clearly prove the guilt of those whose conduct is quite the opposite. Beyond that, it is certainly right to include this praise, the only reward that brave men have for the dangers they faced, in speeches at public trials about our common interest, since they paid with their lives to preserve our common safety. [47] These men stood against the enemy on the borders of Boeotia[35] and fought for the freedom of the Greeks. They did not place their hopes for safety in fortifications, nor did they let the enemy destroy their land. Instead, they thought that courage was a firmer bulwark than walls of stone, and they were ashamed to see the land that nourished them put to the torch. Rightly so. [48] Just as all fathers do not feel the same degree of affection for their adopted sons as they do for their natural children, so too men feel less attachment to land that does not naturally belong to them but has been acquired later in their lives. With these thoughts in mind they faced their share of dangers equal to the best, but they did not have the same share of success. They derived no benefit from their bravery while alive, but when they died, they bequeathed us their fame. They were not defeated but died where they were ordered to stand, defending our freedom. [49] I must tell you something paradoxical yet still true: these men died victorious. The reason is that in death they won both freedom and valor, which for good men are the prizes of war. Furthermore, one cannot say that they were defeated, since they did not cower in fear when the enemy attacked. No one

---

[34] The manuscripts here say "trials about public matters," but editors alter this to "arguments at public trials."

[35] Chaeronea is situated on the western border of Boeotia near Phocis.

would have the right to say that men who died nobly in war have been defeated, since they chose a noble death and avoided slavery. [50] The valor of these men made this fact clear. They alone of all men held the freedom of Greece in their hands. These men departed from life at the same time that Greece passed into slavery; the freedom of the rest of Greece was buried along with their bodies. They have taught the entire world this lesson by fighting not for themselves but by facing danger to secure our common freedom. As a result, gentlemen, I would not be ashamed to say that their lives are our country's crown of glory.

[51] Their conduct was not without reason, because you, men of Athens, alone of all the Greeks, know how to honor good men. In other places you will find statues of athletes erected in the marketplace; in your city you will see statues of successful generals[36] and men who have killed tyrants.[37] It is not easy to find even a few men of this kind in all of Greece, whereas it easy to see men who have won contests for a wreath[38]—they are in many places. Just as you award the greatest honors to your benefactors, so too justice demands that you punish with the most extreme penalties those who have betrayed and brought shame on our country. [52] Consider this, gentleman, if you are to do the right thing, you cannot acquit this man Leocrates here. His crime has already been judged and condemned. The Council of the Areopagus (please do not jeer when I mention its name—in my opinion, the Council was the greatest reason for our survival in that crisis) arrested and put to death men who at that time fled the country and abandoned it to the enemy. Certainly, gentlemen, do not think that men who are responsible for judging cases of murder, cases of the greatest religious importance, would violate the legal rights of any citi-

[36] The first general to have a statue erected in his honor was Conon, who decisively defeated the Spartan fleet at Cnidus in 394 (Dem. 20.70). Later, Timotheus, Iphicrates, and Chabrias received the same honor.

[37] Harmodius and Aristogeiton killed Hipparchus, the brother of the tyrant of Hippias in 514. Sometime after the overthrow of the tyranny in 510, the Athenians erected statues of Harmodius and Aristogeiton. These statues were taken as booty during the Persian invasion of Attica in 480, but new statues were erected after the Persian Wars.

[38] I.e., athletes.

zen. [53] On the contrary, you yourselves convicted and punished Autolycus for sending his sons and wife abroad, even though he himself remained here to face danger.[39] If you condemned a man who was guilty only of sending abroad people who were unfit for military service, what punishment must a man suffer who did not repay his fatherland for raising him?[40] Moreover, the people of Athens thought the situation serious and voted that those who fled the danger threatening the country were guilty of treason and deserved the harshest punishment. [54] When this kind of crime has been condemned by the most just tribunal, led to a conviction by you who were sitting as judges, and agreed by the people to deserve the harshest punishment, will your verdict be different from theirs? If it is, you will be the greatest fools in the world and will find hardly any men at all willing to risk their lives to defend you.

[55] It is clear that Leocrates is subject to punishment for all the charges brought against him. I know he will try to trick you by saying that he sailed as a merchant and that he went away to Rhodes for business reasons. If he says this, look at how easily you will catch him lying. First of all, men who sail for trade do not leave by the back gate and board their ships at Akte but inside the harbor, where they are sent off in full view of their friends. Furthermore, they do not leave with a mistress and several slave women, but alone with one slave to serve them. [56] Beyond that, why would he need to live for five years as a merchant in Megara, have his ancestral images sent to him, and sell his house here if he had not convicted himself of betraying the city and doing the greatest injustice to its citizens? It would be the strangest thing of all, if you who have the power of the vote would acquit him of the crimes for which he himself expected to be punished. But apart from this reason, I think one should not accept this defense. [57] For surely it is outrageous that when others who were abroad to

---

[39] Autolycus was a member of the Areopagus who was prosecuted by Lycurgus and condemned for sending his family abroad during the crisis after Chaeronea. See Lyc. Fr. 3, *Against Autolycus.*

[40] All Athenians were legally required to provide their elderly parents with food and shelter. If they failed to do so, their parents could bring a private action against them. Here, Lycurgus compares Leocrates' desertion of Athens to a failure to look after one's parents in old age.

trade hurried home to help the city, he alone sailed away on business during the crisis when no one else was seeking to increase his wealth but only to save what he already possessed. I would like him to tell me what kind of business would make him more useful to the city than reporting to the generals for duty and fighting at your side to drive back our attackers? I do not see any help as important as this one. [58] And it is not only his actions that deserve your anger but also his words, for he has clearly had the audacity to lie to you. He had never before practiced this line of trade but bought blacksmiths,[41] nor did he import anything to Athens from Megara, though he lived abroad for six years straight. Finally, he happened to have an interest in the 2 percent tax,[42] which he would not have abandoned and gone abroad on trade. If he says anything along these lines, I think you will not allow him to get away with it.

[59] Perhaps he will come forward and rely on the argument that some of his supporters have advised him to use, namely, that he is not guilty of treason since he was not in charge of the shipyards, or the city gates, or the army camps, or any part of the city at all. My opinion is that men in those positions can betray part of our forces, but this man handed over the entire city to the enemy.[43] The treason of the former harms only the living, but this man's treason robbed even the dead and the temples in the countryside of their ancestral rites. [60] If the former had turned traitors, our city would have fallen into slavery but would still be inhabited, but if everyone acted like Leocrates, the city would be a wasteland. After a setback, cities have a strong chance of recovery, but after complete destruction, they lose even the hope common to all cities. Just as any man who is alive has a hope of improving his fortunes, but after he dies, loses all means of enjoying prosperity, so too with cities: once they are destroyed, their misfortune is permanent. [61] If one must speak the truth, destruction is the death of a city. This is the greatest proof: a long time ago our city was a slave to tyrants,[44] later to the Thirty when its walls were torn down by the

[41] I.e., slaves who were trained as blacksmiths.

[42] For the 2% tax, see above, 19n.

[43] A similar argument is found at Lys. 31.26.

[44] An allusion to the rule of the Peisistratids, who were overthrown in 510.

Lacedaimonians.[45] Yet after both of these, we won back our freedom and earned the right to be the guardians of Greek prosperity. [62] This is not true for cities that have been destroyed. If I can mention the more distant past, who has not heard about Troy? It was the greatest of all cities at that time and ruled over all of Asia, but after the Greeks leveled it to the ground, it has been a wasteland ever since. And then there is Messene, which has finally been settled again after five hundred years by a bunch of nobodies.[46]

[63] Perhaps one of his supporters will dare to minimize his crime and say that one man could not be responsible for these disasters. They are not ashamed to make this kind of defense for which they deserve to be put to death. If they agree that he left his country, after admitting this, let them allow you to decide how serious it was. If he did none of these things at all, isn't it insane to claim that he could not have caused this by himself? [64] My opinion, gentlemen, is very different from theirs: the city's safety was this man's responsibility. Every individual has his own personal share in managing and protecting the city, and when someone neglects his duty in one way, he may not realize it, but he neglected it in all ways. You will easily discover the truth of this if you consider how the ancient lawgivers thought about the issue. [65] These men did not assign death as a penalty for the person who stole a hundred talents and a lesser penalty for the man who stole ten drachmas. Nor did they put a man to death for committing a great sacrilege and punish a man who committed a smaller one with a lesser penalty. And they did not punish the man who killed a slave with a fine and the one who killed a free man with loss of rights, but they imposed the death penalty for all offenses, even the smallest ones. [66] Each of these men looked not at the individual character of the crime nor at the seriousness of the crimes but considered this alone: was the crime likely to harm people if it grew more widespread?

---

45 When the Athenians surrendered to the Spartans in 404, they were required to tear down the walls surrounding their city. Later that year the Thirty Tyrants seized power, only to be overthrown the next year by the democratic forces.

46 Messene was the capital of Messenia, which was conquered by the Spartans in the Archaic period and its inhabitants enslaved. The Theban general Epaminondas invaded the Peloponnese in 369, liberated Messenia from Sparta, and founded the city of Messene as its capital.

It is ridiculous to look at the matter in any other way. Consider, gentlemen, if someone should walk into the Metroon[47] and erase one of the laws, then defend himself by claiming his action had no effect on the city, wouldn't you put him to death? And rightly so, in my opinion, if your aim was to protect the other laws. [67] You must punish this man in the same way if you intend to make the other citizens better people. You will not think about whether he is one isolated individual, but look at what he did. I think it is our good fortune that there are not many such men in Athens. This man therefore deserves to suffer a greater penalty, since he alone of all the rest of the citizens wanted safety for himself, not for the city.

[68] I get very angry, gentlemen, whenever I hear one of his associates say that it is not treason if someone leaves the city. For example, your ancestors once left the city when they were fighting against Xerxes and crossed over to Salamis.[48] This man is so foolish and holds you in such complete contempt that he thinks it right to compare the most glorious of deeds with the most shameful. [69] Where is the valor of these men not well known? What man is so grudging or so completely lacking in ambition that he would not pray to have taken part in their great deeds? They did not desert the city but only moved from one place to another as part of their brilliant plan to confront the danger that faced them. [70] Eteonicus the Spartan,[49] Adeimantus the Corinthian,[50] and the entire Aeginetan fleet[51] were on the point of seeking their own safety during the night; but our forefathers, even

---

[47] The Metroon was the public archive of Athens where texts were kept of all laws and decrees.

[48] After the Persian army under Xerxes defeated the Greeks at Thermopylae in 480, the Athenians abandoned Attica and moved to the island of Salamis.

[49] Lycurgus gets the name of the Spartan commander of the Greek fleet wrong; it was Eurybiades (Herod. 8.2.2). Eteonicus was the name of a Spartan leader during the Peloponnesian War (Thuc. 8.23.4).

[50] According to Herodotus (8.94), the allegation that Adeimantus fled at the start of the battle of Salamis and the rest of the Corinthian ships followed him was nothing more than an Athenian slander.

[51] Herodotus (8.74) reports that the Aeginetans agreed with the Athenians and Megarians that the Greeks should fight at Salamis. In the battle they fought better than all the other Greeks (8.93).

though deserted by all the Greeks, preserved freedom for themselves and for the others by using force to compel the Greeks to fight the barbarians at sea near Salamis. Alone they triumphed over both enemies and allies in the right way, by helping the latter and routing the former in battle. Was this in any way similar to the man who fled his country on a four-day voyage to Rhodes? [71] Would any of these men of old have perhaps tolerated such a crime? Wouldn't they have stoned to death the man who brought shame on their own courage? All those men loved their country so much that when Alexander came as an ambassador for Xerxes,[52] they almost stoned him to death because he demanded earth and water although he had been their friend before this? Since they considered it justified to take revenge for just a speech, wouldn't they certainly have punished with the harshest penalties the man who by his actions betrayed his country into the hands of the enemy? [72] With such thoughts in mind, therefore, they maintained their position as leader of the Greeks for ninety years,[53] sacked Phoenicia and Cilicia, won victories in battle on land and sea at Eurymedon, captured one hundred triremes from the barbarians, and sailed around Asia on raids.[54] [73] This was the crowning point of their triumph: they were not satisfied with setting up a trophy at Salamis but fixed a boundary for the barbarians to protect the freedom of Greece and stopped them from crossing it.[55] They made a treaty

[52] According to Herodotus (8.140–144), Alexander I of Macedon conveyed a message from the Persian general Mardonius offering to return Attica to the Athenians in exchange for an alliance. Herodotus says the Athenians rejected the offer, but he does not say they almost stoned Alexander. Demanding "earth and water" was a way of demanding submission.

[53] The Athenians led a large alliance of Greeks for seventy-four years from the establishment of the Delian League in 478 until their defeat in 404. Lycurgus exaggerates the length of their leadership for rhetorical purposes.

[54] The Athenians and their allies under Cimon defeated the Persians on land and sea at Eurymedon in Pamphylia probably in 466. For the date, see E. Badian, *From Plataea to Potidaea* (Baltimore and London 1993), 4–9. By "Asia," Lycurgus means "Asia Minor," modern-day Turkey.

[55] By the terms of the Peace of Callias in 449 BC, the Persians recognized the freedom of the Greeks and pledged not to send warships beyond Cyaneai, a set of islands near the Bosporus, and Phaselis, a city in Lycia near Pamphylia.

that forbade them from sailing beyond Cyaneai and Phaselis in a warship and established the right of the Greeks to conduct their own affairs not only for the Greeks living in Europe but also for those living in Asia. [74] Do you think any of these fine deeds would have happened or that you would still live in this country if they thought like Leocrates and fled? Just as you praise and honor good men, in the same way you must punish cowards, especially Leocrates, who neither feared nor respected you.

[75] But consider your traditions and opinions on this matter. Although you already know, it is still worthwhile to go through them. By Athena, the ancient laws and values of the men who originally established them are a source of pride for the city. If you pay attention to them, you will act justly and gain a reputation for being righteous and worthy of the city. [76] You have an oath that all the citizens swear when they are enrolled on the list of citizens and become ephebes: not to dishonor your sacred arms, not to abandon your post, to defend your fatherland and hand it down greater.[56] If Leocrates swore this oath, he has clearly perjured himself and has not only wronged you but also has committed impiety against the divinity. If he did not swear it, he was clearly not prepared to perform any of his duties. For this you would be justified in taking revenge both for your own sake and for the gods. I want you to hear the oath. Read it, clerk.

[OATH] [57]

[77] Gentlemen, this is certainly a fine and sacred oath. All of Leocrates' actions have violated it. Indeed, how could a man be more

[56] When Athenians reached the age of eighteen, they were enrolled on a list of citizens in their deme and performed military service as ephebes for two years.

[57] The Ephebic Oath is not preserved in the manuscripts of this speech, but several texts of the oath have been preserved in other sources. The most reliable is the one found on a fourth-century stele from the Attic deme of Acharnai (see M. N. Tod, *A Selection of Greek Historical Inscriptions*, II, *From 403 to 323 B.C.* [Oxford, 1948], no. 204), which runs as follows: "I shall not disgrace my sacred weapons nor shall I desert the comrade at my side, wherever I stand in the line. I shall fight in defense of things sacred and holy and shall hand down to my descendants a fatherland that is not smaller but larger and stronger to the best of my ability and with the help of all, and I shall obey those who on any occasion are governing

sacrilegious or more of a traitor to his country? How could anyone disgrace his arms more than by refusing to take them up and repel the enemy? How has the man who has failed to report for duty not abandoned his comrade and his post? [78] How has the man who did not face danger defended what is holy and sacred? With what greater treason could he have abandoned the country? For his part, the country was deserted and left in the hands of the enemy. Well, then, won't you put to death this man who is guilty of every crime? If not, whom then will you punish? Those who committed just one of these crimes? Then it will be easy to commit great crimes if you are clearly more angry about small ones.

[79] Here is another point, gentlemen: you must realize that what preserves our democracy is the oath. There are three elements of a state: the magistrate, the judge, and the private citizen. Each of these gives this oath as a pledge and rightly so. Many men, by fooling people and escaping detection, are not only freed from danger for the moment but are also free from punishment for their crimes for the rest of their lives. But the man who swears a false oath does not escape the notice of the gods, nor does he escape their punishment. On the contrary, if not he himself, then the children and the whole family of the perjurer fall into the greatest misfortunes. [80] For this reason, judges, all the Greeks at Plataea gave themselves this pledge when they were in battle formation and about to fight against Xerxes' forces. They did not invent one for themselves but imitated your traditional oath. It is worth hearing. Although their deeds occurred long ago, we can still plainly see their bravery in the words they wrote. Read it out for me.[58]

---

prudently and the established laws and any that may be established prudently in the future. If anyone tries to destroy them, I shall resist to the best of my ability and with the help of all, and I shall honor the ancestral sacred rites. The witnesses are the gods Aglauros, Hestia, Enyo, Enyalios, Ares and Athena Areia, Zeus, Thallo, Auxo, Hegemone, Heracles, and the boundaries of my fatherland, wheat, barley, vines, olives, and figs." Note how closely Lycurgus echoes the language of the oath in the following section.

[58] The version of the Oath of Plataea preserved in Lycurgus' speech is shorter and different in some details from the version on the fourth-century stele found at Acharnai that also contains the Ephebic Oath (see preceding note). Herodotus does not mention the oath in his account of the battle of Plataea, but he says the

[OATH]

[81] I will not put life above liberty, nor will I desert our leaders, living or dead, but I will bury all our allies who die in battle. After we have defeated the barbarians, I will destroy none of the cities that fought for Greece, and I will dedicate a tithe from the spoils of all the cities that took the side of the barbarian. I will not rebuild any of the temples burnt and destroyed by the barbarians, but I will allow them to be left behind as a reminder of the barbarians' impiety.

[82] So strictly, gentlemen, did they abide by this oath that they gained the favor of the gods to help them. Yet out of all the Greeks who demonstrated their valor in the face of danger, your city won the greatest fame. It would be the most terrible thing of all if your ancestors had the courage to die for your city's reputation, but you do not punish those who cover it with shame, but let the city's glory, acquired at the cost of so much effort, be destroyed by the wickedness of such men.

[83] And yet, gentlemen, you alone out of all the Greeks cannot let any of this happen. I want to tell you some brief stories about our past. If you use these as examples, you will make better decisions about both this and other cases. Our city has the great advantage that it is a shining example of noble deeds for the Greeks. Just as our city is the oldest of all in age, so too our ancestors surpassed the rest of mankind in valor. [84] During the reign of Codrus,[59] the Peloponnesians were suffering from famine in their land and decided to march against our city, expel our ancestors, and divide our land among themselves. First, however, they sent to Delphi and asked if they would take Athens. After the god replied that they would take the city if they did not kill Codrus, the king of the Athenians, they marched off against Athens. [85] But Cleomantis, one of the Delphians, found

---

Greeks swore a similar oath before the battle of Thermopylae (7.132.2). Although Diodorus Siculus (11.3.3) agrees with Lycurgus that the Greeks swore an oath before the battle of Plataea, Theopompus (*FGrHist* 115 F 148) claims the stele was a forgery, but some modern scholars believe that the oath is genuine. See R. Meiggs, *The Athenian Empire* (Oxford, 1972), 504–507.

[59] Codrus, according to one tradition, was the last king of Athens and reigned from 1090/89 to 1070/69. His son Medon agreed to hold the position of archon for life, instead of the kingship.

out about the oracle and reported it secretly to the Athenians. Our ancestors, it seems, always enjoyed such goodwill even from foreigners. When the Peloponnesians invaded Attica, what did our ancestors do, gentlemen of the court? They did not abandon the country, as Leocrates did, and flee, nor did they betray the land that had nourished them and its temples to the enemy. No, although few in number, they were cut off and besieged and endured hardship for their country.

[86] So noble were the kings in those days that they chose to die to save their subjects rather than to live and move to another country. The story goes that Codrus instructed the Athenians to pay attention to when he ended his life, then dressed up in beggar's clothes to deceive the enemy, slipped out of the gates and began to gather firewood in front of the city. When two men approached him from their camp and asked for news about the city, he attacked one of them with his scythe and killed him. [87] The one who survived flew into a rage at Codrus and, thinking him a beggar, drew his sword and killed him. After this, the Athenians sent a herald, asked them to return the king's body for burial, and told them the whole truth. The Peloponnesians returned the body but, realizing they would not be able to hold on to our land, returned home. Our city granted Cleomantis the Delphian and his descendants the permanent right to dine in the Prytaneum.[60]

[88] Observe: did those kings have the same love for their country as Leocrates, when they chose to die by deceiving the enemy, to exchange their own lives for the common safety? That is why they alone have given their names to our country and have received divine honors[61]—and rightly so. Even in death they justly inherited a share of the country to which they were so firmly devoted. [89] But Leocrates deserves no share of our country either in life and in death. He alone would rightly be cast out of the country that he betrayed to the enemy.[62] For it is

---

[60] The Prytaneum contained the hearth of the city with the cult of Hestia and was used to entertain official foreign guests of the city. Pausanias (1.18.3) locates it at the edge of the Agora nearest the Acropolis.

[61] Several of the Attic tribes were named after the mythical kings of Athens, though Codrus was not among them.

[62] Athenian law forbid the burial of traitors in Attica.

not right that the same land should cover men who excelled in bravery and the greatest coward of all mankind.

[90] And yet he tried to argue, and perhaps he will repeat to you now, that he would not have subjected himself to this trial had he known that he was committing this kind of crime.[63] As if all thieves and temple robbers do not use this argument! This is not an indication that they did not commit the crime but that they have no shame. This is not what he should say; rather, he should deny that he sailed away, deny he abandoned the city, and deny he settled in Megara. [91] This is the evidence relevant to the case. As for his return to Athens, I think that some god brought him back for punishment so that he would meet with a death without honor for fleeing the danger that would have brought him glory. If he had met with disaster in any other place, it would still not be clear that this was the reason for his punishment. But here among those he betrayed, it is obvious he is being punished for breaking our laws.

[92] The first thing the gods do to evil men is to lead their minds astray.[64] It strikes me that some ancient poets wrote the following iambic verses and left them for us like a prophecy:

> For when the wrath of the gods brings harm on a man,
> This is the first step: it snatches away the good sense
> From his mind and turns his thoughts to the worse
> So that he knows not what wrongs he does.

[93] Which of the older men does not remember, and which of the younger men has not heard, about Callistratus?[65] The city condemned him to death, but he fled into exile; then, when he learned from the

---

[63] Leocrates probably made this argument when Lycurgus initiated his prosecution in the Assembly. For the procedure, see the Introduction to the speech.

[64] This is a traditional idea in Greek tragedy; see, e.g., Aeschylus, *Niobe* Fr. 77. The author of the verses quoted here is unknown.

[65] Callistratus was an Athenian politician who played a leading role in the formation of the Second Athenian League in 378. He was condemned to death after Alexander of Pherae won a victory against the Athenian fleet in 361. For a study of his career, see R. Sealey, "Callistratos of Aphidna and His Contemporaries," *Historia* 5 (1956): 178–203.

god at Delphi that were he to return to Athens, he would receive what he deserved from the laws, he came back and sought refuge at the altar of the Twelve Gods[66] but just the same was put to death. And justly so: punishment is what guilty men deserve from the laws. The god brought the guilty man back so that the people he had wronged could punish him. It would be terrible if the same divine signs appeared to pious men and to criminals.

[94] I believe, gentlemen, that divine providence watches over all human affairs and especially the reverence we show our parents, the dead, and the gods themselves; rightly so. They have given us the beginning of our lives and the greatest share of the blessings we receive; it would be the greatest sacrilege not only to mistreat them but to refuse to devote our lives to helping them. [95] There is a story, which, even if it is rather fantastic, is suitable for all you younger men to hear.[67] Once in Sicily a stream of lava burst out of Aetna. They say it flowed through the rest of the country and even reached one of the cities of the people who lived there. Everyone else took to flight, looking to their own safety, but one of the younger men, seeing that his father, who was rather old and unable to move, would be caught by the lava, lifted him up and carried him away. But because of the additional burden, I think, he himself was also caught. [96] At this point you should observe how the god shows his favor to virtuous men. The story goes that the fire flowed around this spot in a circle, and these two alone were saved. For this reason, the spot is still even now called "The Place of the Holy." But those who retreated in a hurry and left their parents behind all perished. [97] Now that you have the testimony of the gods, you should all agree to punish this man, who for his part is guilty of all the worst crimes: he has robbed the gods of their ancestral honors, betrayed his parents to the enemy, and prevented the dead from receiving their customary rites.

[98] Now pay close attention, for I am not about to turn away from

[66] The Altar of the Twelve Gods was built by Peisistratos, the grandson of the tyrant of the same name, during his archonship in 522/21 (Thuc. 6.54.6). Remains of the altar have been discovered in the northern part of the Agora.

[67] This is the earliest version of a story that was often retold by later writers.

the men of old. Justice demands that you listen to the deeds for which they won respect and take them to heart. The story goes that Eumolpus, the son of Poseidon and Chione,[68] came with the Thracians to lay claim to our land. At this time Erechtheus was king and was married to Praxithea, the daughter of Cephisus. [99] When this large army was about to invade the country, he went to Delphi and asked the god what he should do to gain victory over the enemy. The god prophesied that if he sacrificed his daughter before the two armies met in battle, he would defeat the enemy. In obedience to the god, he performed his command and drove the invaders from his country. [100] Euripides therefore deserves our praise because, in addition to his other poetic virtues, he chose to make a tragedy out of this story, believing that their deeds would serve as an example that citizens could look to and study and thus acquire in their hearts the habit of loving their country. The iambic verses he wrote for the girl's mother are worth hearing, gentlemen of the court, for in them you will see the magnanimity and nobility that made her worthy of our city and to be Cephisus' daughter:[69]

Men look more kindly on one who grants a favor
With noble intent, but those who do a favor,
But take their time, they regard as less honorable.
I will give my own child to be killed.
I have many reasons: first, a city better
Than this one you could not find.
Above all, our people have not come as aliens
From elsewhere, but we are born from this earth.
Other cities, founded by migrations with men imported
From here and there, are thrown together like dice.

---

[68] Eumolpus was the ancestor of the Eumolpids, who held a famous priesthood for the Mysteries at Eleusis. Apollodorus (3.15.4) reports that during the reign of Erechtheus, Eleusis was at war with Athens and called on Eumolpus from Thrace to help them. When Erechtheus consulted the god at Delphi, he was told that he had to sacrifice one of his daughters to save Athens. He followed the god's order and with his help killed Eumolpus in battle.

[69] These verses are from Euripides' lost play *Erechtheus.*

Whoever leaves a city and dwells in another,
Like a poor bolt driven into a piece of wood,
Is a citizen in word, but not in deeds.
And then we bear children for this reason—
To protect the altars of the gods and our country.
The city has one name, but many people live
Within it. Why must I destroy them
When I can give one girl to die for all?
Since I know numbers, what is more and
What is less, one family's loss does not overcome
The fate of an entire city and carry equal weight.
If in our house I had, instead of females,
Male offspring, and the enemy's flames threatened the city,
Would I not send him out into the clash of spears,
Afraid that he would die? No, I wish I had children
Who would fight and shine among men,
Not mere figures of men born in our city for nothing!
A mother's tears, whenever they send children off,
Have made women out of men headed for battle:
I hate women who prefer to have their children live
And give them bad advice rather than what is good.
Indeed, those who die in battle with many others
Win the honor of public burial and an equal renown.
Yet a single crown will be given to this one child of mine
Alone for dying to protect this city! She will save
Both her mother and you as well as her two sisters:[70]
Which one of these gains is it not honorable to receive?
I will give my daughter, who is not mine except by birth,
As a sacrifice for our land. Look, if the city is captured,
What difference will children make for me?
As far as it lies in my power, all will be saved;
Others will rule, but I will be the one to save the city.
That thing which counts the most in public life,

[70] Apollodorus (3.15.4) says that after this child was sacrificed, the other two committed suicide out of sympathy for her.

The ancient laws of our ancestors, no one will
Cast them out against my will while I am still alive.
Nor in place of olive and the golden Gorgon
Will Eumolpus or his Thracian horde crown with garlands
The trident standing upright over the city's
Foundations, or Athena lose her place of honor.
Citizens, take for yourselves the child of my womb,
Save yourselves, win victory! For a single life
It cannot be that I will not save the city for you.
O fatherland, may all who dwell in you
Love you as I do! Thus we would dwell
In you at peace, and you would not suffer harm.

[101] These verses, gentlemen, formed part of our fathers' education. Though all women by nature love their children, the poet portrayed this woman as loving her country more than her children. His point was that if women will have the courage to do this, men have all the more reason to place devotion to their country ahead of everything else. They should not abandon their country and flee or disgrace it in front of all the Greeks, as Leocrates did.

[102] I wish to bring Homer also to your attention and praise his poetry. Your fathers considered him such an important poet that they established a law that every four years at the Panathenaia the rhapsodes recite the poems of this poet alone of all the poets.[71] This was their way of showing the Greeks their admiration for noble deeds. And rightly so, since the laws because of their brevity do not teach but merely order what one should do; the poets, on the other hand, by representing human life and selecting the noblest deeds, persuade men by using both reason and clear examples. [103] When Hector was encouraging the Trojans to fight for their country, he gave this speech:

Keep on then fighting by the ships. He who among you
finds his death and destiny by spear thrown or spear thrust,
let him die. He has no dishonor when he dies defending

[71] The Panathenaea was a festival celebrated every four years at the end of the Attic month of Hekatombaion (July) to honor the goddess Athena.

his country, for then his wife shall be saved and his young children,
and his property and his house shall not be damaged, if the Achaians
must go away with their ships to the beloved land of their fathers.[72]

[104] Your ancestors listened to these verses and were eager to imitate such deeds; they were so courageous that they were willing to die not only for their own country but for all of Greece as if it were their own land. When they took their stand against the barbarians at Marathon and defeated an army from all of Asia, by risking their own lives they gained a security that was shared by all Greeks.[73] Their fame did not make them arrogant but inspired them to live up to their reputation. They made themselves leaders of the Greeks and masters over the barbarians. They did not practice valor by words alone but demonstrated it to all by their actions.

[105] This is why the men who lived in our city then were so remarkable in both their public and private lives that when the Spartans, the most courageous men in the world, were in the past fighting against the Messenians,[74] the god prophesied that they would defeat their enemy by picking a leader from one of us. Indeed, if the god thought that our leaders were better than the two descendants of Heracles who always rule as kings in Sparta,[75] how can anyone doubt that their valor was without a rival? [106] What Greek does not know that they took Tyrtaeus from our city to be their general[76] and that under his command they defeated their enemy and organized their

---

[72] Lycurgus quotes these verses from *Iliad* 15.494–499 with three minor changes. I have adapted the translation of Richmond Lattimore to reflect these changes.

[73] The Athenians, supported only by the Plataeans, defeated a Persian army at Marathon in 490.

[74] For the Spartan conquest of Messenia, see above, 62.

[75] There were always two Spartan kings, each of whom traced his genealogy back to Heracles (Herod. 6.53, 7.204).

[76] Tyrtaeus was a Spartan poet who wrote at the time of the Second Messenian War (ca. 650). The legend that he was actually an Athenian appears first in Plato, *Laws* 629a and is repeated by later authors (Philochorus, *FGrHist* 328 F 215, Pausanias 4.15.6), but most modern scholars consider this an invention of Athenian propaganda.

system of training for their young men, a good policy not only to meet the immediate danger but for all time? He composed elegiac poems and left them behind for them so that they would learn to be courageous by listening to them. [107] They paid no attention to other poets but were so enthusiastic about this man that they established a law that whenever they were on campaign, they must summon everyone to the tent of the king to hear the poems of Tyrtaeus because they think this above all will make them willing to die for their country. Indeed, it is still useful to listen to these elegiac verses so you can understand the sort of deeds that brought men fame in their country:[77]

It is noble for the brave man to die, falling among
 The soldiers in front, fighting for his country.
But it is most wretched of all if he leaves behind
 His city and rich fields and goes begging,
Wandering with his mother and old father, with
 His small children and his wedded wife.
He will be hated by all those whomever he meets,
 Yielding to poverty and hateful need;
He brings shame on his family, disgrace to his noble shape;
 Complete dishonor and wretchedness follow him.
If then no one respects nor cares for the man who flees
 Or for his descendants after him,
Let us fight with spirit for this land, and let us die
 For our children, not sparing even our lives.
But you, young men, stand next to each and fight;
 Don't be the first to turn to shameful flight or fear,
But make great and strong the spirit in your breast,
 And fight among men as if you cared not for life.
Don't flee and abandon the older men, whose legs are
 No longer swift, the revered elders.
For this is indeed shameful: an old man lying fallen
 Among the soldiers in front, ahead of the young,
With his white head and his grey beard, breathing

[77] This elegy is one of the longest fragments of Tyrtaeus (Fr. 10 West) to survive. It is preserved only because Lycurgus quotes it here.

Out his valiant spirit in the dust,
Holding his bloody groin in his hands—
A sight that inspires shame and rage—
His flesh stripped bare. All is seemly for young men,
When they have the splendid bloom of lovely youth:
While alive, he looks handsome to men, lovely to women,
And beautiful as he falls among the soldiers in front.
But let each man go forward and stand firm, planting both feet
On the ground and biting his lip with his teeth.

[108] These are truly fine words and useful for those who are willing to take them to heart. The men who heard them were so inspired to bravery that they competed with our city for leadership and rightly so, for the finest actions were performed by both sides. Our ancestors defeated the first barbarians to invade Attica and proved that courage prevails over wealth and bravery over sheer numbers.[78] The Spartans then made their stand at Thermopylae, where they did not meet with the same success, but they far surpassed all men in bravery.[79] [109] For this reason, you can see written above their graves true testimonies of their courage for all the Greeks. For the Spartans:

O stranger, announce to the Spartans that here
We lie, obedient to their laws.[80]

And for our ancestors:

Fighting for the Greeks, the Athenians at Marathon
Brought low the might of the gold-apparell'd Medes.[81]

---

[78] Another allusion to the Athenian victory over the Persians in 490.

[79] Lycurgus alludes to the battle of Thermopylae in 480, where a small band of Spartans held back the much larger Persian army for several days before they were overwhelmed.

[80] This famous epigram is attributed to the poet Simonides (ca. 555–468) and is quoted by Herodotus (7.228.2), who gives a slightly different text ("obedient to their orders" instead of "obedient to their laws").

[81] This epigram is also attributed to Simonides. After Persian defeat of the Medes in the middle of the sixth century, the cultures of the two peoples were merged. As a result, the Greeks often called the Persians Medes.

[110] These deeds are good to recall; the praise earned by these men and the glory won by our city will be remembered forever. But not what Leocrates did: he willingly disgraced the glory the city has built up through all history. If you put him to death, all the Greeks will think you too hate such kinds of actions. If you do not, you will rob your ancestors of their glory and do great harm to the rest of our citizens. For if they no longer admire the former, they will try to imitate this man, since they will believe that although the men of old honored such deeds, you consider lack of shame, treason, and cowardice the most admirable qualities.

[111] If I cannot make you understand the right attitude to have toward such men, look at how our ancestors punished them. Just as they knew how to practice good actions, in the same way they chose to punish wicked actions. Consider, gentlemen, how angry they were at traitors, whom they treated as the common enemies of the city. [112] When Phrynichus was slain at night by the fountain near the willows by Apollodorus and Thrasybulus,[82] and both men were arrested and put in prison by Phrynichus' friends, the people found out what happened and released them from prison. They then questioned several under torture and through an investigation discovered that Phrynichus had betrayed the city, and his killers had been unjustly imprisoned. [113] The people voted on the motion of Critias[83] to put his corpse on trial for treason, and if it appeared that a traitor had been buried in their country, to dig up his bones and cast them out of Attica so that not even the bones of a man who had betrayed both his country and his city would lie buried in its territory. [114] They also decreed that if any people spoke in defense of the dead man, and the dead man was convicted, they would be subject to the same penalties

---

[82] Phrynichus was one of the leaders of the Four Hundred, a group of oligarchs who seized control of Athens in 411. According to Lysias (13.71), Thrasybulus of Calydon and Apollodorus of Megara plotted against him and on his return from an embassy to Sparta, Thrasybulus assassinated him. Democracy was restored soon afterwards. Thucydides (8.92) also recounts the incident, but does not name the assassin. The decree granting Thrasybulus citizenship for his deed has been preserved in an inscription (*IG* I^3 102).

[83] Critias later became leader of the Thirty Tyrants, who imposed a narrow oligarchy in Athens in 404.

as he was. They thought it wrong even to help those who had betrayed the rest and by the same token that the man who protected a traitor was also guilty of treason. By despising criminals and voting such measures against them, they delivered themselves safely from danger. Clerk, take their decree and read it.

[DECREE]

[115] You hear this decree, gentlemen. Next they dug up the traitor's bones and cast them out of Attica, and put to death the men who defended him, Aristarchus and Alexicles,[84] and did not even allow them to be buried in the country. Now that you have in your hands the very man who has betrayed our country yet still lives, will you use your vote to allow him to go unpunished? [116] Will you fall so far below the standard set by your ancestors? They punished men who helped a traitor only by their words; will you acquit a man who abandoned the democracy by his actions, not his words, as if he were innocent? Don't do it, gentlemen of the court. It is not in your nature or traditions to cast a vote that is unworthy of you. In fact, if there had been one decree of this kind in the past, one might be able to say that they passed it out of anger rather than from true conviction. But when they inflicted the same punishment on all, how is it not perfectly clear that they are by their very nature hostile to all such actions? [117] Hipparchus, the son of Timarchus,[85] did not wait for his trial for treason in the Assembly but allowed his case to go uncontested.[86] Your ancestors sentenced him to death, but since they did not have his person in custody as a hostage for his crimes, they tore down his statue from the Acropolis, melted it down, and made a pillar on which they voted to

[84] Aristarchus and Alexicles were associates of Phrynichus, but Lycurgus' account is inaccurate. Alexicles was arrested but later released (Thuc. 8.92.4, 93.1). After the fall of the Four Hundred, Alexicles fled to the Spartans at Deceleia (Thuc. 8.98), and Aristarchus went to the fortress of Oenoe, which he betrayed to the Thebans (Xen., *Hellenica* 1.7.28).

[85] The manuscripts give Timarchus as the name of Hipparchus' father, but earlier sources say it was Charmus.

[86] Hipparchus was a relative of the tyrants Peisistratus and Hippias and served as archon in 496/5 but was ostracized in 488/7 (*Ath. Pol.* 22.4). No other sources confirm the story found here, and Lycurgus may well have got it wrong.

inscribe the names of men who were under a curse and traitors. And Hipparchus himself is written upon the stele, along with the other traitors. [118] First, take the decree that ordered that the statue of Hipparchus the traitor be torn down from the Acropolis, then the inscription on the stele and the list of traitors also inscribed on this stele and read them, clerk.

[DECREE]

[119] What do you think, gentlemen? Do you think they passed the same sentence as you on guilty men, and did not, when they could not get their hands on his person, destroy the traitor's monument, punishing him with the harshest available penalties? Their aim was not just to melt down a bronze statue but to leave behind for future generations for the rest of time an example of how they dealt with traitors. [120] Take for them also the other decree about the men who moved to Deceleia[87] when the people were under siege by the Spartans so that they know that their ancestors used to inflict on traitors similar and consistent penalties. Read it out, clerk.

[DECREE]

[121] You hear this decree too, gentlemen, condemning those who moved to Deceleia in wartime and granting the right to any Athenian who wished, if someone was caught returning, to arrest him and bring him before the Thesmothetae, who were instructed to take him into custody and hand him over to the public executioner.[88] Well, then, this was the way they punished men who moved from one part of Attica to another; will you not put to death the man who left the city and the country, fled to Rhodes in time of war, and betrayed the people? How then will you appear to be the descendants of these men?

[122] It is also worthwhile for you to hear the decree about the man who was put to death on Salamis.[89] When this man tried to betray the city by only a speech, the Council took off their wreaths and killed

[87] The Spartans occupied Deceleia in 413 and used it as a base to make raids on Attica. Some Athenians who were sympathetic to Sparta joined them there.

[88] Lit. "the man in charge of the pit." One form of execution in Athens was for the condemned man to be thrown into a deep pit.

[89] According to Herodotus (9.4–5), the Persian general Mardonius sent Murychides to the Athenians on Salamis with a proposal that they join in an alliance

him with their own hands. This was a noble decree and one justly worthy of your ancestors. They showed their nobility not only in their character but also in the punishments they inflicted on criminals.

[DECREE]

[123] What then, gentlemen? Since you wish to imitate your ancestors, do you think it your traditional duty not to put Leocrates to death? When they executed a man who betrayed the city only by his words when it was lying in ruins, what do you think it is right for you to do to a man who not by his words but by his actions abandoned the city while it was still inhabited? Shouldn't the penalty you impose exceed theirs? When they inflicted such a punishment on those who tried to rob the city of the safety provided by the people, what is it right for you to do to the man who betrayed the safety of the people themselves? When they punished guilty men in this way to protect their reputation, what should you do to protect our country?

[124] These examples are enough for you to learn about your ancestors' attitude toward men who broke the city's laws; and yet I still want you to hear what the stele set up in the Council-house says about traitors and men who subvert the democracy, since learning from many examples makes your decision easy. After the Thirty, your fathers, who had endured the kind of suffering no Greek ever deserved, soon after their return from exile, shut off all paths to crime, since they knew from experience how the opponents of democracy got their start and made their attack. [125] They voted and swore an oath that if anyone tried to set up a tyranny or destroy the city or subvert the democracy, the person who saw this and killed him was free from pollution.[90] They thought it was better for the guilty to die rather than for them to fall into slavery after investigating the truth of the charges. At first they thought that citizens ought to live their lives in such a

---

with Persia. When Lycidas, a member of the Council, argued that they should accept the proposal, the other members of the Council and some bystanders stoned him to death.

[90] I.e., was not liable for punishment. After the fall of the Four Hundred in 411, the Athenians voted on the motion of Demophantus (see 127) to impose severe penalties for men who tried to set up a tyranny or to overthrow the democracy (And. 1.95–98). Lycurgus mistakenly dates the measure to after the overthrow of the Thirty in 403.

way that none of them would ever come even under suspicion for these crimes. Take this decree for me.

[DECREE]

[126] They wrote these words on the stele and placed it in the Council-house to remind all those who meet there every day and discuss the country's business how they should deal with such men. For this reason, if anyone caught sight of people even just intending to commit these crimes, they swore to kill him and rightly so. Although for other crimes the punishment should come afterwards, in the case of treason and subverting the democracy, punishment should precede the crime. For if you will let the moment slip by when they are still on the point of doing harm to the city, it is not possible to punish them after they have committed the crime. At that point they are in too strong a position for their victims to punish them.

[127] You certainly ought to draw inspiration from this foresight and these deeds; when you cast your votes, do not forget what kind of men your ancestors were, but encourage each other not to leave the court today until you have voted in the very same way they did. You have reminders and examples of their punishments clearly set out in the decrees about criminals. In the decree of Demophantus you have sworn to put to death by word or deed, by your own hand or by your vote, anyone who betrays our country. Don't think you have inherited the property your ancestors have left behind but have not also inherited their oaths and their pledge. Your fathers gave these as security to the gods and thus shared in the city's common prosperity.

[128] Your city was not alone in its attitude toward traitors; the Spartans also shared your convictions. Don't be angry at me for mentioning them many times; it is good to take examples from a city that respects justice and law so that you will cast with greater conviction a vote that is in keeping with justice and your oath. Well, the Spartans caught their king Pausanias betraying Greece to the Persians.[91] When he slipped away and sought refuge in temple of the goddess of the

[91] Pausanias was not the king of Sparta but acted as regent for his cousin Pleistarchus. Lycurgus' account of this incident is very close to that of Thucydides (1.128–134).

Brazen House,[92] they blocked up the entrance, stripped away the roof, and camped around it in a circle, [129] and did not leave until they had starved him to death. They made his punishment a conspicuous lesson to all that even the protection of the gods does not help traitors, and rightly so. For their first offense is often to commit sacrilege by robbing the gods of their traditional rites. But the most important evidence for the Spartans' attitudes is what I am about to describe: they enacted a law explicitly stating that those who refused to risk their lives for their country must die. Thus they imposed the very penalty that cowards happen to fear most and made survival in battle subject to the threat of punishment and shame. So that you may know that I have not told a story without proof but one with true examples, take the law for them.[93]

[LAW OF THE SPARTANS]

[130] Consider, gentlemen, how fine this law is and how useful not only for them but also for the rest of mankind. The fear inspired by one's fellow citizens is very strong and will compel men to face the dangers of the enemy. What man, who sees a traitor punished with death, will leave his country in time of danger? Who will love his own life more than the welfare of his country when he knows that this penalty hangs over his head? There should be no other penalty for cowardice than death, because when men know they will be forced to choose one of the two dangers facing them, they will much rather choose the danger posed by their enemies than the one posed by their laws and their fellow citizens.

[131] It would be far more just to put this man to death than those who deserted the army; the latter return to the city to fight for its defense or to share in the common misfortune of the other citizens, but this man fled from his fatherland to secure his own individual safety and did not even have the courage to defend his own hearth,

---

[92] There was a temple of Athena of the Brazen House on the acropolis of Sparta (Pausanias 3.17.2–3).

[93] This last command is addressed to the clerk (the preceding "you" are, of course, the judges). Lycurgus is the only orator to have the clerk read to the court a law from another city-state. According to Plutarch (*Lycurgus* 13.1), the Spartans did not write their laws down.

but alone of all mankind betrayed the common and binding ties of nature, which even animals, who lack reason, treat as the most important and serious bonds. [132] Birds are endowed by nature with the greatest speed, yet anyone can see that they are willing to die to protect their nest. For this reason the poets have said:

> Not even the wild bird, if it builds a home,
> Thinks it right to bear its nestlings in any other place.[94]

Yet Leocrates went to such an extreme of cowardice that he abandoned his fatherland to the enemy.

[133] For this reason no city has allowed him to live there as a metic, but they have driven him out as if he were worse than a murderer. Men who are in exile for murder and move to another city do not find those who receive them hostile, but what city would accept this man? Someone who did not help to defend his own country would perhaps face danger for someone else's country! Men like this, who will take advantage of a city's benefits, but will not consider it worth defending in adversity, make bad citizens, bad guest-friends,[95] and bad friends in private life. [134] And yet if this man is hated and driven out by men he has not even wronged, what penalty does he deserve from you who have suffered the most? Doesn't he deserve the ultimate penalty? Indeed, gentlemen, if there were a penalty worse than death, Leocrates, of all the traitors there ever were, would most deserve to suffer it. Other traitors were on the point of committing crimes when they were caught and then punished. This man alone, by abandoning the city, accomplished what he attempted to do and is now on trial for it.

[135] I am astonished at the men who intend to speak in his support; what reason will they have to ask for his acquittal? Will it be out of their friendship for him? In my opinion, they have no right to ask for a favor but deserve to die for having this man as a friend. Before Leocrates did this, it was not clear what sort of men they actually were; but now it is clear to all that they cultivate their friendship with him

---

[94] The author of these tragic verses is unknown. Their suitability in this context is questionable, and they have been suspected of being a later addition.

[95] Guest-friends (*xenoi*) are friends in foreign communities and are contrasted here with friends in one's own community.

because they share his character. As a result, they ought to defend themselves rather than ask you to let him off.

[136] I believe that his father, who has passed away, (if indeed the dead have any sense of what happens here) would be the harshest judge of all. This man abandoned his father's bronze statue in the temple of Zeus the Protector for the enemy to loot and deface. This statue, which his father set up as a monument to his own good character, he has made into an object of shame, since now he is called the father of this sort of man. [137] For this reason, gentlemen, many people have come up to me asking why I did not write this in the indictment, that he betrayed the statue of his father dedicated in the temple of Zeus the Protector. I was not unaware, gentlemen, that this crime merits the greatest punishment, but I did not think I should put the name of Zeus the Protector on the indictment when trying this man for treason.

[138] What shocks me most of all is that you do not realize that those who for a fee join in defending men on trial, although they have no connection either by blood or by friendship with defendants, ought to stir your most intense anger. Helping to defend someone's crimes is proof that the advocates would also have a share in their actions. They should use their eloquence not against you but for you, the laws, and the democracy. [139] Some of these men are no longer trying to distract you by arguments but ask you to acquit men on trial because of their own liturgies.[96] This makes me the most angry. They performed these to benefit their own household, yet they ask you to reward them with a public favor! If someone keeps horses or finances a splendid chorus or spends his money on other such activities, he does not deserve this kind of favor from you—for these he wins a crown for himself and brings no benefit to anyone else—but he deserves a favor if he has done a splendid job commanding a trireme or having walls constructed around the country or contributing from his

---

[96] Liturgies were services performed by wealthy Athenians. There were two types of liturgies (Dem. 20.18–23). The first kind was assigned every year and required men to finance a chorus or sponsor an athletic competition. The second type was imposed only in military emergencies and required men to equip and command triremes, pay taxes for the military budget, or make a contribution toward the building of fortifications.

private funds to the common defense. [140] These activities are performed for all of you in common, and in them you can see the virtue of the men who have contributed; in other cases you see only the wealth of men who have spent money. I do not think anyone has brought such immense benefits to the city that he has the right to ask for the extraordinary favor of freeing a traitor from punishment. Nor do I think anyone so foolish as to show his devotion to the city, yet, at the same time, help the man who has destroyed all his devotion has achieved. Unless, by Zeus, these men do not share the same interests as our country.

[141] Even if the law does not require judges to reach their verdicts in any other cases with their children and wives seated next to them, it would be righteous for them to do this in cases of treason, so that they would have right before their eyes the people who share in their danger to remind them that these men do not deserve the pity accorded to all men and to make their verdicts more severe against the criminal. Since neither law nor custom requires this, and you must render your verdicts on their behalf, take revenge on Leocrates and put him to death, and then report to your children and wives that once you had the man who betrayed them in your power, you punished him. [142] It would be a terrible shock if Leocrates, who fled, did not face danger, and failed to protect the city, thinks he should have equal rights as the men who remained here, stayed at their posts, faced danger, and saved the city. But he comes to share the temples, sacrifices, market, laws, and privileges of citizenship, which 1,000 of your citizens died at Chaeronea to preserve, men whom the city buried at public expense. This man showed no shame as he looked on the elegiac verses written on their tomb when he returned to the city; on the contrary, he thought he could strut around shamelessly in full sight of those who were mourning their misfortunes.

[143] Soon he will ask you to hear his defense in accordance with the laws.[97] Ask him, which laws? The ones he betrayed when he fled? He will ask you to let him live inside the walls of his country. Which walls? The ones he alone of all the citizens did not help defend? Next he will call on the gods to save him from danger. Which gods? Not

[97] Another allusion to the Dicastic Oath, which required the court to hear both accuser and defendant before voting.

the ones whose temples, shrines, and precincts he betrayed. He will plead and beg for pity. Whom is he asking? Not those he did not have the courage to join in contributing to our defense. Let him beg the Rhodians; he thought safety lay in their city rather than in his own country. [144] What man at any age could take pity on this man? The older men? He did his best not to care for them in old age and to deprive them of burial in the free soil of their country. The younger men? What young man who remembers his comrades, who took their positions next to each other at Chaeronea and shared the same dangers, could protect the man who betrayed their graves? Which of them could with the same vote condemn as madmen those who died for freedom and acquit without punishment, as if he were perfectly sane, the man who betrayed his country? [145] If you do, you will grant to anyone who wishes the license to harm by word and deed both you and the people. For when a man who has abandoned the city, sentenced himself to exile, lived in Megara with a patron for five or six years, then moves around freely in our city, not only does this mean that exiles are returning but that a man, who decreed by his clear vote that Attica be turned into a pasture for sheep to graze in, will live together with you in this land.

[146] Before I step down, I wish to say a few words and introduce a decree that the people passed about religious piety. You men who are about to cast your votes will find it useful. Read it for me.

[DECREE]

Well, for my part, I am denouncing the man who is destroying all these things to you who have it in your power to punish him. It is your duty to punish him both for your own sake and for the gods. Before they come to trial, only the men who have committed the crimes are guilty; once there is a trial, those who fail to prosecute them as justice demands are also guilty. You know well, gentlemen, that although you cast your vote in secret, each of you will make his decision clear to the gods.[98] [147] In my opinion, gentlemen, you are casting one vote today to punish all the greatest and most terrible crimes,

---

[98] The idea that even though their vote is secret, the gods will know what the judges decide is a commonplace in Attic oratory. See Lys. 6.53, Dem. 19.239, Pseudo-Dem. 59.126.

for you can see Leocrates is guilty of every one of them: treason because he left the city and put it in the hands of the enemy; subverting the democracy because he did not face danger in defense of freedom; impiety because he is guilty of doing all he could to ravage the sacred precincts and destroy the temples; mistreatment of parents by destroying their tombs and robbing them of their ancestral rites; and desertion and cowardice for refusing to report to the generals for duty. [148] Who then will vote to acquit him or show sympathy for his deliberate crimes? Is anyone so foolish as to save this man and thereby entrust his own safety to men who wish to betray us? Or to pity him and thereby choose to die unpitied at the hands of the enemy?

[149] By defending our country, our temples, and our laws, I have conducted this case in a fashion both just and correct, without attacking the rest of this man's life or making irrelevant charges. Each of you must now realize that a vote to acquit Leocrates is a vote to condemn our country to death and destruction. There are two urns placed before you, one for treason, the other for survival,[99] and you are casting your votes either to destroy our country or to keep it safe and prosperous. [150] If you acquit Leocrates, you will vote to betray the city, the temples, and the fleet; if you put him to death, you will encourage the defense and protection of the country, its revenues, and its prosperity. Imagine then, men of Athens, that the land and the trees are

---

[99] Originally, judges were given one pebble and voted by putting it in either of the two urns, one for the accuser, the other for the defendant. Later, judges were given two ballots in the shape of a disk with a peg in the center. The peg of the ballot for the accuser was pierced, that for the defendant was unpierced. In this system, all the votes that counted were placed in one urn: judges voted for the accuser by placing the pierced ballot in this urn, for the defendant by placing the unpierced ballot in the same urn. After voting they placed the ballot they did not use in the other urn. Lycurgus appears, however, to refer to the earlier system, which was discontinued by 346/45 (Aes. 1.79). A. Boegehold (*Classical Philology* 80.2 [1985]: 132–135) notes that the words describing the voting procedure form two-thirds of a tragic iambic trimeter and suggests that Lycurgus is quoting from a play, possibly Euripides' *Palamedes.* See, however, A. R. W. Harrison, *Law of Athens: Procedure* (Oxford, 1971), 165, n. 2, for an alternative explanation.

imploring you; the harbors, the shipsheds, and the city walls are asking you; and the temples and the shrines are pleading with you to defend them. Make an example out of Leocrates; remember the charges against him, for pity and tears do not have a stronger claim than the preservation of the laws and the people.

FRAGMENTS

The ancient lexicon called the *Suda* lists the titles of fourteen speeches attributed to Lycurgus, but the *Life of Lycurgus* says there were fifteen speeches attributed to him. Harpocration gives the titles of fourteen speeches by Lycurgus, one of which (*Against Aristogeiton*) may comprise two speeches. Harpocration mentions a speech (*Defense of His Career in Politics*) not found in the list of titles found in the *Suda* and a speech (*Against Dexippus*) that may actually have been written by Lysias. Most of the fragments are preserved in ancient lexica and are often very brief, sometimes only a word or a phrase. I have included only the fragments that give some indication about the content of the lost speech and have omitted the titles of the speeches in the entries from the lexica. For an excellent discussion of the fragments, see N. C. Conomis, "Notes on the Fragments of Lycurgus," *Klio* 39 (1961): 72–152. The numbering and the text of the fragments are taken from N. C. Conomis, *Lycurgi Oratio in Leocratem cum Ceterarum Lycurgi Orationum Fragmentis* (Leipzig, 1970).

N.B. I have given the context in which each fragment is found and have indicated what are thought to be Lycurgus' actual words in italics.

FRAGMENT I. DEFENSE OF HIS CAREER IN POLITICS

The biography of Lycurgus in the *Lives of the Ten Orators* (Pseudo-Plut., *Moralia* 842f) relates that Lycurgus, when about to die, asked to be carried to the Council to present his accounts. When no one except Menesaichmus dared to accuse him, Lycurgus refuted his charges and was then carried home, where he died. This information dates the speech to around 324, the year of Lycurgus' death. Lycurgus may have been called upon to account for his financial management, such as how he raised revenues from the sale of hides of sacrificial animals and how he spent money on the navy. The speech may have provided much of the information about Athenian finances found in the *Life of Lycurgus.* Fragment 1.5 may refer to Lycurgus' successful opposition to the revolt of Agis III of Sparta against Alexander in 331–30.[1]

1.1. Harpocration: *hide-money* (*dermatikon*). The speaker could call the money remaining from the sale of the hides (of sacrificial animals) "hide-money."[2]

1.2. Harpocration: *furnish with benches*—for placing seats.[3] Benches (*hedolia*) are also seats on ships.

1.3. Harpocration: *Hekatompedon.*[4] The Parthenon was called by some the Hekatompedon (lit. "hundred-feet long") because of its beauty and proportion, not because of its size.

1.4. Harpocration: *dockyards and shipsheds.* The entire place where triremes are dragged on shore and dragged to the sea again is sometimes called dockyards, as Lycurgus indicates . . .

1.5. Rutilius Lupus 1.7:[5] *For when the youth were stirred up, rashly seizing arms, and trying to injure the Thessalians, who were at peace, I forced the Council to restrain the violence of the young men with its authority. I prevailed upon the treasurers not to provide them with funds for their campaign. I blocked the way when the arsenal was opened and pre-*

---

[1] Aeschines (3.167) alludes to an attempt of Demosthenes to interfere in Thessaly during the revolt of Agis III.

[2] The revenues from the sale of hides could be considerable. A fragment of an inscription dated to the Lycurgan period (*IG* II[2] 1496) reveals that the total for 334/33 was over five thousand drachmas.

[3] Lycurgus is probably referring to the marble seats he installed in the theater of Dionysus. See. A. W. Pickard-Cambridge, *The Theatre of Dionysus in Athens* (Oxford, 1946), 136–144.

[4] Documents from the fifth and fourth centuries BC use the word Hekatompedon to refer to certain parts of the Parthenon. Lycurgus may have been the first author to apply the word to the entire building.

[5] Here and elsewhere, Rutilius Lupus gives a Latin version of Lycurgus' Greek.

vented arms from being removed. Thus by my efforts alone, as you know, an unnecessary war did not break out.

FRAGMENT 2. AGAINST ARISTOGEITON

Lycurgus and Demosthenes cooperated in a prosecution of Aristogeiton for exercising certain political rights while he was listed as a public debtor. Two speeches by Demosthenes (*Against Aristogeiton* [25, 26]) have been preserved in their entirety, though their authenticity has been questioned; only fragments survive from Lycurgus' speech. Since Lycurgus was older, he delivered the first speech. According to Demosthenes (25.14), Lycurgus dealt with the charge against Aristogeiton, the facts of the case, and the main legal arguments. This left Demosthenes with topics normally only appropriate to the *epilogos,* or final part of a court speech, such as the defendant's reputation and general reasons to punish criminals and to uphold the law. Dinarchus (2.13) states that Lycurgus brought the main charge and proved that Aristogeiton was guilty. Despite his apparent conviction, Aristogeiton somehow managed to resume his political career and was prosecuted again in 322 for receiving money from Harpalus.[6] The speech must have been delivered before the Harpalus affair in 324, but it is difficult to determine its date more precisely.

2.1. Harpocration: *Metroion. Having inscribed the laws, they placed them in the Metroion.*

2.2. Harpocration: *nonregistration.* A kind of suit is called by this name and is brought against men who owed money to the public treasury and were listed for this reason, but whose names were erased before they paid.

2.3. Harpocration: *age group of the city.* Instead of "those in an age group," "the young men."

2.4. Harpocration: *pit.* The place where wrongdoers are punished at Athens is given this specific name.

2.5. Harpocration: *three-cornered court.* The name of a court, perhaps because it is in the shape of a triangle.[7]

---

[6] See Din. 2 in this volume.

[7] This court is mentioned by several authors. Homer Thompson (*Hesperia* 23 [1954]: 61 with n. 50) places it in the southwest corner of the Agora.

2.6. Harpocration: *punished with a thousand.* Instead of "owing a thousand drachmas."[8]

2.7. Harpocration: *false registration.* The name of a suit that those who are registered as debtors to the public treasury bring when someone has falsely registered them on the plaque placed next to the goddess.[9]

FRAGMENT 3. AGAINST AUTOLYCUS

In 1.53, Lycurgus mentions a citizen named Autolycus, who was caught sending his family away from Attica during the panic after the Athenian defeat at Chaeronea and as a result was condemned and punished. The *Life of Lycurgus* and Harpocration (*s.v.* Autolycus) reveal that it was Lycurgus who brought the case against Autolycus. He probably did so not long after the battle of Chaeronea, that is, late in 338 or soon afterwards. The fragments of this speech suggest that Lycurgus used several of the same topics and phrases that he did in *Against Leocrates.*

3.1. Scholion on Demosthenes 54.1. The proemium of the speech grasps of the main subject: *Although many great trials have come before you, you have never come to judge a case of such importance.*

3.2. *Suda: Land for sheep to graze in.* Which the enemy has made into farmland, which cattle graze on. *But he abandoned Attica as land for sheep to graze in.*"[10]

3.3. Harpocration: *burial mound.* Burial mounds are graves, as the orator himself makes clear.[11]

---

[8] Lycurgus is probably alluding to the penalty for bringing a frivolous prosecution. See note 6 in *Against Leocrates.* The word also occurred in Fragment 9 (*Against Cephisodotus*) (see below).

[9] The goddess is Athena. The names of public debtors were listed on tablets kept near the temple of Athena on the Acropolis.

[10] A similar expression occurs in 1.145.

[11] Lycurgus may have accused Autolycus of abandoning the graves of his ancestors in the same way that he accused Leocrates of this crime when he left Attica (1.9, 59, 97, 147).

FRAGMENT 4. DEFENSE AGAINST DEMADES AT HIS RENDERING OF ACCOUNTS

On Demades, see Fragment 9.

4.1. Harpocration: *Dismounter* and *to dismount* and *dismounter's wheels.* "The dismounter" is a kind of equestrian contest, and "to dismount" is to compete in "the dismounter" and "dismounter's wheels" take their name from this contest.[12]

4.2. Harpocration: *He will play the tragic parts created for other men.* Didymus says that this is a proverbial expression used about men who adapt themselves to different circumstances and put on haughty airs.[13]

FRAGMENT 5. ON HIS ADMINISTRATION

The speech appears to have been a defense of Lycurgus' management of Athenian finances and may have been delivered when he rendered his accounts for one of his terms as financial administrator.

5.1a. Harpocration: *scrutinized.* This word was used in regard to politicians, even if they had not held any office. *There are three scrutinies according to the law, one which examines the nine archons; another, the speakers; and a third, the generals.* In the same speech he also says *scrutiny of horses.*

5.1b. Scholion on Aeschines 1.195. Lycurgus says that *it is necessary to scrutinize not all men about prostitution but only the speakers who are active in politics and propose decrees.*

5.2. Harpocration: *crowning the victors. But indeed you crowned Callisthenes with a crown worth one hundred minas.*[14]

5.3. Harpocration: *Epicrates.* Lycurgus . . . says that there was a bronze statue of him set up because of his law about the ephebes.[15] They say he acquired a fortune of six hundred talents.

---

[12] This contest was part of the Panathenaea in honor of Athena. The contestants jumped off a chariot. Lycurgus may have compared Demades to a participant in this contest because he constantly changed (or "jumped away from") his policies to suit circumstances. For the charge of inconsistency, see Fragment 4.2.

[13] The meaning of the phrase is not altogether clear.

[14] Callisthenes may have been a politician who opposed Macedon, if he is the same person who moved a decree to counter Philip's threatened invasion of Attica in 343 (Dem. 18.37–38, 19.86).

[15] On Lycurgus' reform of the *ephebeia,* see the Introduction to Lycurgus.

5.4. Bekker, *Anecdota* 145.30: *From the sacred funds, which we supervised.*

5.6. Harpocration: *Temple of Good Fortune.*[16]

5.7. Harpocration: *goatskins.* They called the nets made from woolen threads goatskins.[17]

FRAGMENT 6. ON THE PRIESTESS

The largest number of fragments from a lost speech of Lycurgus comes from *On the Priestess.* Fragment 6.1 indicates the speech was delivered in court about a public charge but does not reveal the nature of the charge nor whether Lycurgus spoke for the prosecution or the defense. Since 6.11 mentions the *genos* (kinship group) of the Eteobutadai, to which Lycurgus belonged and that provided the priestess of Athena Polias on the Acropolis; 6.4 mentions the duties of a priestess; and 6.8 alludes to a sacrifice to Athena, Lycurgus may have delivered the speech in defense of a priestess of Athena Polias from his own *genos* against charges that she had somehow failed to perform her duties or misappropriated funds for sacrifices.[18] This interpretation would explain the references to sacrificial practices and to the cult of Athena Nike, which was also located on the Acropolis (6.13). The fragments reveal Lycurgus' detailed knowledge of religious practices.

6.1. Harpocration: *If this trial were about a private matter, I would have asked you to give me a favorable hearing.* A little later he says: *As it is, I think you will do this even without my request.*

6.2. Harpocration: *to make an extra sacrifice* and *extra sacrifice.* This appears to be used for a sacrifice performed for all. *Moreover, these sacrifices were performed last and were extra sacrifices in addition to the other sacrifices.*

---

[16] There was a sanctuary of Good Fortune in the western part of Athens. A decree moved by Lycurgus concerns religious property used in this cult (*IG* II^2 333). Lycurgus may have defended his management of this cult.

[17] Statues of Athena were often adorned with a goatskin (see *IG* II^2 333, line 11). The priestess of Athena might carry this goatskin in religious processions.

[18] Priestesses had to submit their accounts for public examination (Aes. 3.18).

6.3. Harpocration: *They punished Micon the painter (with a penalty) up to thirty months.*[19]

6.4. *Suda: So that it is required by decree for the priestess to mark the records with a sign.*[20]

6.6. Harpocration: *Alope.* The daughter of Cercyon, who gave birth to Hippothoon, the son of Poseidon, after whom the tribe Hippothontis is named.

6.9. Harpocration: *monthly sacrifices.*[21]

6.10. Harpocration: *sacrificial hearth.*[22]

6.11. Harpocration: *Eteobutadai.* A *genos* among the Athenians, that is, they are the true descendants of Boutes.

6.12. Harpocration: *tablets* (*kyrbeis*).[23]

6.13. Harpocration: *Athena Nike* (*Victory*).

6.15. Harpocration: *pelanos* (*liquid offering*).

6.16. Harpocration: *Plynteria.*[24]

6.17. Harpocration: *Polygnotus.*[25]

---

[19] Micon was a famous painter. According to some, he painted the Battle of Marathon in the Painted Stoa. Something is wrong with the Greek text, but no satisfactory solution has yet been proposed. One scholar has suggested that "months" should be emended to "*minas,*" that is, a sum of Attic money. (See below, Fr. 6.17n.)

[20] Priests and priestesses kept accounts of the funds they administered for sacrifices and had to provide them to the Logistai every year. See Aes. 3.18. For the use of seals by priests as a security device, see *IG* I[3] 52. This fragment may indicate that the priestess was accused of financial impropriety when she rendered her accounts.

[21] Certain sacrifices in Athens were offered every month, while others were given only once a year. See J. Mikalson, *The Sacred and Civil Calendar of the Athenian Year* (Princeton, 1975): 13–24.

[22] This type of altar was normally used for sacrifices to heroes. Lycurgus may be referring to rites for the hero Butes, the ancestor of the Eteobutadai, of which he was a member.

[23] The laws of Solon were written on these *kyrbeis,* which included religious calendars, to which Lycurgus may have referred.

[24] According to Plutarch (*Alcibiades* 34.1), the Plynteria was a festival for Athena celebrated on Thargelion 25, that is, in the spring of each year.

[25] Polygnotus was a painter from Thasos, who received Athenian citizenship for painting the Battle of Marathon in the Painted Stoa (Plut., *Cimon* 4). (See above, Fr. 6.3n.)

6.18. Harpocration: *preliminary offering.*

6.19. Harpocration, *s.v. skiron.* Lycurgus in *On the Priestess.* Those who have written about festivals and months at Athens . . . say that the *skiron* was a large sunshade that was held over the priestess of Athena, the priest of Apollo, and the priest of Helios as they went from the Acropolis to a certain place called Skiron. The Eteobutadai carry this.

6.20. Harpocration: *table setter.*[26]

6.21. Harpocration: *tritomenis* (*third day of the month*).[27]

6.22. Harpocration: *Athena of Health.*[28]

FRAGMENT 7. ABOUT THE PRIESTHOOD

Many of the priesthoods in Attica were held by kinship groups called *gene.* This speech apparently concerned a dispute between two of these *gene* called the Croconidai and the Coironidai over privileges attached to a priesthood, probably that of Dionysus Theoinos. Lycurgus appears to have argued that the Coironidai were descended from Coiron, who was a bastard half-brother of the Crocon, the legitimate son of Triptolemus, and thus the Croconidai had the better claim.[29]

7.1. *Suda, s.v. procharisteria.* The day on which all those in office would sacrifice to Athena when the crops began to grow and winter was already ending.[30] *The most ancient sacrifice for the arrival of the goddess, which was called the Procharisteria for the sprouting of growing crops.*

7.2. Harpocration, *s.v. Coiranidai.* There is a speech of Lycurgus that is given this title: *Dispute of the Croconidai with the Coiranidai,* which several think is the work of Philinus. . . . The person who wrote

---

[26] This was the name of a priestess who assisted the priestess of Athena Polias.

[27] Lycurgus appears to refer to the festival for the birth of Athena, which was celebrated on the third day of each month.

[28] Aristonicus of Marathon, an associate of Lycurgus, passed a decree about sacrifices for Athena of Health during the 330s (*IG* II^2 334 = Schwenk no. 17).

[29] See R. Parker, *Athenian Religion: A History* (Oxford, 1996): 302–304.

[30] Harpocration says the sacrifice was offered to Persephone.

the speech, whoever he is, says they were called by three names: Coironidai, Philieis, and Perithoidai.[31]

7.3. Harpocration: *Theoinia.* The festival of Dionysus in the demes was called Theonia, during which the member of *gene* used to offer sacrifices. They used to call Dionysus Theoinos, . . .

7.4. Harpocration: *Cynnidai.* A *genos* among the Athenians.

7.5. Athenaeus 10.425b. These *oinoptai* used to keep an eye on matters at banquets to see that the participants drank equal amounts. It was a minor magistracy, as the orator Philinus says in *The Dispute of the Croconidai: And there were three oinoptai, who used to provide lamps and wicks to diners.*[32]

7.6. Harpocration: *Skambonidai.* It is a deme of the tribe Leontis.[33]

FRAGMENT 8. AGAINST ISCHYRIAS

We do not know of any politicians named Ischyrias during Lycurgus' lifetime, but there is an Ischyrias who passed a decree in 306/5 about money to be paid by the Treasurers of Athena (*IG* II^2 1492, lines 108, 114). The sole fragment from the speech (Harpocration: *cross beam*) does not help us to determine the nature of the case.

FRAGMENT 9. AGAINST CEPHISODOTUS CONCERNING THE HONORS TO DEMADES

The fragment from the prologue reveals that the speech was delivered by Lycurgus when prosecuting Cephisodotus for passing an illegal decree of honors for Demades. Lycurgus may have claimed that Cephisodotus was disenfranchised and thus unable to propose a decree. He also appears to have argued that Demades was not worthy of honors and contrasted his actions with the achievement of Pericles

---

[31] Toeppfer (*Attische Genealogie* [repr. New York, 1973], 101–110) suggested that Perithoidai was the name of the deme; Philieis, the name of the phratry; and Coironidai, the name of the *genos.*

[32] This fragment is attributed to Lycurgus because Harpocration (*s.v.* Coironidai) says some believed this speech of Lycurgus was written by Philinus.

[33] Lycurgus may have mentioned this deme because its inhabitants claimed Crocon was the first to live there (Pausanias 1.37.5).

(9.1, 2). Cephisodotus may have proposed his decree for Demades' role in securing peace with Philip after the Athenian defeat at Chaeronea in 338, since Lycurgus mentioned the Macedonian king in his speech (9.3). On the other hand, the honors may have been voted after Demades persuaded Alexander not to invade Attica in 335. Lycurgus apparently lost the case (Din. 1.101). In addition to the fragments given here, see also Fragment 2.6.

9.1. [Cornutus], *Art of Rhetoric* 167. The prologue grasps (the main topic) even in the beginning, as Lycurgus (says): *I will show that the decree is illegal and that the man does not deserve the grant (of honors).*

9.2. Lexicon from Patmos (= *Lexica Graeca Minora* 160): *Pericles, after capturing Samos and Euboea and Aegina, building the Propylaea, the Odeion and the Hekatompedon, and depositing ten thousand talents of gold on the Acropolis, was crowned with an olive wreath.*

9.3. Athenaeus 11.476d. The orator Lycurgus says in *Against Demades* that King Philip drank a toast in a horn to those whom he considered his friends.

FRAGMENTS 10–11. AGAINST LYCOPHRON I–II

On the background to this pair of speeches, see the Introduction to Hyperides 1 in this volume.

10–11.1. Harpocration: *I am amazed if we impose the death penalty on enslavers, who only deprive us of our slaves.*[34]

10–11.2. *Suda: For it is not righteous to let a man go unpunished who has broken the laws, which preserve the democracy, and has been an expounder*[35] *and legislator of other evil practices.*

10–11.3. Stobaeus, *Anthology* 4.22.63 (Hense): *When a wife no longer lives in harmony with her husband, the rest of her life becomes unlivable.*

---

[34] Lycurgus is probably contrasting the harsh penalty for enslavers (*Ath. Pol.* 52.1) with a relatively light penalty for another more serious offense. Lycurgus' definition of the term "enslaver" may not be the standard one; the term normally seems to refer to someone who enslaved free persons.

[35] The manuscripts read "expounder," but Conomis and others propose changing this word to "introducer."

10–11.4. Harpocration: *houseless.*[36] Instead of "uninhabited."

10–11.6. Harpocration: *Hipparchus, the son of Peisistratus. . . .*[37]

10–11.7. Harpocration: *basket bearers.*[38]

10–11.8. Harpocration: *shrine of Melanippus.* A hero shrine of Melanippus, the son of Theseus, . . .

10–11.10. Harpocration: *Hyakinthides.* They are daughters of Hyacinthus of Sparta.[39]

10–11.11. Stobaeus, *Anthology* 3.2.30 (Hense).[40] *Those men who use the advantages given by nature for evil ends find that good fortune is their enemy. For instance, if a man is courageous and prefers to be a pirate rather than a soldier or if a man is strong and prefers to live as a robber . . . to give advice, or if a man is good-looking and prefers to seduce women rather than marry them, this man is a traitor to the gifts given him by nature.*

10–11.12. Athenaeus 6.266f–267a. The Athenians, out of concern for the condition of slaves, passed a law that charges of outrage (*hybris*) could also be brought on behalf of slaves. Hyperides the orator in fact states this in *Against Mantitheus.* Lycurgus makes similar statements in his first speech *Against Lycophron* . . .

---

[36] Lycurgus may have claimed that Lycophron broke up the house of the woman he seduced.

[37] Hipparchus was the son of the tyrant Peisistratus and the younger brother of Hippias, who became tyrant after his father's death. Hipparchus was killed by Harmodius and Aristogeiton for insulting the former's sister. Lycurgus may have compared Lycophron to Hipparchus, since both men insulted a woman's honor.

[38] These "basket bearers" were upper-class women who carried baskets containing ritual items during the Panathenaea. Lycurgus may have mentioned them in connection with the insult to Harmodius' sister (see preceding note). Hipparchus and Hippias invited her to be a "basket bearer," then refused to allow her to participate, claiming she was somehow unworthy (Thuc. 6.56).

[39] Hyacinthus was a Spartan who sacrificed his daughters for Athens. Lycurgus may have contrasted his devotion to Athens with Lycophron's seduction of a married woman.

[40] Stobaeus does not attribute this passage to the *Against Lycophron,* but the topic fits the context of the speech.

10–11.13. Harpocration: *kitchen.* A certain part of the house is so called, the part we call the "cook's room."[41] *Against Lycophron* II.

10–11.14. Harpocration: *enclosure.*[42]

FRAGMENT 12. AGAINST LYSICLES

The main Athenian forces at the battle of Chaeronea were led by Lysicles and Stratocles; the general Chares commanded a force of mercenaries. Stratocles may have died in battle, and Chares appears to have fled into exile after the battle. Lycurgus prosecuted the remaining general, Lysicles, either at his *euthynai* or by *eisangelia.* The fragments of the speech do not indicate the nature of the charge, but Lycurgus probably accused Lysicles of treason or bribery, the standard charge brought against unsuccessful generals. Lycurgus won a conviction, and Lysicles was executed (Diodorus Siculus 16.88).

12.1. Diodorus Siculus 16.88.2: *You were a general, Lysicles, and after a thousand citizens died and two thousand were captured, after a trophy was erected to mark the defeat of the city, and all Greece fell into slavery, and after all these events took place under your command and generalship, you have the audacity to live and look on the light of day and thrust your way into the marketplace, when you serve as a reminder of our country's shame and reproach.*

12.2. Harpocration: *Lebadeia.*[43]

12.3. Harpocration: *battle at Delium.*[44] Delium is an area in Boeotia. The Athenians fought there and were defeated by the Boeotians.

---

[41] Lycurgus may have accused Lycophron of meeting his lover in this part of her house.

[42] Greek houses were often surrounded by an enclosure wall. Lycurgus may have accused Lycophron of breaking through this wall to reach the woman he allegedly seduced.

[43] Lycurgus appears to have mentioned the city because the Athenians retreated there after their defeat and sent heralds to ask Philip to return the bodies of their soldiers who died in battle.

[44] Lycurgus may have compared the Athenian defeat at Delium in 424 BC (Thuc. 4.89–99) with their defeat at Chaeronea. He may also have contrasted the Athenian general Hippocrates, who died at Delium, with Lysicles, to accuse the latter of cowardice.

FRAGMENT 13. ON THE ORACLES

The date and occasion are unknown. Some scholars have suggested the speech concerned oracles about the defeat at Chaeronea (see Din. 1.98); others believe the oracles related to the founding of a new ritual or the restoration of an old cult.

13.1a. *Suda: In a democracy you must say other things. . . .*[45] *The actions you boast about, others are ashamed of.*

FRAGMENT 14. AGAINST MENESAICHMUS

Menesaichmus was a prominent politician, who took over Lycurgus' position as director of Athenian finances. He attacked Lycurgus at Lycurgus' last *euthynai* (see Fr. 1) and prosecuted the sons of Lycurgus after the latter's death (Plut., *Moralia* 842e). Lycurgus appears to have brought a charge of impiety against Menesaichmus by the procedure of *eisangelia.* The fragments of the speech suggest Menesaichmus infringed some ritual connected with the annual pilgrimage (*theoria*) to Delos. Lycurgus won the case, but we do not know what penalty the court imposed on Menesaichmus. The punishment could not have been death, exile, or loss of citizen rights, since Menesaichmus remained active in politics.

14.1. Berlin Papyrus 11748: *Men of the court, (to show) that it is not even possible to sacrifice in the way Menesaichmus says without committing impiety, he (i.e., the clerk) will read you the testimony of Theogenes, who acted as herald for Diodorus, who knows that if a private individual sacrifices and Diodorus is not present. . . .*[46]

14.2a. Lexicon from Patmos (*Lexica Graeca Minora* 159), *s.v. eiresione.* Branches of olive and daphne placed in front of houses, full of many ripe fruits tied together. People used to do this when there was a plague and the god made a prophecy. "*And adorning a large branch with all the fruits that the seasons produced at the time, they dedicated it to Apollo in front of their doors, calling it* eiresione. *They made an offer-*

[45] The text is damaged here, and no satisfactory emendation has been proposed.

[46] The papyrus becomes fragmentary at this point. It appears to have been illegal to offer certain sacrifices without official supervision. Compare the case mentioned at Pseudo-Dem. 59.116–117.

ing of first fruits from all that grew out of the earth, since the suppliant bough dedicated to Apollo brought an end to the barrenness of our land.[47] Codex Darmstadt 2773, fol. 250: *And so each our ancestors is said to have placed each by his own door a suppliant branch to Apollo, now (called)* eiresione.

14.3. Harpocration: *And we call this festival Pyanopsia, but the rest of the Greeks Panopsia, since they saw all the fruits by sight* (*opsis*). All those who have written about festivals at Athens say that the Pyanopsia is celebrated on the seventh day of Pyanopsion. During this, they boil beans, and the *eiresione* is celebrated.

14.4. *Suda: Proerosia.* The sacrifices occurring before plowing for the coming harvest for the purpose of celebrating initiations. *For now I owe you many great honors and am eager to perform the* Proerosia *before all the Greeks who consult oracles.*

14.5a. Scholion on Gregory of Nazianzen. The orator Lycurgus says . . . that when there was a plague among the Hyperboreans, Abaris worked as a hired laborer for Apollo. After learning prophecies from him, he went around Greece prophesying, holding the shaft of Apollo as a token.[48]

14.5b. Harpocration. They say that when there was a plague over the entire world, Apollo prophesied to the Greeks and barbarians who consulted the oracle that the Athenian people should offer prayers on behalf of all men. When many nations sent envoys to them, they say that Abaris came from the Hyperboreans as an envoy . . . [49]

14.7. Harpocration: *Deliasts.* The pilgrims who went out to Delos.[50]

14.8. Harpocration: *island of Hecate.*[51]

14.10. Harpocration, *s.v.* groats (*prokonia*)[52] Lycurgus in *Against Menesaichmus.*

---

[47] An entry in the *Etymologicum Magnum* (303.34) appears to summarize this passage.

[48] The token Abaris carried was an arrow of Apollo; see Herod. 4.36.

[49] Harpocration does not cite Lycurgus, but the scholion on Gregory of Nazianzen suggests he may have taken this information from the orator.

[50] The annual pilgrimage set out of Prasiai in Attica and is described at Plut., *Nicias* 3.

[51] This was a small island between Delos and the nearby island of Rheneia.

[52] These groats were made from fresh or unroasted barley and probably used in a ritual.

MISCELLANEOUS FRAGMENTS

15.1. Stobaeus, *Anthology* 3.9.47 (Hense): *Wealth is perhaps something to be desired; justice, however, is honored and admired.*

15.2. Stobaeus, *Anthology* 3.27, 10 (Hense): *One must help friends and relatives, provided one does not swear false oaths.*

15.3. Stobaeus, *Anthology* 4.31.113 (Hense): *It is a not a noble thing to be wealthy but to be wealthy from noble deeds.*

15.4. Rutilius Lupus 1.2: *The guilty man, judges, is not free from the deepest sorrow, but many things trouble him: the present is full of anxiety; the future is full of fear; the law confronts him with an imminent punishment; his crimes force him to commit more crimes; his enemy is looking for a chance to denounce his offense. These things violently torment his soul every day.*

15.5. Rutilius Lupus 1.13: *I am not amazed that a very hard-working man has reached such a high degree of wealth.*[53] *For whoever has a strong will must be hard-working. From hard work comes knowledge. From knowledge comes eloquence and intellectual ability. From this ability arises the true and lasting blessing of praise. The benefit of good fortune does not betray fervent devotion to virtue.*

15.6. Rutilius Lupus 1.18: *All the parts of his body are most suitable for vice: his eyes for lust, his hands for plunder, his belly for gluttony; those parts that we cannot mention with dignity for every type of degeneracy; his feet for desertion; indeed, one cannot tell whether his vices come from his body or he himself is the product of these vices.*

15.7. Rutilius Lupus 2.11: *For the moment, judges, I will keep silent about the extremely evil deeds he committed without the people's approval; I will say nothing about the forged letters, which he sent to the Council; I will leave out the threats you made against him. You are familiar with all these matters, and you should learn as soon as possible about his most recent actions, which are far more serious.*

15.8. Rutilius Lupus 2.18: *But you, judges, you ought to do this. For when you carelessly acquit the guilty when casting your votes, you encourage impious men to want to commit crimes.*

---

[53] One editor has suggested changing "wealth" to "honor."

INDEX